Carolina Blessings

Recipes from friends of The Children's Home Society of North Carolina

Dedication

Carolina Blessings is dedicated to those many, many lives that The Children's Home Society of North Carolina has blessed and will bless.

The Children's Home Society
of North Carolina

The Children's Home Society of North Carolina promotes the right of every child to a permanent, safe, and loving home. Proceeds from the sale of Carolina Blessings provides funding to help make this mission a reality.

Carolina Blessings
Published by
The Children's Home Society of North Carolina

For additional copies, use the form
provided in the back of the book. Or, write or telephone

Carolina Blessings
The Children's Home Society of North Carolina
Post Office Box 14608
Greensboro, North Carolina 27415-4608
1-800-632-1400

International Standard Book Number 0-9643051-0-0

First Printing, April 1995: 10,000 copies

*This book contains tested recipes contributed by families and
friends of The Children's Home Society of North Carolina. Not all recipes
are original, but all have the hearty endorsement of their
contributors. The Cookbook Committee regrets that due to space limitations and
duplications, the cookbook does not contain every recipe submitted.*

Printed in the USA by

WIMMER
The Wimmer Companies, Inc.
Memphis • Dallas

A Mission of Hope and Blessings

At the 1994 Annual Meeting of The Children's Home Society of North Carolina, Ms. Claire Hurst, a retired Children's Home Society social worker, spoke about the organization's mission. Her speech formed the basis of this essay.

The Children's Home Society of North Carolina is committed to a single mission - that every child has the right to a permanent, safe, and loving home. To fulfill this mission of hope, The Children's Home Society serves many people.

It serves couples whose hearts and arms ache to love and hold a child. Their cherished desire, undimmed by years of disappointment, is to have the opportunity to pass on to their child the devotion and values they hold so dear.

The Children's Home Society serves birth parents who are confused and frightened about the decisions that face them. Their sincere longing, clearly evident through their turmoil, is to provide their child with the love and security that all children need.

The Children's Home Society serves often defenseless children who have endured the circumstances of their births or early childhoods. They earnestly yearn for nothing more than families who love them and care for them as they triumph over their sometimes painful beginnings.

The Children's Home Society serves babies who, because of their tender ages, cannot make their wishes known. Their unwavering trust kindles the steadfast responsibility of finding them loving parents and secure homes.

Through its mission of hope and dedication to service, The Children's Home Society of North Carolina brings blessings to the lives of countless individuals.

The CHS Adoption Resource Center Programs

- Pregnancy Support Services
- Adoption Services
- Child Care Program
- Post Adoption Services
  (Workshops, Seminars, Counseling)

For additional information, please telephone 1-800-632-1400.

Acknowledgments

The Children's Home Society of North Carolina
gratefully acknowledges the generous contributions
by those volunteers whose resources, time, and talent created,
produced, and marketed *Carolina Blessings,*

and

the contribution of the first printing by
Sandy and Marshall Pittman
in honor of their cherished children,
Lee Anna and Dean.

About the Artist

A North Carolina resident, Cynthia Hiatt Poole believes that her artistic skill derives from a combination of inherited ability and instructional influence. Encouraged artistically by her mother, Poole showed, at a young age, unusual understanding of composition, form, and color. Her early work in graphite and oils led to the unique creative style and identity demonstrated in her watercolors.

As exhibited on the cover and divider pages of *Carolina Blessings*, Poole's art reflects her love of life, heritage, and family. Her portraiture captures the character and inner spirit of her subjects, while her scenic work reflects the majesty of the natural world.

Receiving much support and inspiration from her husband and two young daughters, Poole has won numerous awards in juried competition throughout the eastern United States and has received several corporate commissions.

Table of Contents

Menus

Opened in 1944, The Children's Home Society of North Carolina's first central "receiving" home in Greensboro provided a welcoming environment for infants and children as they waited for permanent homes with new families.

The Children's Home Society of North Carolina promotes the right of every child to a permanent, safe, and loving home.

Breakfasts and Brunches

Breakfast for Mom and Dad

- *Cranberry, Pear, and Grapefruit Juice - 36*
- *Swedish Oatmeal Pancakes - 57*
- *Baked Apples with Cream Cheese - 199*
- *Crispy Bacon*
- *Coffee, Tea*

New Year's Day Brunch

- *Scallop Puffs - 20*
- *Sweet Potato Biscuits - 53*
- *Honey-baked Ham*
- *Cheese Grits - 127*
- *Black-eyed Pea and Cabbage Slaw - 89*
- *Raspberry Cranberry Mold - 105*
- *Chocolate Chip Cream Cheese Bars - 240*
- *Praline Confections - 269*
- *Apple Cider Punch - 34*

Breakfast for a Leisurely Morning

- *Freshly Squeezed Orange Juice*
- *Grilled Link Sausages - 165*
- *Scrambled Eggs with Cream Cheese and Chives - 132*
- *Roasted Rosemary Potatoes - 192*
- *Rainbow Row Baked Fruit - 202*
- *Coffee, Tea*

Lunches

Spring Garden Luncheon

- Fuzz Buzz - 37
- Sesame Cheese Straws - 17
- Chicken Salad with Pecans - 82
- Marinated Asparagus - 95
- Fresh Fruit Compote - 201
- Sour Cream Blueberry Muffins
    with Orange Butter - 48
- Tipsy Almond Trifle - 258

Christening Luncheon

- Champagne Punch - 33
- Sausage and Linguine Torte - 118
- Marinated Vegetables - 102
- Herb Rolls - 50
- Strawberries with Sherry Crème - 265

Spirited Tailgate Picnic

- Grilled Chutney Chicken - 166
- Curried Rice - 128
- Black Bean Salad with Feta Cheese - 96
- Mother's Angel Biscuits with Country Ham - 52
- Chocolate Sour Cream Pound Cake - 231
- Buttermilk Pie - 247

Dinners

First Dinner of Spring

- *Warm Mushroom Puffs - 22*
- *Roast Leg of Lamb with Scallion Sauce - 159*
- *Lemon Chive Fettucine and Asparagus - 125*
- *Triple Sec Fruit Salad - 107*
- *Broccoli Timbales with Ginger Orange Carrots - 186*
- *Out-of-this-World Lemon Pie - 255*

Farmer's Market Feast

- *Garden Cheese Spread with Bagel Crisps - 24*
- *Tomato-Vidalia Onion Pie - 197*
- *Posh Squash - 195*
- *Sweet-and-Sour Green Beans - 185*
- *Corn on the Cob with Basil Butter - 187*
- *Bacon Potato Salad - 99*
- *Polka Dot Peach Pie - 256*

Harvest Moon Dinner

- *Cream of Butternut Squash Soup*
  with Cranberry Port Pureé - 73
- *Pork Loin Stuffed with Dried Cherries - 161*
- *Southern Pecan Pilaf - 129*
- *Bundles of Steamed Green Beans*
- *Sour Cream Apple Pie - 244*

Tree-Trimming Dinner

- *Avocado Pinwheel - 31*
- *Tortilla Chips*
- *Spinach Romaine Salad - 93*
- *Sassy Black Bean Soup - 66*
- *Beef and Artichoke Stew - 62*
- *Confetti Muffins - 51*
- *White Chocolate Macadamia Brownies*
  with Hot Fudge Sauce - 242

Special Anniversary Dinner

- *Bourbon Pecans - 23*
- *Caesar Salad - 91*
- *Medallions of Veal with Apple Brandy*
  and Mushroom Sauce - 153
- *Garlic Mashed Potatoes - 192*
- *Green Beans with Sunflower Seeds - 183*
- *Chocolate Cherry Cheesecake - 220*

Simply Sunday Supper

- *Grilled Shrimp - 146*
- *Fireworks Coleslaw - 88*
- *Scallion Rice - 129*
- *Spider Cornbread - 50*
- *Frozen Nutty Buddy Pie - 264*
- *Iced Tea Punch - 34*

Children's Celebrations

Valentine's Day Tea Party

- *Heart-shaped Sandwiches*
  with Simple Pimento Cheese Spread - 24
- *Blueberry Oatmeal Scones - 54*
- *Fresh Fruit Slices*
- *Strawberry Dip - 32*
- *Party Vanilla Cupcakes - 234*
- *French Chocolates - 267*
- *Gelatin Punch - 34*

Little League Victory Celebration

- *Hot Dogs with Hot Dog Chili Sauce - 207*
- *Baked Beans - 181*
- *Day-before Broccoli Salad - 98*
- *Watermelon Wedges*
- *Chocolate Sandwich Cookie Freeze - 264*
- *M&M® Party Cookies - 237*
- *Lemonade*

Cookies for Santa

- *Gingersnaps - 238*
- *Holly Wreaths - 269*
- *Peanut Butter Balls - 268*
- *Tea Cakes - 239*
- *Almond Crunch Cookies - 235*
- *Hot Chocolate - 37*

Appetizers and Beverages

Located in Raleigh, the Executive Mansion
is a striking example of Victorian architecture with
its decorative slate roof, gables, and dormer windows.

Children delight in feeding two of the many pigeons that have found a home on the Executive Mansion grounds.

Sesame Cheese Straws

½ pound extra-sharp Cheddar
  cheese, shredded
1 (2¼-ounce) jar sesame seeds
1 stick butter or margarine,
  softened

1¼ cups all-purpose flour
1 teaspoon salt
⅛ teaspoon cayenne pepper

Preheat oven to 400° F. Allow shredded cheese to reach room temperature.
Toast sesame seeds in a heavy skillet, stirring constantly over low heat about
20 minutes or until golden brown; cool and set aside. Combine cheese,
butter, flour, salt, and cayenne pepper; work dough until mixture is
thoroughly blended. Add sesame seeds. Roll dough to ⅛-inch thickness; cut
into 4x½-inch strips, and place on baking sheet. Bake straws for 12 to 15
minutes or until golden brown; cool on wire rack. Place in airtight container.
Kept in airtight container, straws stay fresh for several weeks. Yield: 5 dozen.

Parmesan Puffs

¼ cup milk
¼ cup water
4 tablespoons unsalted butter
¼ teaspoon salt
½ cup all-purpose flour

2 large eggs
1 cup freshly grated Parmesan
  cheese
Black pepper to taste

Preheat oven to 400° F. Butter a baking sheet. In a small heavy saucepan,
combine milk, ¼ cup water, butter, and salt. Bring mixture to a boil over high
heat. Reduce heat to moderate, add flour, and beat mixture with a spoon until
it leaves the side of the pan and forms a ball. Transfer mixture to a bowl;
whisk in eggs, 1 at a time, whisking well after each addition. Stir in Parmesan
cheese and pepper to taste.

Drop the batter in 16 mounds on prepared sheet. Bake puffs in the upper third
of oven for 15 minutes, or until they are crisp and golden.

Serve puffs as an appetizer or as an accompaniment to soups, meats, and
poultry. Yield: 16 puffs.

Mini Bacon Quiches

8 slices bacon, cooked until crisp
   and drained on paper towels
1 medium tomato
½ small onion
3 ounces Swiss cheese, grated

1 egg, beaten
½ cup mayonnaise
1 teaspoon dried basil
1 (10-ounce) can refrigerated flaky
   biscuits

Preheat oven to 375° F. Chop bacon, tomato, and onion. Mix all ingredients, except biscuits, and set aside. Separate each biscuit horizontally into 3 thinner biscuits. Place each biscuit slice over a mini muffin pan cup. Make an indentation in the middle of each biscuit. Fill cups with cheese mixture. Bake for 10 to 12 minutes or until golden brown. Yield: 30 appetizers.

Olive Quiche Appetizers

Quiche may be baked a day ahead and refrigerated.
To reheat, bake at 375° F. for 10 minutes or until
thoroughly heated.

Pastry for double-crust 9-inch pie
6 ounces medium to sharp cheese
   of your choice
6 eggs
2 cups sour cream

1 cup pimiento-stuffed olives,
   chopped fine
1 teaspoon dried whole oregano
   (optional)
Sliced pimiento-stuffed olives for
   garnish

Preheat oven to 425° F. Roll pastry to fit bottom and sides of a 15x10x1-inch jellyroll pan; set aside.

Shred cheese. Beat eggs in a large bowl. Add sour cream, olives, oregano, and cheese. Mix well. Pour into crust. Bake for 15 minutes. Reduce temperature to 375° F. and continue baking for 20 to 25 minutes or until center is set. Cool slightly, and cut into 1½ x1¼-inch bars. Garnish with sliced pimiento-stuffed olives, if desired. Yield: about 6 dozen.

Savory Cheesecakes

¼ cup breadcrumbs
3 (8-ounce) packages cream cheese, softened
6 eggs
½ large onion, sautéed

1 teaspoon salt
2 teaspoons black pepper
⅛ teaspoon minced or granulated garlic

Preheat oven to 350° F. Butter an 8-inch springform pan, and lightly coat the bottom and sides with breadcrumbs.

In a bowl with electric mixer, blend cream cheese and eggs. Add onion, salt, pepper, and garlic. Add variation ingredients. Pour mixture into prepared pan. Bake for 40 minutes or until center is firm.

Variation #1: 6 strips bacon, fried and crumbled; 1 cup Cheddar cheese, grated.

Variation #2: 4 artichoke hearts, drained and chopped; 4 tablespoons pesto; 5 sun-dried tomatoes.

Ranch Dressing Pinwheels

4 (12-inch) flour tortillas
2 (8-ounce) packages cream cheese, softened
1 (.7-ounce) package ranch buttermilk dressing mix

2 scallions, minced
½ cup diced red bell pepper
½ cup diced celery
1 (2.5-ounce) can sliced black olives, drained

Center each tortilla on a square of aluminum foil. Combine cream cheese, dressing mix, and scallions. Spread cheese mixture on tortillas, covering each tortilla completely. Sprinkle red bell pepper, celery, and black olives on each tortilla, leaving a ½-inch border. Roll up tortilla, and wrap the roll in foil. Refrigerate rolls for at least one hour. Remove foil, and cut rolls into 1-inch slices. Yield: 3 dozen.

Scallop Puffs

3 tablespoons butter or margarine
1 pound bay scallops, cut into quarters
2 teaspoons finely minced lemon zest
3 cloves garlic, minced
3 tablespoons chopped fresh dill

2 cups grated Swiss cheese
1½ cups mayonnaise
Black pepper to taste
12 dozen (1-inch-thick) slices from a fresh baguette or Italian bread loaf
Paprika, for garnish

Melt butter in a medium skillet over medium heat. Add scallops, lemon zest, and garlic. Cook, stirring constantly, until the scallops are just barely cooked through, 2 to 3 minutes. Add dill, and cook 30 seconds longer. Let mixture cool to room temperature.

Add cheese, mayonnaise, and black pepper to scallop mixture, and stir to combine well. Refrigerate in a covered bowl for up to 1 week.

Before serving, preheat broiler. Place bread rounds ½-inch apart on baking sheets. Top each round with scallop mixture, and sprinkle lightly with paprika. Broil until puffed and golden, for 2 to 3 minutes. Serve hot. Yield: 12 dozen.

Sausage Palmiers

Sausage rolls freeze well unbaked; remove from freezer, and bake.

1 (8-ounce) can refrigerated crescent roll dough
½ pound hot bulk sausage

3 to 4 tablespoons Dijon or brown mustard
¼ to ½ cup shredded Cheddar cheese

Preheat oven to 375° F. Unroll crescent roll dough into 2 rectangles. Place them side by side to make 1 long rectangle. Pinch all seams with your fingertips. Turn dough over, and pinch remaining seams. Combine sausage, mustard, and cheese until well blended. Spread sausage mixture over dough. Roll dough in a single roll, starting at the long end. Cut the roll into ½- to ¾-inch slices. Take each small slice, and place cut side up, and 1-inch apart, on an ungreased cookie sheet. Gently press the roll onto the sheet. Bake for 15 minutes or until dough is browned. Yield: 6 to 8 appetizer servings.

Marinated Seafood

½ cup canola oil
½ cup soy sauce
½ cup lime juice
½ cup wine vinegar
1 teaspoon black pepper
1 clove garlic, minced
3 teaspoons Worcestershire sauce

3 teaspoons dry mustard
2 pounds shrimp or other seafood, cooked, peeled, and deveined
1 onion, chopped
1 green bell pepper, chopped
2 stalks celery, chopped

In blender, combine canola oil, soy sauce, lime juice, wine vinegar, black pepper, garlic, Worcestershire sauce, and dry mustard. Pour mixture into large container. Add shrimp and remaining ingredients. Marinate, covered, in refrigerator for 24 hours. Drain marinade from shrimp and vegetables, and serve them cold. Yield: 4 servings.

Italian Marinated Vegetables

The quantity of vegetables may be increased, but they must be stirred more often.

½ to 1 pound fresh mushrooms
1 green bell pepper, cut in 1-inch strips
1 yellow bell pepper, seeded and cut into thin rings
3 carrots, peeled and cut into thin circles
1 (16-ounce) can artichoke hearts, drained and halved

6 green onions, each including 1 inch of green top
½ cup pimiento-stuffed green olives
1 broccoli bunch, cut into flowerets
Cherry tomatoes
1½ cups red wine vinegar
1 teaspoon sugar
2 teaspoons dried oregano leaves
¾ cup olive oil
Minced parsley

In a large serving bowl, combine mushrooms, green and yellow bell peppers, carrots, artichoke hearts, green onions, pimiento-stuffed green olives, broccoli, and cherry tomatoes. Heat vinegar in a saucepan. Stir in sugar and oregano. Cool slightly. Add olive oil, and pour over vegetables. Mix well. Cover and refrigerate for 24 hours, stirring occasionally. Garnish with parsley.

As an appetizer, serve with hors d'oeuvre toothpicks. Yield: 15 servings.

Warm Mushroom Puffs

Pastry:

1 (3-ounce) package cream cheese, softened

½ cup butter

1½ cups flour

In a bowl, mix cream cheese and butter. Stir in flour, and blend well. Chill 30 minutes before rolling.

Filling:

1 small onion, minced

3 tablespoons butter

½ pound mushrooms, minced

¼ teaspoon thyme

½ teaspoon salt

Black pepper to taste

2 tablespoons flour

¼ cup sour cream

In a skillet, sauté onion in butter. Add mushrooms, and cook for 2 minutes. Add thyme, salt, and black pepper. Blend. Cook for an additional minute. Sprinkle flour over mixture. Add sour cream and cook, stirring, until thickened.

Preheat oven to 450° F. On a floured surface, roll out chilled dough until very thin. Cut 3-inch rounds, and place approximately ¾ teaspoon filling on each round. Fold edges over and press together with the tines of a fork. Bake on an ungreased cookie sheet for 15 minutes. Yield: 40 to 50 puffs.

Quick Pesto-Stuffed Mushrooms

1 (12-ounce) package small fresh mushrooms

Olive oil for brushing mushrooms

1 (4-ounce) jar commercial pesto or homemade pesto

12 to 16 slivers of sun-dried tomatoes

¼ cup freshly grated Parmesan cheese

Salt and freshly ground black pepper, to taste

Preheat oven to 400° F. Clean mushrooms, and remove stems. Brush them with olive oil. Spoon pesto into stem cavities. Place tomato sliver on each mushroom, and place mushrooms ½-inch apart on baking sheet. Sprinkle Parmesan cheese over mushrooms. Top with salt and pepper. Bake for 10 to 15 minutes, or until bubbly. Yield: 12 to 16 mushrooms.

Stuffed Mushroom Delight

24 large fresh mushrooms
1 pound sausage
½ cup chopped onion
2 tablespoons minced parsley

⅛ teaspoon salt
½ teaspoon black pepper
1 (8-ounce) package cream cheese, softened

Clean mushrooms with damp paper towels. Remove and chop stems. Set caps aside. Preheat broiler. Combine chopped stems and sausage in large skillet. Cook over medium heat, stirring to crumble. Drain. Add onion, parsley, salt, and black pepper. Cook over low heat until onion is tender. Add cream cheese, and stir until blended. Stuff blended mixture into mushroom caps. Place on cookie sheet. Broil for 5 minutes. Yield: 2 dozen.

Bourbon Pecans

3 ounces bourbon
1 pound pecan halves
½ cup sugar
1 tablespoon Worcestershire sauce
1 tablespoon corn oil

½ teaspoon cayenne pepper
½ teaspoon salt
¼ teaspoon black pepper
1 teaspoon ground cumin

Preheat oven to 350° F. In a small saucepan, boil bourbon until it reduces in amount to 3 tablespoons. Blanch pecans for 1 minute in boiling water. Drain. Combine the reduced bourbon, sugar, Worcestershire sauce, and corn oil. Pour warm nuts in a bowl, and toss with bourbon mixture. Let stand 10 minutes, and then spread on a jellyroll pan. Bake for 30 to 50 minutes, stirring nuts every 10 minutes. When nuts are crisp and lightly browned, and liquid has evaporated, put nuts into a bowl. In a separate bowl, combine cayenne pepper, salt, black pepper, and cumin. Stir spice mixture into nuts, coating them completely. Remove nuts to another sheet pan to cool in a single layer. Sprinkle with sugar, if desired. Store nuts in an airtight container for up to 2 weeks. Yield: 1 pound.

Hot Cheese Loaf

1 (2-pound) round loaf sourdough
  bread
2 cups grated sharp cheese
1½ cups sour cream
1 tablespoon Worcestershire sauce
1 (4-ounce) can green chiles

1 bunch green onions, chopped
1 (4.5-ounce) jar dried beef
1 (2-ounce) jar diced pimientos,
  drained
Tortilla chips

Preheat oven to 350° F. Carefully slice top off bread. Remove bread from
center of loaf, and cut into square chunks. Place chunks on cookie sheet, and
toast for 15 minutes. Set chunks aside. Reduce oven to 325° F. Combine
remaining ingredients, except tortilla chips. Fill hollowed loaf with cheese
mixture. Place top slice on loaf, and wrap in foil. Bake for 1 to 1½ hours.
Serve warm with toasted bread and tortilla chips for dipping.

Garden Cheese Spread

1 cup medium Cheddar cheese,
  grated
1 cup Monterey Jack cheese, grated
½ cup mayonnaise
½ cup scallion, sliced

¼ cup green bell pepper
¼ cup red bell pepper
1 clove fresh garlic, minced
Bagel crisps for spreading

Combine all ingredients, except bagel crisps. Add mayonnaise to desired
texture. Refrigerate for at least 1 hour before serving. Serve on bagel crisps.
Yield: 3½ cups.

Simple Pimiento Cheese Spread

1 pound Cheddar cheese, grated
1 (8-ounce) package low-fat cream
  cheese
½ small onion, minced
1 (4-ounce) jar diced pimientos,
  drained

¾ cup light or regular mayonnaise
¼ teaspoon sugar
Salt and black pepper to taste
Hot pepper sauce to taste
Assorted crackers

Combine all ingredients, and mix well. Serve with crackers. Yield: 3 cups.

Cheddar Cheese Ring with Blackberry Jam

1 pound sharp Cheddar cheese,
  grated
¾ cup mayonnaise
½ teaspoon garlic juice
1 cup chopped pecans

1 medium onion, grated
½ teaspoon hot pepper sauce
1 cup blackberry jam
Assorted crackers for spreading

Combine all ingredients, except jam and crackers; mix well. Press into a ring-shaped mold lined with plastic wrap. Refrigerate for several hours. When ready to serve, unmold ring on a platter and fill the center with blackberry jam. Serve with crackers. Yield: 12 servings.

Marinated Cheese

1 (.7-ounce) envelope Italian salad
  dressing mix
½ cup vegetable oil
¼ cup white vinegar
2 tablespoons water
2 tablespoons minced green onions
1½ teaspoons sugar
1 (8-ounce) package Monterey Jack
  cheese

1 (8-ounce) package sharp Cheddar
  cheese
1 (8-ounce) package cream cheese,
  very cold
1 (4-ounce) jar diced pimientos,
  drained
Fresh parsley sprigs for garnish
Assorted crackers

Combine salad dressing mix, vegetable oil, white vinegar, water, green onions, and sugar in a small jar; cover tightly and shake vigorously to blend; set aside. Cut Monterey Jack cheese crosswise into ¼-inch strips. Cut each strip in half to form 2 rectangles; set aside. Cut Cheddar cheese and cream cheese in same manner.

Assemble cheese slices like dominoes in two rows in a 4-quart dish, alternating Monterey Jack cheese, cream cheese, and Cheddar cheese. Pour marinade over cheese. Cover and refrigerate overnight. Drain and arrange on a platter in rows. Top each row with diced pimientos. Garnish with parsley. Serve with crackers. Yield: 50 appetizer servings.

Sherry Cheese Pâté

2 (3-ounce) packages cream cheese, softened
1 cup grated sharp Cheddar cheese
4 teaspoons dry sherry
½ teaspoon curry powder

1 (8-ounce) jar chopped chutney
3 to 4 scallions with green tops, finely chopped
Sesame or wheat crackers

Combine cream cheese, Cheddar cheese, sherry, and curry powder; mix thoroughly. Spread mixture, ½-inch thick, on a serving platter. Chill thoroughly. Spread chutney over cheese mixture. Sprinkle with scallions to cover. Serve with crackers. Yield: 8 servings.

Brie Cheese with Brown Sugar and Almonds

1 (14-ounce) package Brie cheese
3 tablespoons butter
2 tablespoons packed light brown sugar

½ cup slivered almonds
French bread or crackers

Preheat oven to 300° F. Place Brie cheese on lightly buttered 9-inch quiche dish or pie plate. Bake for 15 minutes. Preheat broiler. In a small saucepan, melt butter. Stir in brown sugar and almonds. Pour butter mixture over Brie cheese. Broil until toasted. Serve with French bread or crackers.

Artichoke Dip

1 (14-ounce) can artichokes (not marinated)
1 tablespoon finely chopped onion
1 tablespoon lemon juice
2 tablespoons crisply fried bacon, crumbled

½ teaspoon Worcestershire sauce
½ teaspoon salt
½ teaspoon hot pepper sauce
⅓ cup mayonnaise
Bland crackers

Drain and chop artichokes. Combine artichokes, onion, lemon juice, bacon, Worcestershire sauce, salt, and hot pepper sauce. Add mayonnaise, and stir until mixture reaches dipping consistency. Refrigerate for several hours. Serve with crackers. Yield: 2 cups.

Layered Mexican Dip

*Recipe may be doubled. If you double the recipe, use
a 9¹/₂x13-inch decorative dish.*

1 (8-ounce) package cream cheese, softened
1 (8-ounce) jar hot picante sauce
¼ cup finely chopped green bell pepper
¼ cup finely chopped onion

¼ cup finely chopped tomatoes
1 (4-ounce) can chopped or sliced black olives
1 (8-ounce) package finely shredded taco cheese
Sturdy tortilla chips

Combine cream cheese and picante sauce. Spread mixture in 8x8-inch decorative dish. Layer bell pepper, onion, tomatoes, and black olives on top of cream cheese mixture. Top with taco cheese. Refrigerate for several hours. Serve with tortilla chips. Yield: 4 to 6 servings.

Chunky Guacamole

8 small or 4 large ripe avocados
4 ripe medium tomatoes, diced into ¼-inch pieces
1 small red onion, coarsely chopped
2 fresh jalapeño peppers, seeded and finely chopped

½ cup fresh lime juice
3 tablespoons fresh coriander leaves
3 tablespoons mayonnaise
Salt to taste
⅓ cup sour cream
Tortilla chips

Peel and pit avocados; place avocado pulp in a medium-sized mixing bowl. Using a fork, mash pulp to a chunky consistency. Do not use a food processor or blender. Add tomatoes, onion, and jalapeño peppers to avocados, and stir to combine. Stir in lime juice and coriander. Fold in mayonnaise. Add salt to taste. Transfer mixture to serving dish; make an indentation in the center of the dip. Spoon sour cream into the indentation. Serve with tortilla chips. Yield: 4 to 4½ cups.

Salsa

*Prepare salsa up to one week in advance
and refrigerate.*

5 fresh medium tomatoes, chopped
1 quart home-canned tomatoes,
  chopped with juice (a 28-ounce
  can tomatoes may be substituted)
½ bunch green onions, diced
½ teaspoon lemon juice
2 teaspoons soy sauce
2 teaspoons sugar

1 tablespoon salt
1 tablespoon black pepper
¼ cup vegetable oil
2 tablespoons vinegar
1 teaspoon oregano
1 (3-ounce) jar jalapeño peppers,
  chopped
Tortilla chips

Combine all ingredients, except tortilla chips. Chill, if desired. Serve with
tortilla chips. Yield: approximately 5 cups.

Southwestern Holiday Dip

1 (8-ounce) package cream cheese,
  softened
½ cup sour cream
1 (3-ounce) package pepperoni or
  salami, chopped

1 (4-ounce) can green chiles,
  undrained
1½ tablespoons dried minced onion
2 teaspoons chopped chives
½ cup chopped pecans
Tortilla chips

Preheat oven to 350° F. In a bowl with an electric mixer, beat cream cheese
and sour cream until well blended. By hand, stir in pepperoni, green chiles,
onion, and chives. Spread mixture in 8x8-inch baking dish. Sprinkle with
pecans. Bake for 20 minutes. Serve hot with tortilla chips. Yield: 4 to 6
servings.

Hot Clam Spread

1 (6.5-ounce) can minced clams,
   drained
1 (8-ounce) package cream cheese
1 teaspoon Worcestershire sauce
½ cup sour cream

2 tablespoons mayonnaise
½ medium onion, chopped
8 ounces (½-pound) mild Cheddar
   cheese, grated and divided
Butterfly-shaped butter crackers

Preheat oven to 350° F. Combine clams, cream cheese, Worcestershire sauce, sour cream, mayonnaise, and onion. Add half the Cheddar cheese, and mix well. Place mixture in a 9-inch pie plate. Top with remaining cheese. Bake for 20 minutes. Serve with crackers. Yield: 4 to 5 cups.

Shrimp Spread

This is a flavorful and economical way to serve shrimp. It can be prepared a day ahead and refrigerated. Do not freeze.

1 (8-ounce) package cream cheese,
   softened
Juice of 1 small lemon
1 small onion, grated
1 stalk celery, finely chopped
½ cup mayonnaise
¼ cup ketchup
¼ teaspoon salt

1 pound shrimp, cooked, shelled,
   and chopped
Dash of sherry (optional)
Dash of Worcestershire sauce
   (optional)
Dash of hot pepper sauce (optional)
Dash of freshly ground black pepper
   (optional)
Assorted crackers

Blend cream cheese with lemon juice. Stir in onion, celery, mayonnaise, ketchup, and salt. Add shrimp. For more flavor, add a dash each of sherry, Worcestershire sauce, hot pepper sauce, and black pepper. Serve with crackers. Yield: 25 servings.

Hot Spinach Spread

2 or 3 jalapeño peppers, seeded and
  chopped
1 medium onion, chopped
2 tablespoons vegetable oil
1 (4-ounce) can chopped green
  chiles
2 tomatoes, peeled, seeded, and
  chopped
1 (10½-ounce) package spinach,
  thawed and dried

1½ tablespoons red wine vinegar
1 (8-ounce) package cream cheese,
  softened
2½ cups grated Monterey Jack
  cheese
1 cup half-and-half
Salt and black pepper to taste
Paprika
Tortilla chips

Preheat oven to 400° F. Grease a round 10-inch baking dish. Sauté jalapeños
and onion until soft in vegetable oil. Add chiles and tomatoes. Cook, stirring
constantly, for 2 minutes. Remove from heat; transfer to mixing bowl. Stir in
spinach, vinegar, cream cheese, Monterey Jack cheese, half-and-half, salt, and
black pepper. Pour into prepared baking dish. Sprinkle with paprika. Bake for
25 minutes. Serve with tortilla chips. Yield: 30 servings.

Mushroom-Almond Pâté

This pâté keeps well in the refrigerator and also
freezes well.

3 tablespoons butter or margarine
1 onion, finely chopped
3 cloves garlic, finely chopped
¾ cup mushrooms, chopped
½ teaspoon dried thyme
1 cup whole almonds, toasted in
  oven

3 tablespoons olive oil
¼ cup balsamic vinegar
½ teaspoon salt, or to taste
½ teaspoon freshly ground black
  pepper
Crackers or French bread

Melt butter in medium skillet. Gently sauté onion, garlic, mushrooms, and
thyme in butter until onions are soft. Chop almonds coarsely; place almonds
and olive oil in blender and process to desired consistency. Add onion mix,
vinegar, salt, and black pepper. Blend well. Chill for several hours. Serve on
crackers or French bread. Yield: about 2 cups.

Avocado Pinwheel

*Pinwheel may be prepared one day in advance and
chilled until ready to garnish.*

¼ cup cold water
1 (.75-ounce) envelope unflavored gelatin
3 avocados, mashed (1 cup)
1 tablespoon lemon juice
1 (.6-ounce) package dry Italian dressing mix
2 cups sour cream

3 tablespoons parsley, chopped
Dash of hot pepper sauce
3 to 4 drops green food coloring (optional)
Garnishes: chopped scallions, chopped tomatoes, chopped or sliced ripe olives, chopped yellow, green, or red bell pepper

Brush an 8-inch springform pan with oil. Line with plastic wrap, and brush lightly with oil. In a small saucepan, combine cold water and gelatin. Set aside to soften. In the bowl of a food processor, combine avocados, lemon juice, dressing mix, sour cream, parsley, hot pepper sauce, and food coloring, if desired. Blend thoroughly. Melt gelatin mixture over low heat, and blend into avocado mixture. Pour into prepared pan, and chill until set. When ready to serve, unmold onto platter. Arrange selected garnishes in concentric circles on top of mold. Serve with tortilla chips. Yield: 18 to 20 servings.

Avocado Dip

*To maintain fresh green color, place avocado pit in
dip while chilling.*

2 tablespoons chopped onion
2 avocados, peeled and pitted
1½ teaspoons fresh lemon juice
1½ cups (12 ounces) sour cream

¼ cup blue cheese, crumbled
Salt and black pepper to taste
Tortilla chips, crackers, or crudités

Purée onion, avocados, and lemon juice in food processor. Blend with sour cream, blue cheese, salt, and black pepper. Chill for 1 hour. After chilling, adjust seasoning to taste, and serve with tortilla chips, crackers, or crudités. Yield: about 2½ cups.

Piña Colada Fruit Dip

1 (8-ounce) can crushed pineapple, undrained
¾ cup milk
½ cup sour cream

1 (3½-ounce) package instant coconut pudding and pie filling
Fresh fruit slices

In food processor or blender, combine all ingredients, except fruit. Cover; blend for 30 seconds. Refrigerate for several hours. Serve with fresh fruit slices for dipping. Yield: 2 cups.

Pineapple Cheese Spread

Be sure to leave leaves on pineapple since they enhance the presentation. Cheese mixture can be prepared a day ahead and refrigerated. Do not freeze.

2 (8-ounce) packages cream cheese, softened
3 tablespoons chutney, chopped coarsely
2 teaspoons curry powder

6 ounces slivered almonds
1 tablespoon dry mustard
1 pineapple half, leaves intact
4 ounces roasted peanuts, crushed
Shredded wheat crackers

Combine cream cheese, chutney, curry powder, almonds, and mustard. Blend until smooth. Scoop fruit out of pineapple half; reserve for another use. Fill pineapple shell with cheese mixture and cover with crushed peanuts. Serve with crackers. Yield: 20 servings.

Strawberry Dip

1 (8-ounce) jar strawberry preserves
1 (8-ounce) package cream cheese, softened

1 (8-ounce) container frozen whipped topping
Fruit slices

Mix preserves and cream cheese together. Use large mixing spoon or spatula to fold in whipped topping. Refrigerate for at least 6 hours before serving. Serve with fruit slices for dipping. Yield: 3 cups.

Fresh Fruit Dip

2 (8-ounce) packages cream cheese
4 tablespoons butter or margarine
1 cup sifted confectioners' sugar
2 tablespoons orange juice
1 tablespoon grated orange zest, or
  more to taste

½ teaspoon vanilla extract
Chopped pecans for garnish
Apple and pear slices, shortbread
  cookies, and gingersnaps

Blend cream cheese, butter, and sugar. Add orange juice, zest, and vanilla
extract. Beat until smooth. Transfer to serving bowl. Chill at least half an hour.
If refrigerated for several hours, allow to soften before serving. Garnish with
pecans. Serve with sliced apples and pears, shortbread cookies, and
gingersnaps. Yield: 2 cups.

Fruited Champagne Punch

1 (46-ounce) can unsweetened
  pineapple juice
1⅓ cups orange juice
⅔ cup lemon juice
⅓ cup lime juice

1 cup sugar
1 (1-liter) bottle ginger ale, chilled
½ bottle champagne (optional),
  chilled
1 prepared ice ring

Combine pineapple, orange, lemon, and lime juices, and chill. Just before
serving, dissolve sugar in a small amount of hot water. Pour chilled juices into
a punch bowl. Add dissolved sugar, and stir. Slowly add the ginger ale and
champagne. Add ice ring. Yield: 4½ quarts.

Champagne Brandy Punch

Recipe may be halved.

1 pint brandy
1 quart club soda
1 quart orange juice

4 bottles champagne
Prepared ice ring or block

Place ice ring in large punch bowl. Add brandy, club soda, and orange juice,
and stir. Slowly add champagne. Do not stir. Yield: 55 to 60 cups.

Apple Cider Punch

1 quart apple cider
2 cups cranberry juice
1 cup orange juice
1 (12-ounce) can apricot nectar

1 cup sugar
2 sticks cinnamon
Orange slices studded with whole
   cloves, for garnish

Combine all ingredients, except orange slices, in a large saucepan or crock pot. In saucepan, simmer 20 minutes; in crock pot, simmer until hot. Garnish punch with orange slices. Yield: 2 quarts, or 20 to 25 servings.

Gelatin Punch

1 (6-ounce) package strawberry or
   lime gelatin
2 cups sugar
1 quart boiling water
1 (12-ounce) can frozen orange
   juice concentrate

1 (12-ounce) can frozen lemonade
1 (46-ounce) can pineapple juice
2 quarts cold water
2 (28-ounce) bottles ginger ale

Mix gelatin, sugar, and boiling water until dissolved. In a separate bowl, mix orange juice, lemonade, pineapple juice, and water. Combine mixtures, and freeze in large plastic container. Five hours before serving, thaw mixture. Add ginger ale. Yield: 7 quarts.

Iced Tea Punch

½ gallon strong brewed tea
½ cup sugar
1 (6-ounce) can frozen lemonade
   concentrate

2 (12-ounce) bottles of ginger ale
Mint sprigs and lemon slices, for
   garnish

Mix tea and sugar, and chill. Just before serving, add lemonade concentrate and ginger ale. Garnish each serving with mint sprigs and lemon slices. Yield: 10 servings.

Holiday Wassail

*Serve wassail at an open house during the holidays or
enjoy all winter long.*

1 orange	3 (3-inch) sticks cinnamon
1 lemon	½ cup sugar
1½ teaspoons whole cloves	2 cups orange juice
1 gallon apple cider	1 cup lemon juice

Carefully peel orange and lemon, keeping each rind intact in a single strip.
Insert cloves into each strip. Combine cider, rinds, cinnamon, and sugar in
large saucepan or stockpot. Bring to a boil, reduce heat, cover, and simmer
for 10 minutes. Remove from heat, and cool completely.

To serve, add orange and lemon juices, and reheat thoroughly. Leftovers can
be stored in refrigerator. Reheat before serving. Yield: about 5 quarts.

Sherry Wassail

2 quarts apple cider	3 whole cloves
½ cup brown sugar	3 whole allspice
⅓ cup frozen lemon juice concentrate, thawed	1½ teaspoons ground nutmeg
	2 fifths dry sherry
⅓ cup frozen orange juice concentrate, thawed	Orange slices studded with whole cloves, for garnish
6 cinnamon sticks	

Combine cider, brown sugar, and fruit concentrates in a kettle. Add the
cinnamon, cloves, allspice, and nutmeg. Bring mixture to a boil; cover and
simmer for 20 minutes. Remove whole spices. Add sherry, and heat just to
boiling. Garnish with orange slices. Serve hot in mugs. Yield: 20 (6-ounce)
mugs.

Virginia Milk Punch

4 ounces bourbon	4 ounces vanilla ice cream
4 ounces milk	Ground nutmeg, for garnish

Mix all ingredients, except nutmeg, in a blender. After pouring into glass,
sprinkle mixture with nutmeg. Yield: 1 serving.

Russian Tea

8 cups water
3 cinnamon sticks
1 teaspoon whole cloves
1½ cups sugar

5 tea bags
2 cups orange juice
½ cup lemon juice
2 cups unsweetened pineapple juice

Boil water, cinnamon, and cloves for 15 minutes. Remove from heat, and add sugar and tea bags. Let stand 5 minutes. Remove spices, and add orange, lemon, and pineapple juices. Serve hot. Yield: 3 quarts.

Boiled Custard

6 eggs, well beaten
3 quarts whole milk
1 cup sugar

2 (14-ounce) cans sweetened
   condensed milk
2 teaspoons vanilla extract

In a large metal container, combine all ingredients. Place container in a kettle of simmering water. Cook mixture for 2 to 3 hours, stirring every 15 minutes, until mixture is the consistency of thick buttermilk. Cool before serving in punch cups. Serve warm or cold. Yield: 5 quarts.

Use this recipe for delicious custard ice cream, too. Add extra flavoring, if desired, after mixture is completely cooked. Freeze mixture in an ice cream maker, following manufacturer's directions. For flavoring, add crushed fruit, crushed peppermint candy, or melted unsweetened chocolate to taste.

Cranberry, Pear, and Grapefruit Juice

2 cups cranberry juice
2 cups pear nectar

1 cup grapefruit juice

In a pitcher, stir juices together. Chill well. Yield: 6 servings.

Fuzz Buzz

Great at the beach on a hot summer afternoon!

1 (6-ounce) can frozen lemonade
1 empty lemonade can filled with
   vodka or gin

1 tray of ice cubes
1 whole peach, unpeeled
Pinch of sugar

Blend all ingredients at high speed. Yield: 2 cups.

Hot Chocolate

6 cups milk, divided
12 ounces semi-sweet chocolate,
   grated

1 teaspoon vanilla extract
3 cups half-and-half
8 (4-inch) cinnamon sticks

Combine 3 cups milk, chocolate, and vanilla extract in a heavy saucepan. Stir over moderate heat until chocolate is dissolved. Stir in remaining milk and half-and-half. Bring mixture to a boil, letting it froth slightly. Pour hot chocolate into 8 mugs, and garnish with a cinnamon stick. Yield: 8 cups.

Breads

*Antique shops and artists' lofts abound
at Lexington Park in Asheville.*

Children always enjoy examining the many charming
antique toys featured in Lexington Park shops.

Oatmeal Yeast Bread

This is a heavy-textured and delicious bread.

2 cups boiling water
1 cup dry rolled oats
2 (¼-ounce) packages yeast
⅓ cup lukewarm water
1 tablespoon salt

½ cup honey
2 tablespoons melted butter
4 to 5 cups unbleached flour
1 egg yolk
Poppy seeds

Pour boiling water over oats. Let mixture stand for ½ hour, or until oats soften. Soak yeast in lukewarm water. Add salt, honey, and melted butter to oats. Stir in yeast mixture. Gradually add enough flour to form a soft dough. Knead 5 to 10 minutes, adding flour as necessary, until dough is smooth and elastic. Rub a large bowl with butter, turn dough into it, brush top of dough with vegetable oil, and set bowl in a warm place to rise.

When dough has doubled in bulk, punch it down, divide in two, and shape into 2 loaves. Put each loaf into a greased 8x4-inch bread pan. Preheat oven to 325° F. Mix a few drops of water with egg yolk; use this mixture to coat tops of loaves. Sprinkle poppy seeds on the bread, and bake for about 50 minutes. When done, brush tops with butter. Yield: 2 loaves.

Fabulous Overnight Crescent Rolls

1 cup milk
1½ sticks butter or shortening*
¼ cup sugar
½ teaspoon salt
1 (¼ ounce) package yeast

¼ cup warm water (110° F.)
4 cups unbleached flour, measured
   by spooning into cup
2 eggs, room temperature
Melted butter

Heat milk, butter, sugar, and salt until butter melts; remove from heat, and
cool slightly. Dissolve yeast in warm water in large bowl of mixer. When milk
mixture is lukewarm, beat into yeast. Add 2 cups flour and beat first at slow
speed, then at medium speed for 2 minutes. Beat in eggs, and scrape bowl.
Slowly add 1 cup flour, beat at low speed 2 minutes. Remove beaters, stir in
¾ cup flour and beat with wooden spoon until dough is smooth and elastic.
Dough will not be stiff. Rub a large bowl with oil, turn dough into it, brush top
of dough with vegetable oil, and cover with plastic wrap. (Dough may be
refrigerated at this point for up to two days. Punch dough down every 9 to 10
hours). Set aside, and let rise until doubled in bulk, about 2 hours.

Preheat oven to 400° F. Punch down dough, and beat out all air bubbles by
kneading. Divide dough into 4 parts. Sprinkle remaining ¼ cup flour on
board, and roll each piece in a ⅛-inch thick circle. Brush with melted butter;
then cut each circle into 8 wedges. Roll each wedge up from wide to narrow
end to form crescent. On a lightly oiled baking sheet, place rolls far enough
apart for them to triple in size. Brush rolls with more melted butter. Cover
with plastic, set in warm place to rise for about 1 hour. Bake for 10 to 12
minutes. Yield: about 32 large rolls.

Butter makes richer rolls; shortening makes fluffier rolls.

Refrigerator Rolls

*To freeze, cool baked rolls and place in
plastic bags; seal tightly.*

1½ cups boiling water
½ cup sugar
1 teaspoon salt
¼ cup shortening
1 (¼-ounce) package active dry
  yeast

½ cup lukewarm water (110° F.)
1 egg, beaten
5 to 6 cups all-purpose flour
Melted butter

In a large mixing bowl, combine boiling water, sugar, salt, and shortening. Stir
mixture until completely dissolved. Set aside, and allow mixture to cool until
it is lukewarm. Dissolve yeast in lukewarm water; add to cooled mixture. Add
egg, and mix well. Stir in enough flour to make a soft dough. Cover, and store
in refrigerator at least 8 hours. Dough keeps well, refrigerated, for 1 week.

When ready to use, punch down dough, and roll out to ½-inch thickness on
floured board. Cut with floured biscuit cutter, or shape into desired rolls.
Place on greased baking sheet or shallow pan. Brush rolls with butter. Let rolls
rise until doubled in size, about 1 hour. Preheat oven to 425° F. Bake for 20 to
25 minutes. Yield: 24 rolls.

Apricot Bread

This bread is delicious toasted, buttered, and served
with coffee. It also freezes well.

1½ cups dried apricots, cut into
   bite-size pieces
1 stick butter, softened
1 cup sugar
2 eggs
¾ cup orange juice
2 cups sifted all-purpose flour

3 teaspoons baking powder
¼ teaspoon baking soda
¾ teaspoon salt
1 teaspoon orange zest
1 cup chopped nuts (English walnuts
   preferred)

Soak apricots in enough water to cover for 30 minutes. Drain and chop.
Preheat oven to 350° F. Grease a 9x5-inch loaf pan, and line it with greased
foil, brown paper, or wax paper. Cream butter and sugar. Beat eggs, and add
alternately to butter mixture with orange juice. Add flour, baking powder,
baking soda, and salt. Stir in apricots, orange zest, and nuts. Pour into prepared pan. Bake for 1½ hours. Cool for 10 minutes in pan; remove from pan,
and cool completely on wire rack. Yield: 12 servings.

Whole Wheat Banana Bread

This bread keeps and freezes well.

1 cup whole wheat flour
1 cup all-purpose flour
¼ cup wheat germ
1 teaspoon baking soda
½ teaspoon salt
1½ cups mashed ripe bananas

½ cup sugar
¼ cup oil
2 eggs (or 1 whole egg plus 2 egg
   whites)
1 teaspoon vanilla extract

Preheat oven to 350° F. Spray a 9x5x3-inch loaf pan with cooking spray.
Combine flours, wheat germ, baking soda, and salt in large bowl; mix well.
Form a well in the center of mixture. Combine banana, sugar, oil, eggs, and
vanilla extract in medium bowl, and mix well. Make well in flour mixture;
pour banana mixture into it, and stir until just moistened. Spoon batter into
prepared pan. Bake for 1 hour or until toothpick comes out clean. Cool for
10 minutes in pan; remove from pan, and cool completely on wire rack.
Yield: 1 loaf.

Chocolate Tea Bread

This bread freezes well.

2⅔ cups all-purpose flour
1½ cups sugar
¾ cup applesauce
½ cup cocoa powder
1 stick butter, softened
½ cup water

3 eggs
1½ teaspoons baking soda
1 teaspoon salt
1 teaspoon vanilla extract
¾ cup chopped pecans
1 cup chocolate mini-morsels

Preheat oven to 350° F. Grease and flour 4 small loaf pans or 2 (9x5x3-inch) loaf pans. Beat together flour, sugar, applesauce, cocoa powder, butter, water, eggs, baking soda, salt, and vanilla extract for three minutes. Stir in pecans and mini-morsels. Bake for 50 minutes or until wooden pick comes out clean. Watch carefully at the end of cooking time because bread browns quickly. Cool for 10 minutes in pan; remove from pan, and cool completely on wire rack. Yield: 2 loaves or 4 small loaves.

Orange Nut Loaf Bread

1 medium orange, with zest
1 cup white raisins
2 tablespoons vegetable oil
1 teaspoon vanilla extract
1 egg
2 cups all-purpose flour

¼ teaspoon salt
1 teaspoon baking powder
½ teaspoon baking soda
1 cup sugar
½ cup chopped nuts

Preheat oven to 350° F. Grease a 9x5x3-inch loaf pan. Squeeze juice from orange into measuring cup, and add enough boiling water to reach 1 cup. Grind orange zest and raisins. Add diluted orange juice; stir in oil, vanilla extract, and egg. Sift flour with salt, baking powder, baking soda, and sugar, and add to orange mixture. Beat well, and stir in nuts. Bake for 1 hour. Cool for 10 minutes in pan; remove from pan, then cool completely on rack. Refrigerate a day or two before serving. Yield: 1 loaf.

Pumpkin Bread

1 (16-ounce) can pumpkin
3 cups all-purpose flour
2 cups sugar
2 teaspoons baking soda
¾ teaspoon cloves
1 teaspoon cinnamon
1 teaspoon nutmeg (optional)

1 teaspoon salt
½ teaspoon baking powder
½ teaspoon ginger
¼ cup raisins
⅔ cup oil
3 eggs
Streusel Topping

Preheat oven to 350° F. Grease and flour 2 (9x5x3-inch) loaf pans. Combine all ingredients, except topping. Pour mixture into pans. Sprinkle streusel topping over mixture. Bake for 1 hour or until done. Cool for 10 minutes in pan; remove from pan, and cool completely on wire rack.

Streusel Topping:
⅓ cup all-purpose flour
3 tablespoons brown sugar
2 tablespoons chopped nuts

1 teaspoon cinnamon
1 tablespoon margarine

Mix flour, sugar, nuts, cinnamon. Cut in margarine. Yield: 2 loaves.

Zucchini Bread

3 cups all-purpose flour
2 teaspoons baking soda
1½ teaspoons cinnamon
3 eggs
2 cups sugar
1 cup applesauce
2 teaspoons vanilla extract

2 cups shredded zucchini
1 (15-ounce) can crushed
    pineapple, drained
1 teaspoon salt
½ teaspoon baking powder
¾ cup chopped nuts

Preheat oven to 350° F. Grease and flour 2 (9x5x3-inch) loaf pans. Combine flour, baking soda, and cinnamon; set aside. Beat eggs lightly. Add sugar, applesauce, and vanilla extract; beat until creamy. Stir in zucchini and pineapple. Add salt, baking powder, and nuts; stir until moistened. Pour into prepared pans. Bake for 1 hour. Cool for 10 minutes in pan; remove from pan, and cool completely on rack. Yield: 2 loaves.

Oat Bran Banana Muffins

These muffins freeze well.

2¼ cups oat bran, blended in food processor or blender to flour-like consistency
2 tablespoons baking powder
½ cup brown sugar
1½ cups skim milk

2 to 3 very ripe bananas (3, if small)
2 tablespoons vegetable oil
2 egg whites
¼ cup chopped walnuts
½ cup raisins

Preheat oven to 425° F. Spray 12 muffin tins with nonstick vegetable spray, or line them with paper baking cups. Mix oat bran, baking powder, and brown sugar in large bowl. Mix milk, bananas, oil, and egg whites in blender or processor. Batter will be soupy. Stir in walnuts and raisins. Fill each tin two-thirds full with batter. Bake for 17 minutes. Remove from muffin tins imme–diately. Cool. Yield: 12 muffins.

Happy Day Berry Muffins

Children's Home Society families often refer to the
day they received their child as their "happy day."

1 egg
½ cup milk
¼ cup canola oil
1½ cups all-purpose flour
½ cup sugar

2 teaspoons baking powder
½ teaspoon salt
½ teaspoon vanilla extract
¾ cup cranberry halves or blueberries

Preheat oven to 400° F. Spray 12 muffin tins with nonstick vegetable spray, or line them with paper baking cups. Beat egg with milk and oil. Mix remaining ingredients, except berries; stir until flour is moistened. Batter will be lumpy. Fold in berries. Fill muffin tins two-thirds full. Bake for 20 to 25 minutes. Remove from muffin tins, and serve warm. Yield: 12 muffins.

Sour Cream Blueberry Muffins
with Orange Butter

2 eggs
1 stick butter, melted
1 cup sugar
1 cup sour cream
2 cups all-purpose flour

1 teaspoon baking powder
¼ teaspoon baking soda
½ teaspoon salt
1½ cups fresh blueberries

Preheat oven to 375° F. Grease 12 muffin tins. Mix eggs, butter, sugar, and sour cream. Sift together flour, baking powder, baking soda, and salt. Fold egg mixture into flour mixture until well blended. Gently stir in blueberries. Spoon batter into muffin tins. Bake for 25 minutes. Remove from muffin tins imme–diately. Spread orange butter over warm muffins.

Orange Butter:
1 stick unsalted butter, room
   temperature
1 (3-ounce) package cream cheese,
   room temperature

¼ cup powdered sugar
1 tablespoon grated orange zest

Blend all ingredients. Butter may be chilled and shaped for gifts. Yield: 12 muffins.

Healthful Bran Muffins

3 cups bran
¾ cup boiling water
1 stick butter
¾ cup honey
2 eggs

¾ cup wheat germ
2½ teaspoons baking soda
½ teaspoon salt
2 cups buttermilk or plain yogurt
1¾ cups whole wheat flour

Preheat oven to 400° F. Grease and flour 24 muffin tins. Combine bran, boiling water, and butter; set aside. In a separate bowl, combine remaining ingredients. Fold into bran mixture. Fill muffin tins three-fourths full. Bake for 20 to 25 minutes. Yield: 24 muffins.

Orange Muffins

1 stick butter, softened
1 cup sugar
2 eggs
2 cups all-purpose flour
Dash of salt
¾ cup buttermilk

½ teaspoon baking soda
1 cup chopped dates
½ cup chopped pecans
1 tablespoon grated orange rind
Orange Sauce

Preheat oven to 350° F. Grease and flour 24 miniature muffin tins. Cream butter and sugar in large mixing bowl. Mix in remaining ingredients, except orange sauce. Fill muffin tins two-thirds full, and bake for 18 minutes. Put hot muffins on wax paper. Pour orange sauce over muffins. Cool completely, and allow sauce to harden before storing muffins.

Orange Sauce:
1 cup sugar
½ cup orange juice

1 tablespoon orange zest

In a small saucepan, heat together all ingredients until sugar is melted. Yield: 2 dozen miniature muffins.

Biscuit Ring

1 stick butter or margarine

3 (10-ounce) cans buttermilk
      biscuits

Preheat oven to 400° F. Melt butter in tube or Bundt pan. Separate biscuits. Place biscuits on their sides, evenly distributing them in pan. Bake for 20 to 25 minutes. Yield: 12 servings.

Cheese Boxes

*Cheese boxes can be frozen after they are assembled
on cookie sheet. Allow them to reach room
temperature before baking.*

2 sticks butter
½ pound sharp Cheddar cheese,
  grated
1 egg white, unbeaten

1 tablespoon milk
½ teaspoon salt
Hot pepper sauce to taste
1 loaf white bread, unsliced

Preheat oven to 375° F. Cream butter and cheese until smooth. Add egg
white, milk, salt, and hot pepper sauce. Chill until mixture is spreadable.
Remove crust from bread; cut into 1-inch slices. Cut each slice into 4 squares.
Place squares on a cookie sheet. Spread tops and sides of each slice with
cheese mixture. Bake for 15 minutes or until golden brown. Yield: 48 cheese
boxes.

Herb Rolls

1 stick butter or margarine
1½ teaspoons dried parsley flakes
½ teaspoon dried onion flakes
½ teaspoon dried dillweed

1 tablespoon grated Parmesan
  cheese
1 (10-ounce) can buttermilk biscuits

Preheat oven to 425° F. Melt butter in a 9-inch pie pan. Add all ingredients,
except biscuits, to melted butter, and mix well. Cut biscuits into quarters. Coat
quartered biscuits with butter mixture. Place coated biscuits, with sides
touching, in pie pan. Bake for 12 to 15 minutes. Yield: 40 small rolls.

Spider Cornbread

¼ cup butter
1 cup cornmeal
⅓ cup all-purpose flour
1 teaspoon salt

2 teaspoons baking powder
2 tablespoons sugar
1 egg
1¾ cups milk, divided

Preheat oven to 350° F. Melt butter in 9x9-inch baking pan. Sift cornmeal,
flour, salt, baking powder, and sugar together; set aside. Mix egg and 1 cup
milk together. Stir into dry ingredients. Pour mixture into pan, and then pour
remaining ¾ cup milk on top. Do not stir. Bake for about 45 minutes. Yield: 4
to 6 servings.

Topper Cornbread

1 large onion, chopped
4 tablespoons butter
1 (8.5 ounce) box corn muffin mix
1 egg, beaten
⅓ cup milk
1 can creamed corn

1 cup sour cream
½ teaspoon salt
¼ teaspoon dillweed
1 cup grated Cheddar cheese,
divided

Preheat oven to 400° F. Grease an 8x8-inch baking pan. Sauté onion in butter; set aside to cool. Combine corn muffin mix, egg, milk, and corn. Pour into pan. Combine onions, sour cream, salt, dillweed, and ½ cup cheese. Spread over batter, and sprinkle with remaining cheese. Bake, uncovered, for 25 to 30 minutes. Yield: 5 servings.

Confetti Muffins

2 cups all-purpose flour
1½ teaspoons baking powder
½ teaspoon baking soda
¼ teaspoon cayenne pepper
1 teaspoon salt
½ cup yellow cornmeal
2 cups grated sharp Cheddar cheese

½ cup thinly sliced scallion,
including tops
1 cup finely chopped red bell
pepper
¼ cup vegetable shortening
2 tablespoons sugar
2 large eggs
1½ cups buttermilk

Preheat oven to 450° F. Butter 18 (⅓-cup) muffin tins. In a bowl, mix together flour, baking powder, baking soda, cayenne pepper, salt, and cornmeal. Add cheese, scallion, and red bell pepper, mixing well. In a large bowl, cream together shortening and sugar. Add eggs, and whisk mixture until it is smooth. Whisk in buttermilk, add flour mixture, and stir batter until just mixed. Divide batter among prepared muffin tins. Bake for 15 to 18 minutes, or until golden brown. Turn the muffins onto racks. Serve warm with butter. Yield: 18 muffins.

Mother's Angel Biscuits

This biscuit dough keeps about a week in the
refrigerator. Baked biscuits freeze well.

5 cups self-rising flour
¼ cup sugar
¾ cup shortening

1 package yeast, dissolved in 2
tablespoons warm water
2 cups buttermilk
Melted butter

Sift flour, add sugar, and cut in shortening. Add yeast that has been dissolved in warm water. Add buttermilk; knead lightly, and place in refrigerator several hours or overnight. Preheat oven to 425° F. Roll dough to ⅓-inch thickness, and cut with a 2-inch biscuit cutter.* Prick dough with a fork, and brush with melted butter. Bake biscuits for 12 to 15 minutes. Yield: 80 biscuits.

Alternatively, roll dough to ¼-inch thickness and fold, or roll it to ½-inch thickness and stack.

Easy Yeast Biscuits

6 cups self-rising flour
1 cup shortening
1½ cups buttermilk

⅓ cup sugar
1 tablespoon yeast, dissolved in ½
cup water

Preheat oven to 425° F. Combine all ingredients at once in large bowl. Remove dough from bowl, and knead about 4 to 5 minutes on floured surface. Roll out, and cut with biscuit cutter. Place biscuits on cookie sheet, and bake for 10 to 12 minutes. Yield: 72 (1½-inch) biscuits.

Cheese Biscuits

1 tablespoon shortening
1 cup self-rising flour
⅓ to ½ cup buttermilk

½ cup grated extra-sharp Cheddar
cheese

Preheat oven to 425° F. Grease and flour a baking sheet. Blend shortening into flour. Add buttermilk; mix together to form dough. Add cheese and mix well, but do not knead dough excessively. On floured dough board, roll dough to ⅓-inch thickness. Using biscuit cutter, cut out biscuits, and place on prepared baking sheet. Cut biscuits thicker than normal biscuits. Bake for 15 to 20 minutes. Yield: 12 (2-inch) biscuits.

Sweet Potato Biscuits

Serve biscuits with baked ham.

3 cups flour
2 tablespoons sugar
2 teaspoons baking powder
½ teaspoon baking soda
Dash of salt

¼ cup shortening
¾ cup mashed, cooked sweet
 potatoes
1 cup buttermilk
¼ cup chopped pecans (optional)

Preheat oven at 450° F. Lightly grease a baking sheet. Combine flour, sugar, baking powder, baking soda, and salt in a large mixing bowl; stir well. Cut in shortening with pastry blender until mixture resembles coarse meal. Stir in sweet potatoes. Add buttermilk, stirring with a fork until dry ingredients are moistened. Stir in pecans, if desired.

Turn dough out onto a lightly floured surface, and knead 4 to 5 times. Roll to ½-inch thickness, and cut with a 1½-inch biscuit cutter. Place biscuits on prepared baking sheet. Bake for 8 to 10 minutes or until lightly browned. Serve hot. Yield: about 2½ dozen biscuits.

Honey Bun Cake

1 (18.25 ounces) box yellow cake
 mix
4 eggs
⅔ cup oil

8 ounces sour cream
1 cup brown sugar
3 tablespoons cinnamon
Icing

Preheat oven to 325° F. Grease and flour a 13x9-inch baking pan. With an electric blender, blend cake mix, eggs, oil, and sour cream for 4 minutes, and put half the batter in prepared pan. In a small bowl, mix brown sugar and cinnamon together, and sprinkle over batter. Spread remainder of batter over filling mixture, using the back of a spoon dipped in warm water. Bake for 30 to 40 minutes. Remove from oven, and pour icing over top.

Icing:

1 cup powdered sugar
1½ tablespoons milk

1 teaspoon vanilla extract

Mix all ingredients together well. Yield: 16 to 18 servings.

Blueberry Oatmeal Scones

1 cup all-purpose flour
1 cup self-rising flour
1¼ cups oatmeal
¾ cup sugar
¼ cup raisins
1 teaspoon cinnamon

⅔ cup melted margarine
¼ cup milk
1 egg
½ cup fresh or partially thawed
  frozen blueberries

Preheat oven to 375° F. Combine flours, oatmeal, sugar, raisins, and cinnamon in medium bowl. Add margarine, milk, and egg. Stir until mixed. Pat the dough onto a lightly floured surface. Form into a circle. Spread berries evenly over the circle. Fold the circle in half. Reshape dough into another circle. Cut into 8 wedges. Place on ungreased baking tray. Bake for 15 minutes or until lightly browned. Yield: 8 scones.

Raisin Cinnamon Rolls

1 (16-ounce) loaf frozen bread
  dough, thawed
4 tablespoons butter or margarine,
  melted and divided
½ cup sugar
2 teaspoons ground cinnamon

⅓ cup raisins
2 tablespoons chopped almonds,
  toasted
2 teaspoons grated lemon zest
½ cup sifted powdered sugar
2½ teaspoons lemon juice

Lightly grease a 9x9-inch baking pan. Roll dough on a lightly floured surface to a 14x8-inch rectangle. Brush surface of dough with 2 tablespoons melted butter. Combine ½ cup sugar and cinnamon; sprinkle over dough, leaving ½-inch border on all sides. In the same manner, combine and sprinkle raisins, almonds, and lemon zest. Starting with the long side, roll dough into a single roll. Pinch seam to seal, but do not seal ends. Cut roll into 12 slices, and place cut side down on prepared pan. Brush with remaining 2 tablespoons melted butter. Cover and refrigerate 8 hours.

Remove pan from refrigerator, let rolls rise 50 minutes or until doubled in bulk. Heat oven to 350° F. Bake for 20 to 25 minutes. Combine powdered sugar and lemon juice; drizzle over warm rolls. Yield: 1 dozen rolls.

Apple Kuchen

1 stick butter
1 (18.25 ounces) box yellow cake
  mix
½ cup coconut
2½ cups sliced apples

½ cup sugar
1 teaspoon cinnamon
1 cup sour cream
1 egg

Preheat oven to 350° F. In a large bowl, cut butter into cake mix. Add coconut and mix mixture well. Pat mixture into an ungreased 9x13-inch pan. Bake for 10 minutes. Arrange apples over cake mix. Mix sugar and cinnamon; sprinkle over apples. Mix sour cream with egg, and spread over apples. Bake for 25 minutes. Yield: 16 to 18 servings.

Apple Walnut Coffee Cake

2 eggs
1 cup oil
1 cup sugar
1 teaspoon vanilla extract
2 cups all-purpose flour
1 teaspoon salt

1 teaspoon baking soda
1 teaspoon cinnamon
½ cup brown sugar
½ cup walnuts, chopped
2 Granny Smith apples, diced and
  unpeeled

Preheat oven to 350° F. Grease a Bundt pan or a 9x13-inch baking pan. By hand, mix eggs, oil, sugar, and vanilla extract. Sift together flour, salt, baking soda, cinnamon, and brown sugar; add to egg mixture. Stir in walnuts and apples. Bake for 1 hour. Serve warm or cold. Yield: 16 to 18 servings.

Crescent Delight

2 (8-ounce) packages cream cheese, softened
1 cup granulated sugar
1 teaspoon vanilla extract

2 (8-ounce) cans refrigerated crescent rolls
Ground cinnamon to taste

Preheat oven to 425° F. Combine cream cheese, sugar, and vanilla extract. Press 1 can of rolls in 9x13-inch baking pan. Cover bottom of pan. Spread cheese mixture over rolls. Cover with remaining rolls. Sprinkle rolls with cinnamon. Bake for 12 minutes, or until light brown. Cool completely before cutting. Yield: 16 servings.

Blueberry Coffee Cake

2 sticks butter or margarine
1 cup sugar
2 eggs
1 (8-ounce) carton sour cream
1 teaspoon vanilla extract

2 cups all-purpose flour
1 teaspoon baking powder
1 teaspoon baking soda
1 can blueberry pie filling

Preheat oven to 375° F. Grease and flour a 9x13-inch baking pan. Cream butter and sugar. Add eggs, and mix well. Add sour cream and vanilla extract. Mix together flour, baking powder, and baking soda; blend well with sour cream mixture. Spread half of batter in prepared pan. Spread blueberry pie filling over batter. Spread remainder of batter over pie filling. Sprinkle topping over batter. Bake for 45 minutes.

Topping:
⅓ cup flour
½ cup sugar
⅔ cup chopped pecans

4 tablespoons butter or margarine, softened

Mix flour, sugar, pecans, and butter. Yield: 18 to 20 servings.

Wonderful Pancakes

For Christmas presents, place dry ingredients in
plastic bag and tie with a pretty ribbon.

Oil for coating griddle
1½ cups all-purpose flour
1 teaspoon salt (or less)

1 teaspoon baking powder
1 egg
1 to 1½ cups buttermilk

Preheat oven to 200° F. Heat a griddle over moderate heat until it is hot enough to make drops of water scatter over its surface; brush it with oil. Mix flour, salt, and baking powder together. Add egg and buttermilk to taste. Do not store batter in refrigerator. Spoon batter onto the griddle to form 3-inch rounds, and cook pancakes for 1 to 2 minutes on each side, or until golden. Transfer the pancakes as they are cooked to a heatproof platter, and keep them warm in oven. Yield: 12 to 15 pancakes.

Swedish Oatmeal Pancakes

Serve pancakes with hot cooked apples.

Oil for coating griddle
4 cups oats
1 cup all-purpose flour
¼ cup sugar
2 teaspoons baking soda
2 teaspoons baking powder

Pinch of salt
4 cups (1 quart) buttermilk
4 eggs, beaten
1 stick butter, melted
2 teaspoons vanilla extract

Preheat oven to 200° F. Heat a griddle over moderate heat until it is hot enough to make drops of water scatter over its surface; brush it with oil. Combine oats, flour, sugar, baking soda, baking powder, and salt. Add buttermilk, eggs, butter, and vanilla extract. Let stand at least 30 minutes or refrigerate overnight. Spoon batter onto the griddle to form 3-inch rounds, and cook pancakes for 1 to 2 minutes on each side, or until they are golden. Transfer the pancakes as they are cooked to a heatproof platter, and keep them warm in oven. Yield: 8 servings.

Soups

Pier fishing is a favorite pastime at scenic Sunset Beach.

With great anticipation for a reply from a faraway person,
two children stuff a message in a bottle and prepare to
throw it out to sea.

Spicy Oyster-Artichoke Soup

1 pint fresh oysters
½ cup chopped shallots
1 bay leaf
¼ teaspoon red pepper flakes
Pinch of dried thyme
3 tablespoons margarine
2 tablespoons shake-and-blend flour

1 (14½-ounce) can chicken broth
1 (14-ounce) can artichoke hearts, coarsely chopped
2 tablespoons chopped cilantro
½ teaspoon salt
¼ teaspoon hot pepper sauce
½ cup evaporated skim milk

Drain oysters, reserving liquid. Chop oysters into quarters, and set aside. In a saucepan, sauté shallots, bay leaf, red pepper flakes, and thyme in margarine until shallots are tender. Add flour to shallot mixture, and stir with wire whisk until smooth. Gradually add chicken broth and oyster liquid. Simmer for 15 minutes, stirring occasionally with wire whisk. Remove bay leaf, and discard. Stir in oysters, artichoke hearts, cilantro, salt, and hot pepper sauce; simmer, uncovered, for 10 minutes. Stir in evaporated skim milk, and cook until thoroughly heated. Yield: 4 servings.

Manhattan Clam Chowder

¼ cup diced salt pork
3 onions, diced
4 cups stewed tomatoes with Italian seasoning
2 cups diced (1-inch) potatoes

2 cups boiling water
⅛ teaspoon black pepper
1 pint minced clams (fresh or canned), undrained

In a medium saucepan, brown salt pork at medium heat. Add onions, and stir until browned. Add tomatoes, potatoes, boiling water, and black pepper. Cook until potatoes are tender. Stir in clams and juice, and cook mixture for 5 minutes. Yield: 4 servings.

Beef and Artichoke Stew

1 clove garlic, halved
2 large onions, sliced
4 tablespoons oil
1 cup flour
1½ teaspoons salt
½ teaspoon black pepper
2 pounds beef cubes

½ teaspoon dillweed
1 cup red wine
1 (10¾-ounce) can beef consommé
1 (14-ounce) can artichoke hearts
18 fresh mushrooms
4 tablespoons butter or margarine

In a large saucepan or Dutch oven, heat garlic and onion in oil until soft. Remove from pan, and set aside. In a small bowl, combine flour, salt, and black pepper. Dredge beef cubes in flour mixture; brown cubes in oil. Return onion and garlic to pan; add dillweed, wine, and consommé. Cover tightly, and simmer for 1½ hours, or until meat is tender. Add artichoke hearts, and cook for 10 minutes. Preheat oven to 400° F. In a small skillet, sauté mushrooms in butter; combine mushrooms and stew in a 4-quart casserole dish. Bake, covered, for 30 minutes. Yield: 6 to 8 servings.

Beef Taco Soup

This chunky soup is like a taco in a bowl.

½ pound ground chuck
¼ cup chopped onions
1½ cups water
1 (16-ounce) can stewed tomatoes, undrained
1 (16-ounce) can kidney beans, undrained

1 (8-ounce) can tomato sauce
1 (.5-ounce) envelope taco seasoning
1 avocado, peeled, seeded, and cut into chunks
Shredded Cheddar cheese, sour cream, and corn chips, for garnish

In a large saucepan, cook ground chuck and onion until meat is browned; drain off any excess fat. Add water, tomatoes, kidney beans, tomato sauce, and taco seasoning. Mix well. Simmer, covered, for 15 minutes. Add avocado; cook mixture until avocado is just warm. Ladle soup into bowls. Serve with cheese, sour cream, and corn chips. Freezes well without avocado. Yield: 8 servings.

Chili

Serve chili with corn muffins. This dish can be frozen; reheat and add garnishes before serving.

2 large onions, sliced
1 green pepper, chopped
2 garlic cloves, minced
¼ cup cooking oil
2 pounds ground chuck
1 (16-ounce) can whole tomatoes, chopped, plus liquid
1 (8-ounce) can tomato sauce
1½ teaspoons salt
2 to 4 tablespoons chili powder

1 bay leaf
½ teaspoon red pepper flakes
¾ teaspoon oregano
Dash of paprika
Dash of cayenne pepper
2 (1-pound) cans red kidney beans, drained
Grated Cheddar cheese, chopped onion, and sour cream, for garnish

In a large skillet, sauté onion, pepper, and garlic in oil; remove, using a slotted spoon, to platter. Add ground chuck to skillet, and brown. Drain off fat. Return sautéed vegetables to skillet; then add tomatoes and remaining ingredients. Simmer, covered, for 1½ hours. Serve with Cheddar cheese, onion, and sour cream. Yield: 6 servings.

Bean Pot Soup

2 cups dry small white or great Northern beans
4 quarts water
1 (1-pound) can whole tomatoes
2 cups diced celery
2 carrots, diced
2 potatoes, diced

2 medium onions, chopped
½ cup uncooked rice
4 teaspoons salt
1 teaspoon black pepper
4 beef bouillon cubes
1 to 2 pounds lean ground beef

Wash beans well; drain and place in large kettle. Add 4 quarts water, and bring to boil. Boil 2 minutes; remove from heat, and let stand for 1 hour. Return to heat, and cook until beans are almost tender. Add tomatoes, celery, carrots, potatoes, onions, rice, salt, black pepper, and bouillon cubes. Brown beef in skillet, stirring to keep meat crumbly. Add to bean mixture; cover and simmer for 1 hour or until vegetables are tender. Yield: 10 servings.

Brunswick Stew

1 (5-pound) hen
2½ pounds potatoes
2 pounds onions
2 (1-pound) cans tomatoes, drained
2 cups chicken broth
1 (14-ounce) bottle ketchup
1 (8-ounce) can tomato sauce
2 (16-ounce) cans baby butter
    beans, drained

2 (16-ounce) cans white whole-
    kernel corn, drained
1 (16-ounce) can tiny green peas
½ teaspoon salt
1 teaspoon black pepper
1 tablespoon Worcestershire sauce
1 tablespoon sugar
Saltine crackers (optional)

Cook hen in boiling water until done; pick meat from bones, and set aside. Peel and dice potatoes and onions; chop tomatoes. In a 6-quart pot, cook vegetables in chicken broth until tender. Add remaining ingredients, including chicken. Cook over low to medium heat for 1½ to 2 hours or until thick; stir frequently to prevent sticking. If necessary, thicken stew with crushed crackers. Yield: 12 servings.

Spicy Chicken Taco Soup

This recipe freezes well and can be doubled.

3 chicken breast halves, deboned
1½ cups water
2 tablespoons olive oil
1 (.5-ounce) package taco seasoning
1 onion, chopped
1 clove garlic, minced
1 (8-ounce) can tomato sauce

1 (4-ounce) can green chiles,
    chopped
1 (8-ounce) jar green chile salsa
1 (15-ounce) can black beans, with
    liquid
1 (15-ounce) can pinto beans, with
    liquid
4 ounces grated Cheddar cheese

Cover and cook chicken in water until done; then shred, and set aside. In large skillet, combine olive oil, taco seasoning, onion, and garlic. Sauté until onion is tender. Add shredded chicken, tomato sauce, chiles, salsa, and beans; cook until thoroughly heated. Serve hot with cheese sprinkled over each serving. Yield: 4 servings.

Black-eyed Pea and Ham Stew

*The stew improves in flavor if uncovered and
cooled to room temperature; then covered and chilled
overnight. Heat stew over moderately low heat
until it is hot. Do not let it boil.*

1 pound dried black-eyed peas

1 smoked ham hock, blanched in
boiling water for 2 minutes and
drained

8 cups cold water

1 cup chopped onion

1 cup chopped green bell pepper

1 cup chopped celery

1½ pounds cooked ham, cut into
1½-inch pieces

1 bay leaf

1 tablespoon Worcestershire sauce

2 tablespoons ketchup

2½ tablespoons arrowroot

Salt to taste

Hot pepper sauce to taste

½ cup minced fresh parsley leaves

½ cup thinly sliced scallion greens

4 cups cooked rice

In a kettle, combine black-eyed peas with enough cold water to cover them
by 2 inches. Bring water to a boil, and cook peas for 2 minutes. Remove the
kettle from the heat, and let peas soak for 1 hour. Drain and rinse peas in a
colander, and return them to the kettle. Add ham hock, 8 cups cold water,
onion, green bell pepper, celery, ham, and bay leaf. Bring mixture to a boil,
cover, and simmer for 30 minutes, stirring occasionally. Stir in Worcestershire
sauce and ketchup; simmer for 15 to 20 minutes, or until peas are tender.
Remove kettle from heat. In a small bowl, stir together ½ cup of hot cooking
liquid and arrowroot; stir until arrowroot dissolves. Stir arrowroot mixture into
stew, and cook stew over moderately low heat, stirring for 1 minute, or until
thickened. Do not let the stew boil. Season stew with salt and hot pepper
sauce. Stir in parsley and scallion greens. Discard bay leaf, and serve the stew
with rice. Yield: 6 servings.

Black Bean Chili

This chili can be frozen. After reheating, add garnishes.

1 large onion, chopped
1 tablespoon vegetable oil
1 (28-ounce) can tomatoes, undrained
⅔ cup picante sauce
1½ teaspoons cumin
1 teaspoon salt
½ teaspoon basil
3 (16-ounce) cans black beans, rinsed and drained

1 green bell pepper, cut in ¾-inch pieces
1 red bell pepper, cut in ¾-inch pieces
1 large zucchini or yellow squash, grated (about 2 cups)
Rice, chopped cilantro, sour cream, and shredded cheese, for garnish

In large saucepan, cook onion in vegetable oil until onion is transparent. Add tomatoes, picante sauce, cumin, salt, and basil. Cover and simmer for 15 minutes. Stir in black beans, peppers, and zucchini. Cover and simmer until vegetables are tender. Garnish with rice, cilantro, sour cream, and cheese. Yield: 4 servings.

Sassy Black Bean Soup

1 tablespoon olive oil
1 cup chopped onion
2 small cloves garlic, minced
2 (15-ounce) cans black beans, drained
1 (14½-ounce) can stewed tomatoes, undrained and chopped
1 (10½-ounce) can chicken broth

½ cup commercial picante sauce, mild, medium or hot, as desired
¼ cup water
1 teaspoon cumin
2 tablespoons fresh lime juice
Chopped fresh cilantro and sour cream, for garnish

Heat olive oil in a large nonstick saucepan over medium heat until hot. Add onion and garlic; sauté until tender. Add beans, tomatoes, chicken broth, picante sauce, water, and cumin; stir well. Bring to a boil; reduce heat, and simmer, uncovered, for 15 minutes. Remove from heat; stir in lime juice. Ladle soup into bowls; garnish with cilantro and dollop of sour cream. Yield: 4 servings.

Fiery Three-Bean Vegetarian Chili

*To make chili hotter, add additional cayenne
pepper or hot pepper sauce. To improve flavor,
let chili simmer longer; chili tastes even better
after chilling and reheating.*

1 clove garlic, minced
1 large onion, finely chopped
1 medium green bell pepper, finely
  chopped
1 tablespoon vegetable oil
4 tablespoons chili powder
1 tablespoon cider vinegar
¼ teaspoon allspice
¼ teaspoon coriander
1 teaspoon cumin
½ teaspoon salt, or to taste

2 cups canned crushed tomatoes,
  with liquid
1 (16-ounce) can red kidney beans,
  with liquid
1 (16-ounce) can garbanzo beans,
  drained
1 (16-ounce) can pinto beans, with
  liquid
Cayenne pepper or hot pepper
  sauce to taste
Cooked white or brown rice

In a Dutch oven, sauté garlic, onion, and green bell pepper in oil over medium heat until soft but not browned. Add remaining ingredients, except rice.
Bring to a boil. Cover and reduce heat. Simmer chili for 45 minutes, stirring
frequently. Serve over rice. Yield: 6 to 8 servings.

Cream of Broccoli Soup

This recipe is better when made a day ahead, cooled, and stored in the refrigerator. Reheat before serving.

1½ quarts chicken broth
1 (10-ounce) package frozen chopped broccoli
1 cup finely chopped onion
2 teaspoons salt
2 teaspoons monosodium glutamate, if desired
2 teaspoons white pepper

1 teaspoon garlic powder
8 ounces shredded American cheese or mild Cheddar cheese
1½ cups whole milk
½ cup cream
4 tablespoons butter
½ cup cold water
⅓ cup all-purpose flour

In large saucepan, bring chicken broth to a boil. Add broccoli and onion, and boil for 12 minutes. Add seasonings and shredded cheese; stir until cheese melts. Add milk, cream, and butter; stir and heat to boiling. In another pan over medium heat, slowly add cold water to flour, and stir constantly until mixture is smooth and the consistency of heavy cream. Add flour mixture to soup. Yield: 8 to 10 servings.

Mexican Corn Chowder

3 cups corn kernels
1 cup water
2 tablespoons butter
1 cup minced onions
2 cloves garlic, minced
½ cup cilantro
2 cups chopped tomatoes
3⅓ cups milk

1 teaspoon hot pepper sauce
¼ teaspoon black pepper
1 teaspoon cumin
½ pound Monterey Jack or Cheddar cheese, shredded, for garnish
3 tablespoons diced green chiles, for garnish

Blend corn and water in a food processor or blender to make a coarse purée. Melt the butter in a large saucepan. Add onion and garlic; sauté until soft and translucent. Add corn purée, cilantro, and tomatoes; cook over medium heat for 5 minutes, stirring occasionally. Add milk and seasonings. Gently heat through, but do not allow to simmer. To serve, sprinkle with cheese and chiles. Yield: 6 to 8 servings.

Gazpacho

4 large ripe tomatoes
2½ cucumbers, divided
1 large green bell pepper
10 to 12 scallions
1 to 2 cloves garlic
1 teaspoon salt
¼ cup red wine vinegar
⅓ cup olive oil

3 cups tomato juice
1 to 1½ cups beef broth or water
Hot pepper sauce to taste
Worcestershire sauce to taste
Salt and freshly ground black
  pepper
Plain croutons for garnish

Peel, seed, and dice tomatoes and 2 cucumbers into ¼-inch pieces. Wash and trim green bell pepper and scallions, and dice into ¼-inch pieces. Set aside vegetables. With mortar and pestle, mash garlic and salt; transfer garlic mixture to a small bowl. Beat in wine vinegar and olive oil. Combine this dressing with chopped vegetables, and stir in tomato juice. Add broth to the consistency you prefer. Season with hot pepper sauce, Worcestershire sauce, salt, and pepper. Chill. Slice remaining ½ cucumber paper-thin. Serve gazpacho in chilled bowls topped with cucumber slices and garnished with croutons. Yield: 4 to 6 servings.

Fresh Mushroom Soup

1 pound fresh mushrooms, sliced
2 tablespoons butter, melted
2 tablespoons flour
4 cups chicken stock

¼ cup dry sherry
Salt and black pepper, to taste
Chopped fresh parsley, for garnish

Place mushrooms in soup pot (without water or oil). Cover and cook over very low heat for 15 minutes or until only small amount of liquid remains. Add melted butter, and sprinkle with flour. Cook, stirring constantly, for a few minutes longer. Slowly add chicken stock, stirring constantly. Simmer for 10 minutes.

With slotted spoon, remove mushrooms, and transfer to blender or food processor. If preferred, do not process all mushrooms. Add sherry, blending until nearly smooth. If needed, add ¼ cup soup liquid to blender to achieve a smooth purée. Stir puréed (and sliced) mushrooms into soup, reheat, and serve. Season with salt and pepper. Yield: 6 servings.

Creamy Mushroom Soup

1 pound fresh mushrooms	3½ cups chicken broth
1 teaspoon lemon juice	3½ cups water
1 stick butter or margarine	1 teaspoon salt
1 small onion, sliced	¼ teaspoon white pepper
⅓ cup all-purpose flour	1 cup heavy cream

Remove mushroom stems and save. Slice caps thinly; set aside. In 4-quart saucepan, cook mushrooms, lemon juice, and butter until just tender. Remove mushrooms, and cook stems and onions until onions are tender. Stir in flour until blended, and cook 1 minute. Gradually add broth and water; stir until thick. Purée this mixture in blender, and then return mixture to saucepan. Stir in seasonings, cream, and mushroom slices. Reheat to boiling. Yield: 6 servings.

French Onion Soup with Grated Cheese

4 tablespoons butter	3 quarts beef stock, warmed
2 tablespoons vegetable oil	½ cup dry vermouth
2 pounds white onions, thinly sliced	8 slices French bread
1 tablespoon salt	Olive oil for brushing bread
1 tablespoon sugar	Garlic clove, halved
3 tablespoons flour	Grated Swiss cheese, for garnish

In 5-quart pot, melt butter and oil. Stir in onions, salt, and sugar; cook, uncovered, over low heat for 30 minutes or until onions are a rich golden color. Sprinkle flour over onions, and cook, stirring constantly, for 2 to 3 minutes. Remove from heat. Stir in stock and vermouth. Cook, partially covered, for 30 to 40 minutes.

Preheat oven to 300° F. Brush French bread with olive oil, and rub with garlic half. Bake 10 minutes per side. Increase oven heat to 375° F. Pour soup into ovenproof serving bowls. Place bread slices on top. Sprinkle Swiss cheese generously over soup and bread. Bake until cheese melts and browns. Yield: 8 to 10 servings.

Potato Bacon Soup

4 cups peeled, cubed potatoes
1 cup ½-inch-thick celery slices
1 cup chopped onion
2 cups water
1 teaspoon salt
1 cup milk

1 cup cream
3 tablespoons butter or margarine
1 tablespoon dried parsley flakes
⅛ teaspoon black pepper
6 slices bacon, fried until crisp and
  crumbled for garnish

Combine potatoes, celery, onion, water, and salt in large pot. Cover and simmer about 20 minutes or until potatoes are tender. Mash mixture a few times with a potato masher, leaving some vegetable pieces whole. Stir in milk, cream, butter, parsley, and black pepper; return to heat. Stir constantly until hot. Serve in bowls, and garnish with crumbled bacon. Yield: 4 servings.

Potato Bean Soup

Carrots give this light soup a beautiful golden color.

½ cup sliced celery
2 medium carrots, shredded
1 clove garlic, minced
2 teaspoons margarine, melted
4 cups chicken broth
3 medium potatoes, peeled and
  diced
2 tablespoons snipped fresh dill or 2
  teaspoons dried dillweed

1 (15-ounce) can cannellini beans
  or great Northern beans, drained
½ cup low-calorie dairy sour cream
  or plain nonfat yogurt
1 tablespoon all-purpose flour
⅛ teaspoon black pepper
Salt to taste

In a large saucepan, cook celery, carrots, and garlic in hot margarine over medium heat for 4 minutes or until tender; stir often. Carefully stir in broth, potatoes, and dill. Heat to boiling; reduce heat, and simmer, covered, for 20 to 25 minutes or until potatoes are tender. With the back of a spoon, lightly mash about half the potatoes. Add beans to potato mixture.

In a small bowl, stir together sour cream, flour, black pepper, and salt; stir into potato mixture. Cook, stirring, until thickened and bubbly. Cook 1 additional minute. Yield: 4 to 6 servings.

Rich Swiss Potato Soup

12 slices bacon, coarsely chopped
1 onion, coarsely chopped
2 leeks (or 4 scallions), coarsely
  chopped
1 pound cabbage, coarsely chopped
4 potatoes, peeled and diced

6 cups chicken stock
2 cups Gruyère cheese, grated
1 cup light cream
1 tablespoon dillweed
Salt and black pepper to taste
Buttered croutons, for garnish

Sauté bacon in large kettle for 3 minutes. Drain. Add onion, leeks, and cabbage; cook 5 minutes. Add potatoes and chicken stock; bring to a boil, lower heat, and simmer, uncovered, for 40 minutes. Pour mixture into blender a little at a time, and blend until smooth; return mixture to kettle. Gradually add cheese, and stir over medium heat until melted. Do not boil. Just before serving, add cream, dillweed, salt, and black pepper. Serve with buttered croutons. Yield: 10 to 12 servings.

Squash Soup

*Soup may be made a day ahead and
reheated before serving.*

3 medium squash, sliced
1 chicken bouillon cube
¾ cup water
1 pint half-and-half

1 teaspoon salt
1 cup grated sharp Cheddar cheese
Squash slices for garnish

Cook squash and bouillon cube in water until squash is tender. Pour mixture into blender, and purée. Return to saucepan, and add half-and-half, salt, and cheese. Heat until hot, but do not boil. Garnish with squash slices. Yield: 5 to 6 appetizer servings.

Cream of Butternut Squash Soup with Cranberry Port Purée

If chilled and covered, the soup will keep for 1 day, and the purée for 3 days.

1 large onion, chopped
2 carrots, thinly sliced
½ cup unsalted butter
½ teaspoon ground mace
½ teaspoon ground ginger
½ teaspoon allspice
¼ teaspoon ground cinnamon

½ teaspoon white pepper
3 pounds butternut squash, seeded, peeled, and cut into 1-inch pieces
2 sweet potatoes (about 1¼ pounds), peeled, and cut into 1-inch pieces
6 cups chicken broth, divided
Cranberry Port Purée

In a large heavy saucepan, cook onion and carrots in butter over low heat. Stir occasionally until onion is softened. Add mace, ginger, allspice, cinnamon, and white pepper; stir well. Add squash, sweet potatoes, and 4 cups of broth. Simmer, covered, for 30 minutes or until vegetables are very soft. In a blender or food processor, process soup in batches, transferring it into a saucepan as it is processed. Stir in remaining 2 cups broth. Adjust seasonings as necessary. Place in individual bowls, and pipe 1 tablespoon cranberry port purée decoratively onto each serving.

Cranberry Port Purée:
1 (12-ounce) bag cranberries
1 cup Ruby Port wine

½ cup sugar

In a heavy saucepan, combine all ingredients. Simmer mixture, stirring occasionally for 7 to 10 minutes, or until cranberries burst and mixture starts to thicken. In a food processor, purée mixture, and force purée through a fine sieve into a bowl, discarding solids. Spoon purée into a pastry bag fitted with a small plain tip. Yield: 8 to 12 servings.

Tomato Herb Soup

1 large onion, chopped
1 stick butter
½ cup all-purpose flour
2 cups milk
2 cups chicken stock
⅓ cup chopped parsley
⅓ cup chopped fresh basil

8 to 10 fresh tomatoes, peeled,
  seeded, and chopped
1 (46-ounce) can tomato juice
Salt and freshly ground black
  pepper to taste
Shredded Parmesan cheese for
  garnish

Sauté onion in butter in a large skillet. Add flour, stirring constantly. Cook slowly; add milk and chicken stock. Stir in parsley and basil. Place mixture in large stockpot; blend with tomatoes and tomato juice. Heat to boiling; add salt and pepper to taste. Garnish with shredded Parmesan cheese and serve piping hot. Yield: 8 servings.

Zucchini Soup

2 pounds zucchini, thinly sliced
½ cup chopped onion
1½ tablespoons butter
2 cups chicken broth

½ teaspoon curry powder
½ teaspoon lemon juice
Sour cream and chives (optional)

In covered saucepan, sauté zucchini over medium heat with chopped onion and butter. In a separate saucepan, heat chicken broth. Pour broth into a bowl; add curry powder, and lemon juice. Place 1 cup zucchini mixture and 1 cup broth at a time into blender; purée for 1 minute. Repeat until all is blended. Reheat and add salt to taste. Serve hot or cold. Garnish with sour cream and chives, if desired. Yield: 6 servings.

Chilled Nectarine Soup

3½ pounds fresh, semi-ripe
  nectarines, peeled, pitted, and
  thinly sliced
½ cup sugar
3 cups water

2 cups white wine
2 teaspoons vanilla extract
Plain yogurt for garnish
8 fresh mint leaves for garnish

In a large, heavy saucepan, combine nectarines and sugar. Add water, wine, and vanilla extract; bring mixture to a simmer, and cook for about 12 minutes or until nectarines are tender but not mushy. Pour soup into a large bowl, and let cool. Cover with plastic wrap, and chill for at least 3 hours. To serve, ladle soup into bowls, spoon a dollop of yogurt on each serving, and garnish each serving with a mint leaf. Yield: 8 servings.

Cold Strawberry Cream Soup

2 pints fresh strawberries, stemmed
  and washed
2 cups white wine
2 cups water
⅔ cup sugar

2 tablespoons lemon juice
2 tablespoons cornstarch, mixed
  with 2 tablespoons cold water
3 teaspoons grated lemon zest
⅓ cup sour cream

Remove 8 strawberries, and set aside. Slice remaining berries, and place in a large saucepan with wine and water. Simmer, covered, for 10 minutes. Add sugar, lemon juice, and cornstarch mixture. Bring to a boil, and stir until thickened. Stir in lemon zest and sour cream. In batches, transfer mixture to a blender, blend until smooth, and pour into a stainless-steel saucepan. Cook soup, taste for sugar, and chill thoroughly. To serve, ladle soup into glass soup bowls, and top each portion with a whole strawberry. Yield: 8 servings.

Salads

*Colorful foliage and equally colorful roadside
produce stands make the North Carolina mountains
a popular autumn travel destination.*

Two young sports fans savor delicious apples from North Carolina's mountain orchards.

Shrimp Salad

1 cup shrimp, cooked, peeled, and
  deveined
1 cup chopped celery
1 teaspoon lemon juice
Dash of garlic salt
Dash of celery seed

½ cup mayonnaise
1 medium potato, boiled, peeled,
  and chopped
1 hard-boiled egg, grated
Salt to taste
Lettuce leaves

Mix shrimp and remaining ingredients, except lettuce leaves. Chill. Serve salad on lettuce leaves. Yield: 4 servings.

Chicken and Apricot Salad
with Double Mustard Mayonnaise

3 pounds chicken, cooked
1 cup dried apricots, cut in ¼-inch
  strips
⅓ cup sherry
3 celery stalks, chopped
4 scallions, sliced diagonally

1 cup chopped pecans
1 tablespoon fresh rosemary, or
  more, to taste
Double Mustard Mayonnaise
Fresh apricots and rosemary for
  garnish

Remove bones from chicken and cut it into 2x¾-inch strips. Place apricots and sherry in a small saucepan. Simmer for 3 to 4 minutes, and add to chicken. Stir in celery, scallions, pecans, and rosemary. Toss to combine. Mix Double Mustard Mayonnaise with salad. Garnish with fresh apricots and rosemary. Serve chilled.

Double Mustard Mayonnaise:

2 egg yolks or 4 tablespoons egg
  substitute
2 tablespoons fresh lemon juice
2 tablespoons Dijon mustard

¾ cup vegetable oil
⅔ cup olive oil
¼ cup honey mustard
Salt and black pepper to taste

In a food processor, place egg yolks, lemon juice, and Dijon mustard; blend well. With machine running, add oils in a steady stream, and blend mixture until thick. Add honey mustard, and season with salt and pepper. Yield: 6 to 8 servings.

Steak, Mushroom, and Hearts of Palm Salad with Béarnaise Mayonnaise

1 (3-pound) boneless top round steak, 2 to 2½ inches thick
1 tablespoon dried mustard
Salt and freshly ground black pepper to taste
1 bunch scallions, sliced
12 ounces fresh mushrooms, sliced

1 (14-ounce) can hearts of palm, drained and sliced into ½-inch slices
½ cup chopped fresh parsley
Béarnaise Mayonnaise
Sliced tomato and fresh tarragon for garnish

Preheat broiler. Rub steak with dried mustard. Sprinkle steak generously with salt and pepper. Broil steak about 6 inches from the heat, turning once until cooked medium rare. Let cool several minutes; then cut steak into thin strips, 2½ to 3 inches long. Combine steak, scallions, mushrooms, hearts of palm, and parsley in a mixing bowl. Add the béarnaise mayonnaise. Refrigerate from 2 to 12 hours. Garnish with tomato and tarragon before serving.

Béarnaise Mayonnaise:
3 shallots, peeled and minced
2½ tablespoons dried tarragon
½ cup dry white wine
¼ cup tarragon vinegar
2 egg yolks or 4 tablespoons egg substitute

2 tablespoons fresh lemon juice
1 tablespoon Dijon mustard
½ cup olive oil
1 cup vegetable oil
Salt and freshly ground black pepper to taste

Place shallots, tarragon, wine, and vinegar in a small saucepan. Cook over high heat until mixture is reduced to 1 tablespoon; set aside. Place egg yolks, lemon juice, and Dijon mustard in a food processor with steel blade. Process 10 seconds. Add oils, pouring in a steady stream, until mixed well. Add shallot mixture, salt, and black pepper, and process to blend. Yield: 8 servings.

Chicken and Artichoke Salad

1 cup cubed cooked chicken
1½ cups cooked white rice
1 (16-ounce) can artichoke hearts,
  drained and chopped

¼ cup chopped scallion
¼ cup chopped fresh parsley
2 tablespoons dry tarragon
Dressing

Combine chicken, rice, artichoke hearts, scallion, parsley, and tarragon in a medium bowl. Pour dressing over chicken mixture, and blend well. Refrigerate for 8 hours or overnight. Serve cold.

Dressing:
1 teaspoon salt
⅛ teaspoon black pepper
Dash of cayenne pepper

3 tablespoons red wine vinegar
½ cup vegetable oil
¼ teaspoon paprika

Combine all ingredients in a jar. Shake well to blend. Yield: 4 servings.

Carousel Mandarin Chicken Salad

This salad is great for a luncheon or
light summer supper!

2 to 3 cups diced cooked chicken
1 cup diced celery
2 tablespoons lemon juice
1 tablespoon minced onion
1 teaspoon salt
⅓ cup mayonnaise

1 cup seedless green grapes
1 (11-ounce) can mandarin oranges,
  drained
½ cup toasted slivered almonds
Lettuce leaves

Combine chicken, celery, lemon juice, onion, and salt, and chill overnight. Before serving, add remaining ingredients, except lettuce leaves, and mix well. Serve on lettuce leaves. Yield: 4 to 6 servings.

Chicken Salad with Pecans

4 cups diced cooked chicken
(white meat only)
2 cups diced celery
1 cup mayonnaise
½ cup sour cream
2 tablespoons fresh lemon juice

Salt and freshly ground black
pepper to taste
½ cup toasted chopped pecans
4 slices bacon, cooked crisp and
crumbled
Fresh parsley sprigs

Mix together chicken, celery, mayonnaise, sour cream, lemon juice, salt, and black pepper; chill well. Just before serving, stir in pecans. Top each serving with bacon, and garnish with parsley sprigs. Yield: 6 to 8 servings.

Club Chicken Salad

3 pounds chicken breasts
Salt to taste
3 cups cubed Italian bread (¾-inch
cubes)
3 tablespoons olive oil
6 slices lean bacon, chopped
½ cup mayonnaise

½ clove garlic, minced and mashed
to a paste
1 teaspoon dried basil leaves
Salt and freshly ground black
pepper to taste
1 pint cherry tomatoes, quartered
4 scallions, minced

In a large saucepan, combine chicken breasts with enough cold water to cover them by 1 inch. Remove chicken, bring water to a boil, and add salt to taste. Return chicken to the pan, and poach at a bare simmer for 17 minutes. Remove pan from the heat, let chicken cool in liquid for thirty minutes, and drain. Discard the skin and bones. Cut meat into bite-size pieces.

Preheat oven to 350° F. In a bowl, drizzle bread cubes with oil, tossing to coat evenly; season with salt. Spread bread cubes in a jellyroll pan, and toast in the middle of oven for 15 to 20 minutes, or until golden. Remove from oven, and let cool.

Cook bacon in a small skillet over moderate heat, stirring until crisp. With a slotted spoon, transfer bacon to paper towels to drain. In a small bowl, combine mayonnaise, garlic, and basil. Season mixture with salt and black pepper. In a large bowl, combine chicken, tomatoes, scallions, two-thirds of the bacon, mayonnaise, and additional salt and pepper to taste. Divide the salad among 6 plates. Garnish each plate with croutons and remaining bacon. Yield: 6 servings.

Dijon Chicken and Rice Salad

*This salad tastes best when allowed to
warm to room temperature.*

3¾ cups water
1½ cups long grain rice
½ teaspoon salt
2 tablespoons Dijon mustard
2 tablespoons white wine vinegar
¼ cup olive oil

½ to 1 cup diced red, green, and
  yellow peppers
¼ cup pitted black olives, sliced
¼ cup chopped scallions
2 poached chicken breast halves,
  diced, or 1 (8-ounce) can chicken

In a medium saucepan, bring water to a boil. Add rice and salt; reduce heat, cover, and simmer 20 to 25 minutes or until water is absorbed. Place rice on a jellyroll pan to air dry for 10 to 15 minutes; then place rice in a bowl. Combine mustard, vinegar, and olive oil; mix into rice. Add peppers, olives, scallions, and chicken. Combine thoroughly. May be refrigerated for several days. Yield: 6 servings.

Greek Chicken Salad

4 chicken breast halves, skinned and
  deboned
2 medium cucumbers, peeled,
  seeded, and chopped
4 ounces Feta cheese, crumbled
1 (3.8-ounce) can sliced black
  olives, drained

8 tablespoons chopped parsley
½ cup light mayonnaise
½ cup low-fat yogurt
2 tablespoons oregano leaves
⅛ teaspoon garlic powder

In a saucepan, cover chicken with cold water seasoned to taste. Bring to a boil, remove from heat, and cool completely in broth. Drain broth, and cut chicken into ½- to 1-inch pieces; set aside. Combine remaining ingredients in a large bowl; mix well. Toss in chicken. Chill thoroughly. Yield: 6 servings.

Chicken and Spinach Pasta

12 ounces twist pasta
⅛ cup sesame seeds
¼ cup canola oil
⅓ cup soy sauce
⅓ cup white wine vinegar
2 tablespoons sugar

½ tablespoon salt
½ tablespoon black pepper
3 cups chopped cooked chicken
½ cup chopped scallions
8 cups torn fresh spinach
¼ cup fresh parsley, chopped

Cook pasta according to package directions. Rinse, drain, and set aside in a large bowl. Cook sesame seeds and oil in saucepan until golden; combine with soy sauce, wine vinegar, sugar, salt, and black pepper. Pour mixture over pasta. Add chicken, and toss well. Cover and chill 6 hours. Before serving, toss with scallions, spinach, and parsley. Yield: 6 servings.

Cold Chinese Noodles

4 chicken breast halves, skinned and deboned
Salt and black pepper to taste
1 to 2 pounds angel hair pasta, cooked and cooled
2 bunches scallions, chopped
2½ tablespoons sesame oil
¾ cup vegetable oil

2 tablespoons sesame seeds
3 tablespoons ground coriander seeds
¾ cup soy sauce
1 teaspoon chile oil (or to taste)
5 ounces smoked ham, cut into strips
1 cup chopped pecans

In a saucepan, cover chicken with cold water seasoned to taste. Bring to a boil, remove from heat, and cool completely in broth. Drain broth, and cut chicken into strips. Combine chicken and pasta in a large bowl. Mix well. Add scallions; set aside.

In a saucepan, heat sesame oil and vegetable oil. Add sesame seeds and cook until sesame seeds turn a light brown. Remove from heat. Stir in coriander and soy sauce. Add chile oil. Pour dressing over pasta, and mix well. Add ham and pecans. Refrigerate until chilled. Yield: 8 to 10 servings.

Festive Pasta Salad

*This salad is a great mid-summer dish. Use vegetables
fresh from your garden.*

1 pound multicolored rotini
1 bunch broccoli, separated into
   flowerets
1 (4-ounce) jar sun-dried tomatoes
2 red bell peppers, julienned
1 green bell pepper, julienned
2 medium zucchini, diced

8 ounces mozzarella cheese,
   julienned
1 cup grated Parmesan cheese
1 (4-ounce) jar diced pimientos,
   drained
Dressing

Cook rotini according to package directions; rinse in cold water, and set
aside.

Blanch broccoli in boiling water for 3 minutes. Drain and rinse with cold
water. Drain sun-dried tomatoes, and reserve oil; set tomatoes aside. In a
saucepan, sauté the red and green bell peppers in the oil from tomatoes; add
the zucchini. In a serving bowl, toss the rotini, broccoli, peppers, zucchini,
mozzarella, Parmesan cheese, sun-dried tomatoes, and pimientos. Add
dressing, and mix well.

Dressing:
4 cloves garlic
1½ cup olive oil
½ cup red wine vinegar

1 tablespoon Dijon mustard
Salt, black pepper, and basil to taste

Finely chop garlic cloves; whisk together with oil, vinegar, mustard, salt,
pepper, and basil.

Pasta Salad with Walnut Dijon Vinaigrette

Recipe can be halved.

Salad:

1 pound spinach pasta, various shapes

1 pound egg pasta, various shapes

1 bunch broccoli, separated into flowerets

1 pound mushrooms, sliced

2 yellow squash, sliced

2 zucchini squash, sliced

½ (6-ounce) bag radishes, sliced

½ pound green beans, steamed

Walnut Dijon Vinaigrette

1 cup freshly grated Parmesan cheese

1 pound bacon, cooked crisp and crumbled

1½ cups walnuts, coarsely chopped

Lettuce leaves (optional)

Cook pasta in boiling salted water until al dente. Drain and cool. In a large bowl, combine cooled pasta with all the vegetables. Pour half of the vinaigrette over salad, and toss well. Refrigerate 6 to 8 hours or overnight. Before serving, add Parmesan cheese, bacon, walnuts, and additional vinaigrette to taste. Add more salt if seasoning is needed. Serve salad on lettuce leaves, if desired.

Walnut Dijon Vinaigrette:

2 tablespoons minced garlic

½ cup Dijon mustard

1 cup red wine vinegar

2 teaspoons salt

1 teaspoon freshly ground black pepper

1½ cups walnut oil

Process garlic, mustard, vinegar, salt, and black pepper in a blender. Gradually add walnut oil, and process until oil is well blended. Refrigerate. Yield: 24 servings.

Tabbouleh with Feta Cheese

1 pound bulgur wheat
¾ cup fresh lemon juice, plus
  additional to taste
3 cups hot water
2 medium cucumbers, chopped very
  small
4 ripe medium tomatoes, chopped
  very small
1 clove garlic, minced

½ medium red onion, minced
1½ bunches parsley, finely chopped
2 tablespoons fresh mint, minced
1 cup crumbled Feta cheese
¾ cup olive oil
Salt and freshly ground black
  pepper to taste
Pita bread

Place the bulgur in a large mixing bowl. Add lemon juice and hot water. Let stand until the bulgur is tender, 30 to 40 minutes. Drain off any excess liquid.

Add the cucumbers, tomatoes, garlic, onion, parsley, mint, and Feta cheese to the bulgur; toss to combine. Dress with enough olive oil and additional lemon juice to make salad moist but not runny. Season with salt and black pepper. Refrigerate salad for several hours. Serve cold or at room temperature with pita bread. Yield: 8 to 10 servings.

Oriental Slaw

1 (3-ounce) package chicken-
  flavored ramen noodles
6 cups shredded cabbage
4 scallions, chopped
½ cup toasted sunflower seeds
½ cup toasted sliced almonds

½ cup vegetable oil
3 tablespoons white vinegar
2 tablespoons sugar
½ teaspoon salt
½ teaspoon black pepper

Remove and retain seasoning packet from noodles. Crush noodles with rolling pin. Combine noodles, cabbage, scallions, sunflower seeds, and almonds. For dressing, combine contents of seasoning packet with remaining ingredients. Whisk and pour over salad. Cover and chill for at least 3 hours or overnight. Yield: 6 servings.

Fireworks Coleslaw

½ pound white cabbage, cored and
thinly sliced (about 4 cups)

½ pound red cabbage, cored and
thinly sliced (about 4 cups)

1 red bell pepper, thinly sliced

1 yellow bell pepper, thinly sliced

1 green bell pepper, thinly sliced

1 4-inch green hot chile pepper,
seeded and thinly sliced (wear
rubber gloves)

1 carrot, thinly sliced lengthwise
with a vegetable peeler

1 scallion, thinly sliced

3 tablespoons minced fresh parsley
leaves

2 tablespoons snipped fresh dill

Dressing

Salt and black pepper to taste

In a large serving bowl, combine cabbages, bell peppers, chile pepper, carrot, scallion, parsley, and dill. (The vegetables may be prepared up to 3 days in advance, covered, and chilled.)

Just before serving, pour dressing over the vegetables. Toss coleslaw until it is well combined. Season with salt and black pepper.

Dressing:

1 small clove garlic

1 teaspoon caraway seeds

½ teaspoon ground cumin

½ cup sour cream

½ cup plain yogurt

In a blender or food processor, blend garlic and caraway seeds until the garlic is minced and the seeds are ground. Add cumin, sour cream, and yogurt. Blend until well combined. (The dressing may be made up to 3 days in advance and kept covered and chilled.) Yield: 10 to 12 servings.

Waldorf Coleslaw

4 cups coarsely shredded cabbage

2 cups chopped apple

1 cup sliced celery

1 cup chopped toasted walnuts

¼ cup lemon or lime juice, bottled

3 tablespoons honey

2 tablespoons water

1 tablespoon vegetable oil

1 teaspoon Dijon mustard

1 teaspoon garlic salt

Ingredients may be chopped in a food processor. In medium bowl, combine cabbage, apple, celery, and walnuts. In small bowl, combine remaining ingredients; mix well. Pour over cabbage mixture. Cover and chill for 4 hours to blend flavors. Yield: 6 to 8 servings.

Broccoli Refrigerator Slaw

Slaw keeps up to 10 days in refrigerator.

1 large head green cabbage, grated, or 1 (16-ounce) package broccoli, carrot, and red cabbage mix
2 medium onions, sliced
¾ cup sugar, or more, to taste
1 cup white vinegar

2 teaspoons sugar
¾ cup vegetable oil
1 teaspoon dry mustard
1 teaspoon celery seed
1 tablespoon salt

Alternate cabbage and sliced onions in large bowl. Pour ¾ cup sugar over slaw. In a small saucepan, bring vinegar and remaining ingredients to a boil; pour over cabbage. Cool and then refrigerate overnight before serving. Yield: 6 to 8 servings.

Black-Eyed Pea and Cabbage Slaw

Peas may be cooked 2 days in advance and kept covered and chilled. Slaw may be made 1 day in advance and kept covered and chilled.

1½ cups dried black-eyed peas, picked over
1 bay leaf
2 parsley sprigs
¼ cup white wine vinegar
3 tablespoons Dijon mustard
⅓ cup drained bottled horseradish
Salt and black pepper to taste
¾ cup vegetable oil

1 2½ to 3 pound cabbage, coarsely grated in a food processor (about 10 cups)
6 carrots, coarsely grated in a food processor (about 4 cups)
½ cup minced scallion
2 large garlic cloves, minced
1 cup minced parsley leaves
Salt and black pepper to taste

Soak peas overnight in enough water to cover by 2 inches. Drain peas and rinse. In a large saucepan, simmer peas, bay leaf, and parsley sprigs in enough water to cover by 2 inches until tender, about 25 minutes. Drain peas and discard bay leaf and parsley sprigs. In a large bowl, whisk together vinegar, mustard, horseradish, salt, and black pepper. Add oil in a stream, whisking until dressing is emulsified. Add peas, cabbage, carrots, scallions, garlic, minced parsley, salt, and black pepper; toss well. Yield: 12 servings.

Bacon Cauliflower Salad

1 large head iceberg lettuce
1 cauliflower
1 large Bermuda onion, sliced and
  broken into rings
1 pound bacon, cooked crisp and
  crumbled

⅓ cup Parmesan cheese
2 cups mayonnaise
½ cup sugar
Salt and black pepper to taste

Wash, drain, and tear lettuce into bite-size pieces. Place in large bowl. Cut up cauliflower, and toss with lettuce. Add layer of onions, and top with bacon. Set aside or refrigerate.

When ready to serve, mix together mayonnaise, sugar, salt, and black pepper. Add to lettuce mixture, and toss. Yield: 12 to 14 servings.

Greek Salad

For a larger crowd, double the recipe.

1 medium head romaine lettuce
1 pound spinach
½ pound Greek olives
½ pound cherry tomatoes

2 medium cucumbers, peeled,
  sliced, and halved
Pepperoncinis, to taste
½ pound Feta cheese, crumbled
Dressing

Wash and dry lettuce and spinach; tear into bite-size pieces. Toss with remaining ingredients, except dressing. Garnish with additional Feta cheese, if desired, and top with dressing.

Dressing:
½ teaspoon salt
1 teaspoon sugar
4 tablespoons lemon juice

½ cup olive oil
1 clove garlic, crushed
Dash of oregano

Whisk together all ingredients until well blended. Yield: 6 servings.

Caesar Salad

1 clove garlic
¾ cup extra-virgin olive oil, divided
1 head iceberg lettuce
1 head romaine lettuce
¼ cup shredded Parmesan cheese
¼ cup crumbled blue cheese
1 tablespoon Worcestershire sauce

¾ teaspoon salt
¼ teaspoon freshly ground black
   pepper
¼ cup egg substitute
¼ cup fresh lemon juice
2 cups herb-seasoned croutons
Diced anchovies to taste (optional)

The day before serving, peel and quarter garlic, drop into ¼ cup olive oil, cover, and refrigerate. Wash lettuces; pat dry, or dry in lettuce spinner. Refrigerate in plastic bag.

About fifteen minutes before serving, tear greens into bite-size pieces, and place in a large bowl. Sprinkle greens with cheeses. In measuring cup, combine ½ cup olive oil, Worcestershire sauce, salt, and black pepper. Drizzle over greens. Toss mixture gently until every leaf glistens. Top with egg substitute, and pour on lemon juice; toss well.

Place seasoned croutons in a medium bowl. Remove garlic from olive oil, and pour oil over croutons. Toss well; then sprinkle over greens. Toss in anchovies, if desired. Serve immediately. Yield: 8 to 10 servings.

Garden Green Italian Salad

Salad:

1 medium head iceberg lettuce
1 medium head romaine lettuce
1 cup canned artichoke hearts,
  drained and halved

1 medium red onion, sliced thin
½ to ¾ cup grated Parmesan cheese
Dressing

In serving bowl, tear lettuces into bite-size pieces. Add artichokes and red onion. Sprinkle with Parmesan cheese. Pour dressing over all, and toss until dressing coats greens. Chill at least 15 to 20 minutes before serving.

Dressing:

¾ cup olive oil
½ cup red wine vinegar
2 cloves minced garlic

⅓ small red onion, grated
1 (4-ounce) jar diced pimientos

Mix olive oil, wine vinegar, garlic, red onion, and pimientos in a jar. Shake well. Dressing keeps in refrigerator for 6 weeks. Yield: 6 servings.

Spinach Salad

Salad:

2 pounds spinach
Lettuce, if desired
2 cups water chestnuts, sliced
4 hard-boiled eggs, sliced
1 large red onion, sliced

1 pound bacon, cooked crisp and
  crumbled
1 cup fresh bean sprouts, or 1
  (8-ounce) can bean sprouts,
  drained
Dressing

Tear spinach and lettuce into bite-size pieces, and place in a salad bowl. Add remaining ingredients and enough dressing to coat leaves. Toss well, and serve with remaining refrigerated dressing.

Dressing:

1 cup salad or olive oil
¾ cup sugar
½ cup red wine vinegar

2 teaspoons salt
⅓ cup ketchup
1 teaspoon Worcestershire sauce

Whisk all ingredients together. Refrigerate. Yield: 8 servings.

Spinach-Romaine Company Salad

½ head romaine lettuce, torn into bite-size pieces

6 hard-cooked eggs, sliced

1 cup (4-ounces) shredded Swiss cheese, divided

1 pound fresh spinach, torn into bite-size pieces

1 (10-ounce) package frozen baby English peas, thawed and drained

1 small red onion, thinly sliced and separated into rings

1 pound bacon, cooked crisp and crumbled

1 cup mayonnaise

1 cup salad dressing

1 teaspoon sugar

1 cup (4-ounces) shredded Cheddar cheese

In a 13x9x2-inch dish, layer romaine lettuce, eggs, ¼ cup Swiss cheese, spinach, ¼ cup Swiss cheese, peas, ¼ cup Swiss cheese, red onion, ¼ cup Swiss cheese, and bacon. Combine mayonnaise, salad dressing, and sugar in small bowl; mix well. Spread dressing over top of salad, and seal to edge of dish. Sprinkle with Cheddar cheese. Cover tightly, and refrigerate several hours or overnight. To serve, cut salad into squares or toss together before serving. Yield: 12 servings.

Spinach Salad with Mandarin Oranges

Salad:

2 pounds spinach, washed and drained

½ pound bacon, cooked crisp and crumbled

1 (8-ounce) can bean sprouts, drained

1 (11-ounce) can mandarin oranges, drained

2 (8-ounce) cans water chestnuts, drained and sliced

1 medium sweet onion, sliced

4 hard-cooked eggs, sliced

Dressing

Combine spinach and remaining ingredients, except dressing, in a large serving bowl. Toss with dressing.

Dressing:

½ cup red wine vinegar

1 cup salad oil

¾ cup sugar

Freshly ground black pepper to taste

In a jar, combine vinegar, oil, sugar, and black pepper. Shake well. Chill. Yield: 4 to 6 servings.

Spinach Salad with Strawberries

1 pound spinach
1 medium head iceberg lettuce
1 pint strawberries, sliced
1 medium red onion, thinly sliced
Toasted almonds, slivered or sliced
⅓ cup sugar
1 tablespoon sesame seeds

1 tablespoon poppy seeds
1½ teaspoon minced onion
¼ teaspoon Worcestershire sauce
¼ teaspoon paprika
½ cup vegetable oil
¼ cup cider vinegar

Wash and dry greens; tear into bite-size pieces. On individual salad plates, portion out greens. Top with a layer of strawberries, a layer of onion rings, and a layer of almonds. Combine remaining ingredients in a jar; shake well. Spoon dressing over salads. Yield: 4 to 6 servings.

Mandarin Orange and Onion Salad with Poppy Seed Dressing

This salad enhances chicken and quiche dishes.

Salad:
1 large head Boston lettuce
1 (11-ounce) can mandarin oranges, drained
1 large red onion, sliced

1 sliced avocado, optional
Walnut halves, to taste, optional
Dressing

Tear lettuce into bite-size pieces. Place in salad bowl, and add remaining ingredients, except dressing. Toss well; serve with dressing.

Dressing:
2 tablespoons red wine vinegar
1 teaspoon Dijon mustard
½ teaspoon salt
Pinch of cayenne pepper

1 tablespoon honey
3 tablespoons peanut oil
1½ teaspoon poppy seeds

Combine all ingredients; mix thoroughly. Refrigerate at least 1 hour before serving. Yield: 4 to 6 servings.

Artichoke-Rice Salad

1 cup regular long-grain rice
2 cups chicken broth
¼ cup diced green bell pepper
¼ cup sliced scallion
¼ cup sliced pimiento-stuffed green olives
1 (6-ounce) jar marinated artichokes

½ cup mayonnaise
½ teaspoon dillweed
Salt and black pepper, to taste
1 small head iceberg lettuce, torn into bite-size pieces
Tomatoes, for garnish
Olives, for garnish

Cook rice, according to package directions, in 2 cups chicken broth. Spread cooked rice onto baking sheet to air dry. Toss together rice, green bell pepper, scallion, and olives. Drain artichokes, reserving liquid. Dice artichokes, and add to rice mixture. Mix mayonnaise with some of artichoke liquid. Add to other ingredients along with dillweed, salt, and black pepper. Serve salad on lettuce garnished with tomatoes and olives. Yield: 4 servings.

Marinated Asparagus

Asparagus salad keeps well in refrigerator for 3 or 4 days.

4 (15-ounce) cans of asparagus spears, drained
⅓ to ½ cup sugar
¼ cup white vinegar
¼ cup water

3 whole cloves
1 stick cinnamon
½ teaspoon celery seed
½ teaspoon salt
Pimientos, drained, for garnish

Place asparagus spears in a 9x12-inch serving dish. Put remaining ingredients, except pimiento, in small saucepan; bring to boil, and boil 3 to 5 minutes. Pour over asparagus. Chill overnight. Using a turkey baster, drain carefully. Garnish with pimiento. Serve at room temperature. Yield: 6 to 8 servings.

Black Bean Salad with Feta Cheese

2 (16-ounce) cans black beans, rinsed and drained
1 (16-ounce) can white kidney beans, rinsed and drained
6 ounces Feta cheese, crumbled
½ cup red onion, minced
¼ cup fresh mint leaves, minced
⅓ cup olive oil (or less, if desired)
3 tablespoons lime or lemon juice
1 to 2 garlic cloves, finely minced
1 teaspoon celery seed
Freshly ground black pepper to taste

In large bowl, combine beans, Feta cheese, onion, and mint. Fold together gently. Combine oil, lime juice, garlic, celery seed, and pepper; pour over bean mixture. Marinate at least 2 hours in refrigerator before serving. Yield: 8 servings.

Green Bean, Walnut, and Feta Cheese Salad

1½ pounds fresh green beans, cut in half crosswise
¾ cup olive oil
½ cup fresh mint leaves, finely chopped
¼ cup white wine vinegar
¾ teaspoon salt
3 cloves garlic, minced
¼ teaspoon freshly ground black pepper
1 cup chopped toasted walnuts
1 cup diced red onion
1 cup crumbled Feta cheese

Bring 4 quarts salted water to a boil in a 6-quart pot over medium high heat. Add beans, and cook until crisp-tender, about 4 minutes; drain well. Immediately plunge into ice water to stop cooking process. Drain beans again; pat dry.

Combine oil, mint, vinegar, salt, garlic, and pepper in food processor, blend and set dressing aside. Arrange beans in shallow glass serving bowl. Sprinkle with walnuts, onion, and cheese. Just before serving, pour dressing over mixture, and toss. Yield: 4 servings.

Crunchy Pea Salad

1 (10-ounce) package frozen peas,
    thawed
1 cup diced celery
1 cup chopped cauliflower
Bacon, cooked crisp and crumbled,
    to taste

¼ cup diced scallions
1 cup chopped cashews
½ cup sour cream
1 cup ranch salad dressing

Combine all ingredients. Chill well. Yield: 4 to 6 servings.

Broccoli Salad

*Norman Wasson, of Chuckanut Manor in Bow,
Washington, contributed this recipe.*

Salad:
4 cups broccoli flowerets
1 red onion, chopped
1 cup sliced fresh mushrooms
1 cup raisins

6 slices bacon, cooked crisp and
    coarsely crumbled
Dressing

Combine broccoli, onion, mushrooms, raisins, and bacon in large salad bowl.
Toss with chilled dressing.

Dressing:
1 egg
1 egg yolk
½ cup sugar or honey
1½ tablespoons dry mustard
1½ tablespoons cornstarch

¼ cup water
¼ cup white vinegar
2 tablespoons butter
½ cup mayonnaise

Whisk together egg, egg yolk, sugar, dry mustard, and cornstarch. In saucepan, combine ¼ cup water and vinegar; bring to boil. Whisk in egg mixture.
Cook for 1 minute or until thickened. Remove from heat; add butter and
mayonnaise. Let dressing chill for 1 hour. Yield: 8 servings.

Black-eyed Pea Salad

This salad is excellent with pork entrées.

3 (16-ounce) cans black-eyed peas
1 cup chopped green bell pepper
1 cup chopped onion
1 (4-ounce) jar diced pimientos, drained

3 cloves garlic, minced
¼ to 1 cup jalapeño peppers, chopped
1 (6-ounce) bottle zesty Italian dressing

Drain peas; mix with green bell pepper, onion, pimientos, garlic, and jalapeño peppers. Stir well, and pour Italian dressing over mixture. Chill overnight before serving. Yield: 10 to 14 servings.

Day-Before Broccoli Salad

1 cup mayonnaise
¼ to ½ cup sugar
¼ cup white vinegar, or to taste
1½ bunches broccoli, separated into flowerets
1 to 1½ cups chopped walnuts

¼ cup chopped red onion
1 cup white raisins
½ cup unsalted sunflower seeds
8 slices bacon, cooked crisp and crumbled

Mix mayonnaise, sugar, and vinegar together; set dressing aside. Mix rest of ingredients, except bacon. Add dressing. Refrigerate for 6 hours or overnight. Before serving, toss bacon pieces with salad. Yield: 8 servings.

Broccoli and Cauliflower Salad

1 head broccoli
1 head cauliflower
1 cup tiny green peas
1 (16-ounce) can kidney beans, drained

1 (8-ounce) bottle Italian dressing
½ cup mayonnaise or salad dressing
1 pound bacon, cooked crisp and crumbled
Chopped scallions, to taste

In salad bowl, break up broccoli and cauliflower into bite-size pieces. Add peas and beans. In small bowl, mix Italian dressing and mayonnaise together. Pour dressing over salad. Sprinkle with bacon and scallions. Chill thoroughly. Yield: 4 to 6 servings.

Marinated Picnic Carrots

*This colorful salad's flavor improves when it is
marinated overnight.*

2 pounds carrots, sliced diagonally
⅔ cup cider vinegar
½ cup oil
½ cup sugar

½ cup chopped onion
1 (.7-ounce) package Italian
   dressing mix
¼ cup chopped parsley

Boil or steam carrots until tender but crisp. Cool. Blend all other ingredients
except parsley. Pour over cooled carrots, and toss well. Refrigerate for several
hours or overnight. Just before serving, add parsley and toss. Yield: 6 to 8
servings.

Bacon Potato Salad

*This salad may be made up to 3 days in advance
and kept covered and chilled.*

4 pounds baking potatoes, peeled,
   halved lengthwise, and cut
   crosswise into ½-inch slices
Salt to taste
3 cups sliced celery
½ cup chopped scallion
¼ cup minced fresh parsley leaves,
   or 1 teaspoon dried parsley flakes

½ pound sliced lean bacon, cut
   crosswise into ½-inch pieces
1 cup mayonnaise
1 tablespoon Dijon mustard
Salt and freshly ground black
   pepper to taste

In a kettle, cover potatoes with cold water, add salt to taste, and bring water to
a boil. Simmer potatoes for 10 to 12 minutes, or until they are just tender
when pierced with a fork; drain. Transfer potatoes to a serving bowl, allow to
cool, and add celery, scallion, and parsley.

In a skillet, cook bacon over moderate heat, stirring, until crisp. Transfer it
with a slotted spoon to paper towels to drain. In a small bowl, make dressing
by blending the mayonnaise, mustard, salt, and black pepper. Pour dressing
over the potato mixture, add bacon, and toss salad until it is combined. Serve
salad at room temperature. Yield: 6 servings.

Hot German Potato Salad

This recipe may be halved.

12 medium potatoes, boiled in skins
12 slices bacon
1½ cups chopped onion
4 tablespoons flour
2 to 4 tablespoons sugar

1½ to 2 teaspoons salt
1 teaspoon celery seeds
Dash of black pepper
1½ cups water
⅔ cup vinegar

Peel potatoes, and slice thin. Fry bacon slowly in skillet; remove bacon from pan, and drain on paper towels. Sauté onion in bacon grease until golden brown. Blend in flour, sugar, salt, celery seeds, and black pepper. Cook over low heat, stirring until smooth and bubbly. Remove from heat, and stir in water and vinegar. Heat mixture to boil, and stir constantly. Boil 1 minute. Carefully stir in potatoes and crumbled bacon bits. Remove from heat, cover, and let stand until ready to serve. Yield: 12 to 16 servings.

Tomato Vinaigrette

*Tomato vinaigrette must be prepared ahead so that it
has adequate time to chill.*

2 large fresh tomatoes, peeled
3 tablespoons fresh parsley, or 1
    tablespoon dried parsley
½ clove garlic, crushed
3 tablespoons olive oil

1 tablespoon white vinegar
4 teaspoons fresh basil, or ¾
    teaspoon dried basil
½ teaspoon salt
Black pepper to taste

Slice tomatoes into ½-inch-thick slices, and place in a 9x13-inch serving dish. Mix all other ingredients. Pour over tomato slices. Chill at least 3 hours before serving. Yield: 8 servings.

Tuscan Salad

2 large tomatoes (1 pound), chopped
1 large yellow or green bell pepper, cut in ¾-inch pieces
6 ounces fresh mozzarella cheese, cut in ½-inch cubes
⅓ cup coarsely chopped fresh basil

6 tablespoons olive oil
3 tablespoons balsamic vinegar
3 cloves garlic, minced
4 ounces crusty French bread, cut into 1-inch cubes
Mixed salad greens, torn into bite-size pieces

Just before serving, mix all ingredients, except greens. Serve salad over greens. Yield: 4 servings.

Mexican Vegetable Salad

2 large zucchini
2 large yellow squash
3 medium cucumbers
1¼ cups tarragon vinegar
2 medium red onions, chopped
8 ripe medium tomatoes, peeled and diced in ¼-inch pieces

1 red bell pepper, diced
1 yellow bell pepper, diced
1 green bell pepper, diced
½ cup chopped fresh coriander
1½ cups olive oil
Salt and freshly ground black pepper to taste

Trim zucchini and yellow squash, cut lengthwise into long strips, then cut into ¼-inch pieces. Peel and seed cucumbers; then cut into ¼-inch dice. Place squash and cucumber in a large mixing bowl. Add tarragon vinegar, and toss. Set aside, and let marinate at room temperature for 45 minutes. Combine onions, tomatoes, bell peppers, and coriander in another large mixing bowl. Drain squash mixture in a colander. Add to onion mixture, and combine well. Dress salad with olive oil, salt, and black pepper. Taste and add more vinegar if needed. Refrigerate at least 2 hours before serving. Yield: 12 to 16 servings.

Marinated Vegetables

1 cup water
¾ cup white vinegar
½ cup granulated sugar
2 garlic cloves, sliced
1 teaspoon dried tarragon
1 bay leaf
1 teaspoon salt
1 tablespoon mustard seed

2 tablespoons finely chopped fresh dill, or 1 tablespoon dried dill
2 bunches fresh broccoli, separated into flowerets
1 head cauliflower, separated into flowerets
1 cup cherry tomatoes, quartered (optional)

In large saucepan, combine water, vinegar, and sugar. Add garlic, tarragon, bay leaf, salt, and mustard seed. Bring to a boil, stirring constantly. Remove from heat, and add dill. Pour mixture over vegetables and marinate overnight, stirring occasionally. Before serving, drain well. Yield: 12 servings.

Apple and Pear Salad with Feta Cheese and Toasted Walnuts

2 cups romaine lettuce, washed and torn
1 cup red leaf lettuce, washed and torn
½ cup curly endive, washed and torn
½ cup raddichio, washed and torn
½ cup Rome apple, unpeeled and cut into pieces

½ cup Granny Smith apple, unpeeled and cut into pieces
1 cup red pear, unpeeled and cut into pieces
½ cup Feta cheese
½ cup English walnuts, toasted
Vinaigrette

Combine all lettuces, fruit, Feta cheese, and walnuts. Toss lightly, and dress with vinaigrette or your favorite commercial raspberry vinaigrette. Yield: 4 servings.

Vinaigrette:
½ cup extra light olive oil
¼ cup raspberry vinegar

1 teaspoon sugar

Combine all ingredients thoroughly, and refrigerate until ready to serve. Yield: ¾ cup.

Bing Cherry Congealed Salad

2 (3-ounce) packages mixed-fruit
  gelatin
2 cups boiling water
1 (16-ounce) can dark sweet
  cherries, drained
1 (11-ounce) can mandarin oranges,
  drained

1 (15-ounce) can crushed
  pineapple, not drained
½ to ¾ cup orange juice
½ cup nuts, chopped, if desired
Lettuce leaves

Dissolve gelatin in boiling water. Add cherries, mandarin oranges, and
crushed pineapple. Add orange juice and nuts; mix well. Pour into 2-quart
casserole dish, and refrigerate until firm. Cut into 2-inch squares, and serve
each square on a lettuce leaf. Yield: 8 to 12 servings.

Cranberry Salad

2 cups cranberries
1½ cups orange juice
1½ cups sugar
1 (¼ ounce) envelope plain gelatin
1 (14.25 ounce) can crushed
  pineapple, drained and juice
  retained

1 pound seedless grapes, halved
1 cup chopped celery
1 cup almonds, halved
Mayonnaise or sour cream,
  seasoned with nutmeg

In a saucepan, simmer cranberries 10 minutes in orange juice. Add sugar
while cranberries are hot, and strain mixture. Dissolve gelatin with pineapple
juice. Pour gelatin over hot cranberries. Let cool to room temperature. Add
fruits, celery, and almonds. Put in 8 individual molds or a 1½-quart ring mold.
Chill until firm. Unmold salad by briefly dipping mold into hot water. Serve
with mayonnaise or sour cream seasoned with nutmeg. Yield: 8 servings.

Waldorf Cranberry Salad

Prepare salad ahead of time.

2 cups cranberry juice cocktail, divided
1 (3-ounce) package lemon gelatin
¼ teaspoon salt

1½ cups chopped unpared apples
¾ cup chopped celery
¼ cup chopped nuts

Pour 1 cup cranberry juice into saucepan, and bring to a boil. Immediately remove from heat, add gelatin, and stir until dissolved. Add remaining 1 cup juice and salt. Chill until partially firm.

Stir apples, celery, and nuts into gelatin. Pour into 5-cup mold, and chill until firm. Unmold salad by briefly dipping mold into hot water. Yield: 6 to 8 servings.

Frozen Cranberry Salad

1 (16-ounce) can whole-berry cranberry sauce
1 (8-ounce) can crushed pineapple, drained

1 (8-ounce) carton nonfat plain yogurt
¼ cup sifted confectioners' sugar
1 teaspoon vanilla extract
Vegetable cooking spray

Combine cranberry sauce, pineapple, yogurt, confectioners' sugar, and vanilla extract, stirring until sugar dissolves. Spoon evenly into 12 muffin tins coated with cooking spray. Freeze 8 hours. Before serving, let stand at room temperature 5 minutes. Loosen edges with a knife, remove salads from tins, and serve immediately. Yield: 12 servings.

Raspberry-Cranberry Mold

2 (3-ounce) boxes cherry gelatin
1½ cups hot water
1 (8-ounce) can crushed pineapple, undrained
1 (8-ounce) can whole-berry cranberry sauce, undrained

1 (8-ounce) carton sour cream
2 (3-ounce) boxes raspberry gelatin
1½ cups hot water
2 (10-ounce) packages frozen raspberries

Combine gelatin, water, pineapple and juice, and cranberry sauce in a 9x13-inch pan or 2 (8x8-inch) pans. Refrigerate until firm.

When first layer is firm, cover with sour cream. In a separate bowl, mix raspberry gelatin with hot water and frozen raspberries. Refrigerate until mixture is consistency of egg whites. Spread raspberry mixture over sour cream. Refrigerate salad until firm, and cut into squares to serve. Yield: 24 servings.

Raspberry Pear Salad

4 fresh pears, peeled and sliced
1 head Bibb lettuce, torn into bite-size pieces

½ cup fresh red raspberries
½ cup toasted pecans
Vinaigrette

When ready to serve, arrange pears attractively on lettuce. Top with raspberries and pecans. Drizzle vinaigrette over all. Yield: 4 servings.

Vinaigrette:
½ cup extra light olive oil
¼ cup raspberry vinegar

1 tablespoon crème fraiche
1 teaspoon sugar

Whisk together ingredients, and chill for several hours. Yield: ¾ cup.

Lemon Cream with Strawberry or Blueberry Sauce

5 small packages lemon gelatin
5 cups boiling water
1 (12-ounce) can frozen lemonade
  concentrate

1 (12-ounce) container frozen
  whipped topping
Strawberry or Blueberry Sauce

Very lightly oil one 4-quart mold or two 2-quart molds. Dissolve gelatin in boiling water. Refrigerate until mixture is consistency of egg whites. Add thawed lemonade concentrate. Stir in whipped topping, and mix thoroughly. Pour into mold. Refrigerate until set. To unmold, dip mold briefly into warm water. Serve sauce as accompaniment.

Strawberry Sauce:
2 (10-ounce) packages frozen sliced
  strawberries, thawed

2½ tablespoons orange brandy
  liqueur

Heat thawed strawberries and stir in orange brandy liqueur. Chill.

Blueberry Sauce:
1 pint fresh blueberries

2 tablespoons raspberry brandy
  liqueur

Heat blueberries and raspberry brandy liqueur until blueberries start to pop open. Use a fork to mash all the berries. Place in a blender, and blend until smooth. Chill. Yield: 8 servings.

Triple Sec Fruit Salad

Fresh melon balls or blueberries can be added.

2 cups orange juice
2 to 3 tablespoons cornstarch
¼ cup Triple Sec or other orange
  liqueur
1 (16-ounce) can pineapple chunks
1 red apple, chopped

1 yellow apple, chopped
2 cups strawberries
1 (11-ounce) can mandarin oranges
2 cups seedless dark grapes
2 kiwi fruit, sliced
Kiwi or fresh mint for garnish

In saucepan, whisk orange juice into cornstarch. Cook over medium heat until thickened and transparent, stirring constantly. Stir in liqueur. Cool to room temperature. Combine pineapple, apples, strawberries, oranges, grapes and kiwi in mixing bowl. Add dressing; mix gently. Serve in champagne glasses. Garnish with additional kiwi or fresh mint. Yield: 12 servings.

Pink Christmas Frozen Fruit Salad

Salad keeps in freezer for up to 2 months.

1 (8-ounce) package cream cheese,
  softened
2 tablespoons mayonnaise
2 tablespoons sugar
1 (8-ounce) can jellied cranberry
  sauce

1 (8¼-ounce) can crushed
  pineapple and juice
½ cup chopped pecans (optional)
1 cup frozen whipped topping
Lettuce leaves

Line 12 muffin tins with paper liners. With electric mixer, blend cream cheese, mayonnaise, sugar, cranberry sauce, and pineapple with juice. Fold in pecans and whipped topping. Spoon mixture into muffin tins. Freeze until firm. Remove individual salads from pans and liners, and seal salads in a freezer bag. Before serving, remove salads from freezer. Serve on lettuce leaves. Yield: 12 servings.

Mother's Frozen Fruit Salad

Slice salad, put wax paper between each slice, and place slices in plastic bags. Remove slices from freezer about 10 minutes before serving. This salad is also good served as a dessert with pound cake. It keeps well in freezer for about 3 months.

1 pint whipping cream (Do not substitute light cream or frozen whipped topping.)

1 pint mayonnaise, more if desired (Do not substitute light mayonnaise.)

½ pound grated sharp cheese

2 (15¼-ounce) cans fruits for salads

1 (16-ounce) can pears

1 (16-ounce) can fruit cocktail

2 (16-ounce) cans crushed pineapple

1 (10-ounce) jar cherries

6 sliced bananas

2 cups sugar

1 tablespoon lemon juice

1 cup chopped pecans

Lettuce leaves, if desired, for garnish

Whip cream and mayonnaise together; add cheese, and set aside. Drain all fruit; cut into small pieces. Add sugar and lemon juice. Combine fruit mixture with cream mixture; add pecans, and mix well. Pour into clean 1-quart milk cartons, leaving room for expansion. Freeze. When ready to serve, cut cartons down sides to remove frozen salad. Slice while frozen. Serve alone or on lettuce leaves. Yield: about 4 quarts or 24 to 32 servings.

Fruit Salad Dressing

*This dressing stores well in refrigerator for several weeks. Use
with fresh fruit salad of bananas, cantaloupe, honeydew,
watermelon, grapes, cherries, and apples.*

⅓ cup sugar
4 teaspoons cornstarch
¼ teaspoon salt
Juice of 1 lemon
Juice of 1 orange

1 cup unsweetened pineapple juice
2 eggs
2 (3-ounce) packages cream cheese,
   whipped

In a double boiler, mix sugar, cornstarch, and salt. Add lemon juice, orange juice, and pineapple juice. Cook over warm water for 20 minutes, stirring constantly. In a small bowl, beat eggs, add a little cooked mixture to them and blend well. Stir egg mixture into juice mixture. Cook, stirring constantly, 5 minutes more. Cool and blend with cream cheese. Yield: approximately 2 cups.

Poppy Seed Dressing

*This dressing is wonderful on fresh salad
greens or fruit salad.*

1½ cups sugar
2 teaspoons dry mustard
2 teaspoons salt
⅔ cup white vinegar

3 tablespoons onion juice
2 cups vegetable oil
3 tablespoons poppy seeds

Combine all ingredients in blender, and mix at high speed 30 seconds. Store in refrigerator. Mix well before each use. Yield: 1 cup.

Pastas, Grains, Eggs

A futuristic skyline and peaceful parks contribute to Charlotte's reputation as a progressive Southern city.

Two young boys watch the clowns and the crowds at Charlotte's lively Festival in the Park celebration.

Fettuccine Alfredo with Leeks, Italian Sausage, and Mushrooms

1 large leek, thoroughly washed and chopped
8 ounces fresh mushrooms, sliced
2 tablespoons olive oil

1 (12-inch) Italian sausage
Alfredo Sauce
1 (12-ounce) package uncooked fettuccine

In a medium skillet, sauté leeks and mushrooms in olive oil. Cut sausage into ½-inch slices, add to skillet, and sauté until no pink remains. Drain fat, and set mixture aside. Combine alfredo sauce and sausage mixture; keep warm. Cook fettuccine according to package directions, omitting salt. Drain well, place in a large serving bowl. Add sausage mixture. Toss until fettuccine is coated.

Alfredo Sauce:

1 cup freshly grated Parmesan cheese
½ cup half-and-half

1 tablespoon parsley
¼ teaspoon white pepper
½ teaspoon garlic powder

In a saucepan, combine all ingredients, and stir over low heat until thickened. Yield: 6 servings.

Variation: For vegetable fettuccine, omit leek, sausage, and mushroom mixture. Toss together sautéed onions, squash, and zucchini. Add 1 diced fresh tomato.

Baked Macaroni and Two Cheeses

7 tablespoons unsalted butter, divided

6 tablespoons all-purpose flour

4 cups milk

1½ teaspoons dry mustard

⅛ teaspoon cayenne pepper, or to taste

Salt and black pepper to taste

1 pound elbow macaroni

3 cups (about 12-ounces) coarsely grated extra-sharp Cheddar cheese

1⅓ cups (about 4-ounces) freshly grated Parmesan cheese, divided

1 cup fresh breadcrumbs

Preheat oven to 350° F., and grease a 3- to 4-quart shallow baking dish. In a heavy saucepan, melt 6 tablespoons butter over moderately low heat. Add flour, and cook roux, whisking, for 3 minutes. Add milk in a stream, and bring to a boil, whisking constantly. Add mustard, cayenne pepper, salt, and black pepper; simmer sauce, whisking occasionally, until thickened, for about 2 minutes.

In a kettle of salted boiling water, cook macaroni until al dente, for about 7 minutes, and drain well. In a large bowl, stir together macaroni, sauce, Cheddar cheese, and 1 cup Parmesan cheese, and transfer to prepared dish.

In a small bowl, stir together breadcrumbs, and remaining ⅓ cup Parmesan cheese, and sprinkle mixture evenly over macaroni. Cut remaining 1 tablespoon butter into bits and scatter over top. Bake macaroni in middle of oven for 25 to 30 minutes, or until golden and bubbly. Yield: 6 to 8 servings as an entrée, or 8 to 10 servings as a side dish.

Pasta with Smoked Salmon in Dill Dressing

½ cup vegetable oil
2 tablespoons lemon juice
1½ teaspoons minced shallots
⅓ cup fresh dill, chopped
Salt and black pepper to taste
1½ pounds pasta
1 cup ripe cherry tomatoes, halved

¼ cup minced fresh chives
5 ounces smoked salmon, cut into small pieces
1 small red onion, cut into thin rings and separated
1 cup sour cream
Fresh dill sprigs for garnish

Combine oil, lemon juice, shallots, and dill. Season with salt and black pepper. Whisk well; set dressing aside.

Cook pasta until al dente. Drain, rinse in cold water, and drain again. Place in a large serving bowl and cool to room temperature, stirring occasionally to keep pasta from sticking together.

Add tomatoes, chives, and dressing to pasta; mix gently. Arrange salmon, onion, and sour cream on top of pasta. Garnish with dill sprigs. Yield: 6 servings.

Pasta with White Clam Sauce

1 (8-ounce) package linguine or angel hair pasta
2 (6.5-ounce) cans minced clams
¼ cup extra virgin olive oil
¼ cup chopped onion
4 cloves garlic, minced
⅓ cup dry white wine
1 teaspoon fresh lemon juice
2 teaspoons fresh basil, chopped, or ½ teaspoon dried basil

1 tablespoon fresh thyme leaves, or 1 teaspoon dried thyme
¼ teaspoon salt
¼ teaspoon crushed red pepper flakes
¼ cup chopped fresh parsley
¼ cup freshly grated Parmesan cheese

Cook pasta according to package directions until al dente. Drain pasta, and keep warm. Drain clams, reserving juice. In a skillet, heat olive oil over medium heat. Add onion and garlic, and sauté until onion is soft. Add clam juice, wine, lemon juice, basil, thyme, salt, and red pepper. Add clams, increase heat to medium high, and cook until liquid reduces by half, for about 2 to 3 minutes. Toss pasta with clam sauce, and let set a few minutes. Sprinkle with parsley and Parmesan cheese. Yield: 4 servings.

Cajun Shrimp Pasta

This recipe may be doubled.

⅓ pound rotini pasta, cooked al dente

½ pound shrimp, cooked and peeled

½ pound chicken breasts, cooked, skinned, boned, and diced

1 cup chopped broccoli

1 cup halved cherry tomatoes

½ cup vinaigrette dressing

¼ cup sour cream

¼ cup mayonnaise

1 teaspoon tarragon

1 tablespoon blackened redfish spice mix

Mix pasta, shrimp, chicken, broccoli, and tomatoes in a large bowl. In a small bowl, whisk together vinaigrette dressing, sour cream, mayonnaise, tarragon, and spice mix. Pour this mixture over pasta mixture, and toss gently. Serve immediately, or chill for several hours. Yield: 4 servings.

Easy Lasagna

If desired, add 1 pound cooked ground beef between noodles and sauce. Lasagna may be prepared ahead and frozen.

½ (16-ounce) box lasagna noodles (do not cook)

1 (32-ounce) jar meatless spaghetti sauce

1 (16-ounce) carton cottage cheese

1 (8-ounce) package mozzarella cheese

1½ ounces Parmesan cheese

½ cup hot water

¼ cup dry red wine

Preheat oven to 350° F. Spray a 13x9-inch pan with nonstick vegetable spray. Layer ingredients, as listed, in prepared pan. Cover tightly with aluminum foil, and bake for 1 hour. Yield: 6 to 8 servings

Manicotti

½ pound link Italian sausage
1 pound ground chuck
2 medium onions, chopped
5 cloves garlic, minced
2 (14-ounce) cans tomato sauce
1 (16-ounce) can tomatoes, chopped and undrained
1 (12-ounce) can tomato paste
1½ teaspoons dried whole oregano
1 1/4 teaspoons dried whole basil
1 teaspoon sugar
½ teaspoon salt
½ teaspoon black pepper

½ teaspoon dried whole thyme
½ teaspoon dried whole rosemary
¼ teaspoon dried whole marjoram
⅛ teaspoon red pepper flakes
20 manicotti shells
1 (8-ounce) package cream cheese, softened
1 (3-ounce) package cream cheese, softened
1 tablespoon chives
1 pound ricotta cheese
4 cups shredded mozzarella cheese
½ cup grated Parmesan cheese

Remove sausage from casing; crumble. Combine sausage, ground chuck, onions, and garlic in a large Dutch oven. Cook over medium heat until beef browns, stirring to crumble; drain well. Add tomato sauce, tomatoes, tomato paste, oregano, basil, sugar, salt, black pepper, thyme, rosemary, marjoram, and red pepper; bring mixture to a boil. Cover, reduce heat, and simmer, stirring occasionally, for 2½ hours.

Cook manicotti shells according to package directions. Combine cream cheeses, chives, ricotta cheese, mozzarella cheese, and Parmesan cheese in a large bowl; stuff mixture into shells. Preheat oven to 350° F. and lightly grease a 14x11½x2¼-inch baking dish or two 2½-quart shallow casserole dishes. Spoon half of sauce into prepared dish. Arrange stuffed shells over sauce. Spoon remaining sauce over shells. Bake, covered, until heated through. Let manicotti stand for 5 minutes before serving. Yield: 8 to 10 servings.

Sausage and Linguine Torte

1 pound linguine

2 tablespoons butter

½ pound sweet (mild) Italian sausage

½ pound hot Italian sausage

1 tablespoon olive oil

1 medium onion, finely chopped

1 green bell pepper, coarsely chopped

3 teaspoons oregano, divided

1 (3.5-ounce) can sliced ripe black olives

¼ cup finely chopped parsley

½ teaspoon salt

½ teaspoon black pepper

3 eggs, slightly beaten

1 (15-ounce) container ricotta cheese

¼ cup grated Romano cheese

3 tomatoes, thinly sliced

1 cup shredded mozzarella cheese

1 cup shredded Swiss cheese

1 tablespoon grated Parmesan cheese

White Cream Sauce or commercially prepared marinara sauce

In salted boiling water, cook linguine until almost tender. Drain and toss with butter. Cover and set aside. Preheat oven to 375° F. Lightly grease and flour an 11-inch springform pan. Remove and discard sausage casings, and finely chop the sausage. In large pan, brown chopped sausage in olive oil. Pour off fat. Add onion, green bell pepper, and 1 teaspoon oregano. Sauté mixture for 5 minutes. In large bowl, gently toss sausage mixture with olives, parsley, salt, black pepper, and linguine. In separate large bowl, whisk together eggs, ricotta cheese, 2 teaspoons oregano, and Romano cheese until light and fluffy. Stir linguine mixture into egg mixture, and toss gently. Press half of linguine mixture into bottom of springform pan. Arrange half of the tomatoes on top. Sprinkle tomatoes with half of the mozzarella cheese and Swiss cheese. Repeat layers. Sprinkle Parmesan cheese over all.

Cover pan with foil. Bake for 50 minutes, or until set. Remove foil, bake for 5 more minutes. Remove from oven, and let stand for 10 minutes. Top with white cream sauce or purchased marinara sauce. Slice into wedges to serve. Yield: 12 servings.

(continued on next page)

Sausage and Linguine Torte
(continued)

White Cream Sauce:

¼ cup margarine

¼ cup flour

1 cup milk

1 cup heavy cream

Pinch of nutmeg

1 teaspoon salt

⅛ teaspoon white pepper

½ cup Parmesan cheese

In a saucepan, melt margarine. Whisk in flour, gradually add milk and cream. Stir constantly over medium heat until mixture boils and thickens; lower heat, and simmer for 2 to 3 minutes. Add remaining ingredients. Stir until smooth while mixture continues to heat. Serve warm. Yield: 2½ cups

Penne Pasta with Prosciutto and Asparagus

*Serve this light and colorful dish with a salad and
crusty bread. Reheat leftovers in microwave oven.*

4 tablespoons extra virgin olive oil

2 or 3 garlic cloves, finely chopped

2 (⅛-inch-thick) slices imported prosciutto ham, trimmed of excess fat and cut into ¼x2-inch strips

10 asparagus spears, cut in 2-inch pieces

1 red bell pepper, membranes removed, cut in 2-inch slices

6 sliced mushrooms (white button or shiitake)

1 teaspoon crushed red pepper

Salt and freshly ground black pepper to taste

12 ounces dried penne pasta

Grated Parmesan cheese

Heat olive oil over medium heat in a large heavy skillet. Add garlic and sauté for 1 minute. Add prosciutto ham and asparagus, and cook for 5 minutes, stirring constantly. Add red bell pepper, mushrooms, and crushed red pepper; continue cooking for 5 additional minutes, stirring constantly. Add salt and black pepper.

Cook pasta according to package directions until al dente. Drain and place in large bowl. Add ham mixture, and toss. Serve with Parmesan cheese on the side. Yield: 4 servings.

Genuine Italian Spaghetti Sauce and Meatballs

1½ cups chopped onion
2 cloves garlic, minced
⅓ cup olive oil
2 (28-ounce) cans tomatoes
4 (6-ounce) cans tomato paste
2 cups water
2 tablespoons sugar
1 tablespoon salt
½ teaspoon black pepper
2 tablespoons oregano

2 bay leaves
8 slices dry bread
2 pounds ground beef
4 eggs, lightly beaten
1 cup grated Parmesan cheese
¼ cup parsley flakes
2 cloves garlic, minced
2 teaspoons salt
Black pepper
2 pounds spaghetti, cooked

Cook onion and garlic in hot oil until tender, but not browned. Stir in tomatoes, tomato paste, water, sugar, salt, black pepper, oregano, and bay leaves. Simmer, uncovered, stirring occasionally, for 30 minutes.

To make meatballs, soak 8 slices of dry bread in water for 2 to 3 minutes. Squeeze out all liquid. Combine soaked bread with ground beef, eggs, Parmesan cheese, parsley, garlic, salt, and black pepper. Mix well. Form into bite-size balls. Fry meatballs in skillet over medium heat for 5 to 10 minutes, or until browned. Remove from skillet, and drain on paper towels.

Remove bay leaves from sauce. Add meatballs; continue cooking sauce for about 2½ hours. Serve sauce over spaghetti. Yield: 8 servings.

Mexican Stuffed Shells

1 pound ground beef
1 (16-ounce) jar mild or medium
  salsa
¼ cup water
1 (8-ounce) can tomato sauce

1 (4-ounce) can chopped green
  chiles, drained
1 cup shredded Cheddar cheese,
  divided
12 manicotti or jumbo shells,
  cooked and rinsed in cool water,
  separated to drain

Preheat oven to 350° F. Brown ground beef; drain. Combine salsa, water, and tomato sauce; stir ½ cup sauce mixture and chiles into ground beef. Add ½ cup Cheddar cheese; mix well. Pour half of remaining sauce mixture in a 13x9-inch baking dish. Stuff cooked shells with ground beef mixture. Arrange shells in baking dish; pour remaining sauce over shells. Bake, covered, for 30 minutes. Top with remaining Cheddar cheese, and bake, uncovered, for 5 minutes longer. Yield: 4 to 6 servings.

Chicken Fettuccine

1 pound skinned and boned chicken
  breasts, cut into cubes
1 stick butter
½ pound sliced mushrooms
⅔ cup chopped scallions
½ cup dry white wine
2 cups half-and-half

2 (16-ounce) cans whole tomatoes,
  crushed and drained
2 garlic cloves, crushed
1 teaspoon basil
½ teaspoon sugar
1 pound fettuccine
Parmesan cheese
Chopped parsley

In skillet over medium heat, sauté cubed chicken in melted butter for 3 minutes. Remove chicken from skillet. Sauté mushrooms and onion in remaining butter. Add wine, and simmer until liquid evaporates. Stir in half-and-half, tomatoes, garlic, basil, and sugar. Simmer until reduced by half. Add chicken and simmer until chicken is tender.

In a saucepan, cook fettuccine according to package directions. Drain and place on serving platter. Spoon chicken mixture on fettuccine, and garnish with grated Parmesan cheese and parsley. Yield: 4 to 6 servings.

Baked Chicken Fettuccine

4 boneless chicken breast halves,
  cut into strips
1 cup sliced mushrooms
¼ cup minced onions
2 tablespoons butter, divided
1 cup white wine
1 cup heavy cream

¼ teaspoon black pepper
¼ teaspoon garlic powder
8 ounces spinach fettuccine, cooked
  al dente
¼ cup Parmesan cheese
1 cup mozzarella cheese

Preheat oven to 350° F. Sauté chicken, mushrooms, and onion in 1 table-spoon butter in large skillet. (If using canned mushrooms, add with wine.) When chicken is tender and slightly browned, add wine. Cover skillet, and simmer until almost all of the liquid has cooked away. In a small saucepan, scald cream, and add 1 tablespoon butter, pepper, and garlic powder. Stir until blended. Place fettuccine and Parmesan cheese in a 2-quart casserole dish. Pour cream mixture over fettuccine. Add chicken mixture. Sprinkle with mozzarella cheese. Bake until cheese is bubbly and slightly browned, for about 20 to 25 minutes. Yield: 4 servings.

Chicken Breasts Over Pasta with Sour Cream

4 tablespoons all-purpose flour
1 cup sour cream
1 (10¾-ounce) can cream of
  mushroom soup
1 cup white wine
½ cup dry sherry

Black pepper, to taste
Garlic salt, to taste
4 chicken breast halves, skinned and
  boned
1 pound pasta, cooked al dente
1 (10-ounce) package frozen green
  peas, steamed

Preheat oven to 350° F. Mix flour with sour cream. Combine mixture with mushroom soup, white wine, sherry, and garlic salt. Place chicken breasts in a baking dish and pour cream mixture over them. Bake for 1½ hours. Cut baked chicken into slices or cubes. Serve chicken and sauce over pasta. Top with green peas. Yield: 4 servings.

Cold Chicken and Artichoke Pasta

2 to 2½ cups water
2 chicken bouillon cubes
¼ cup chopped onion
4 to 6 boneless chicken breast
  halves, skinned and boned
6 ounces vermicelli
1½ tablespoon grated onion
⅓ cup olive oil

3 tablespoons red wine vinegar
3 tablespoons lemon juice
1½ teaspoon sugar
1½ teaspoon seasoned salt
1½ teaspoon basil
1 (14-ounce) can artichoke hearts,
  drained and chopped
Cherry tomatoes for garnish

In a saucepan, bring water to boil; dissolve bouillon cubes, and add onion and chicken. Cook, uncovered, on medium/medium high heat for approximately 45 minutes, or until chicken is tender. Remove chicken, and chop coarsely. Strain and reserve broth.

Cook vermicelli, according to package directions, in reserved broth with additional water. Drain pasta and set aside.

Combine grated onion, olive oil, red wine vinegar, lemon juice, sugar, seasoned salt, and basil; mix dressing well. Mix drained vermicelli with chicken and dressing. Add artichoke hearts to mixture, and toss with other ingredients. Refrigerate for 2 hours before serving. Garnish with quartered cherry tomatoes. Yield: 4 generous servings.

Fresh Italian Tomato Pasta

6 large vine-ripened tomatoes
½ cup chopped scallions
4 tablespoons extra-virgin olive oil
6 cloves garlic, minced
½ cup sliced ripe olives
2 tablespoons chopped fresh basil

2 tablespoons chopped fresh parsley
½ teaspoon salt
½ teaspoon black pepper
8 ounces thin spaghetti
8 ounces mozzarella cheese, cut into ½-inch cubes

Peel tomatoes and coarsely chop them over a bowl, reserving juice. Add scallions to tomatoes. Combine tomatoes, reserved juice, and olive oil. Add garlic, olives, basil, parsley, salt, and black pepper. Cover and let stand at room temperature for 1 hour. Then, if desired, refrigerate until serving.

Cook pasta according to package directions until al dente, drain. Spoon tomato mixture over pasta, and top with mozzarella cheese. Yield: 4 servings.

Spinach Roll-ups

10 whole wheat lasagna noodles
3 bunches spinach, cleaned, stems removed, and leaves chopped
3 tablespoons grated Parmesan cheese
1 cup low-fat cottage cheese
½ teaspoon nutmeg
1 cup sliced onion

2 cups grated Muenster or Monterey Jack cheese
4 cups tomato sauce
½ teaspoon basil
½ teaspoon marjoram
2 cloves garlic, minced
1 teaspoon oregano

Preheat oven to 350° F. Oil a 9x13-inch baking pan. Cook and drain noodles. Allow to cool to room temperature. Steam the spinach until limp; drain, and place in bowl. Add Parmesan cheese, cottage cheese, and nutmeg. Spread noodles with spinach filling and roll. Stand rolls on end in prepared pan. Sprinkle Muenster cheese and onions on top of noodles. Combine tomato sauce and remaining ingredients, and pour mixture over noodles. Bake for 45 minutes, or until sauce is bubbling. Yield: 4 servings.

Lemon Chive Fettuccine with Asparagus

½ pound fettuccine
½ pound fresh asparagus, trimmed and cut into ½-inch pieces
2 tablespoons butter, melted
2 egg yolks
1 cup heavy cream

½ cup freshly grated Parmesan cheese
1 tablespoon chives
1 teaspoon grated lemon rind
Salt and freshly ground black pepper to taste
1 slice of lemon, quartered

Cook fettuccine until al dente, and drain. Cook asparagus until just tender, for about 3 minutes. Drain asparagus, and add to pasta. Toss fettuccine and asparagus with melted butter, and set aside. Whisk egg yolks in a small bowl; then add cream and Parmesan cheese. Transfer mixture to a large pot, and heat thoroughly until the cheese melts. Stir in chives, lemon rind, salt, and black pepper. Add pasta and asparagus to the pot, and toss until covered in the lemon chive sauce. Serve immediately, garnished with lemon slice quarters. Yield: 4 servings as a first course; 2 servings as an entrée.

Pasta Primavera with Sugar Snaps

1 pound linguine or vermicelli
1 tablespoon chopped garlic
3 or 4 carrots, peeled and cut into thin rounds
½ head broccoli, cut into flowerets
Olive oil for cooking
1 pint ripe cherry tomatoes, halved

½ pound sugar snap peas, trimmed
1 bunch scallions, cut into 1-inch lengths
1 bunch fresh basil, leaves washed and roughly torn
½ cup freshly grated Parmesan cheese
⅓ cup chicken broth, or to taste

Bring a large pot of salted water to a boil, and cook pasta until al dente. Drain, and set aside. Sauté garlic, carrots, and broccoli in a large skillet for 2 to 3 minutes in olive oil until crisp-tender. Add cherry tomatoes, and cook for 2 minutes. Add sugar snaps and scallions; cook for 1 minute. Toss vegetables, basil, pasta, and Parmesan cheese together. Add chicken broth as needed to moisten. Serve immediately. Yield: 4 servings.

Pasta Primavera

1 cup broccoli flowerets, steamed for 5 minutes

1 cup diced asparagus, steamed for 5 minutes

1 cup sugar snap or snow peas, blanched for 1 minute

1 small zucchini or yellow squash, halved and then cut into 1-inch chunks and blanched for 1 minute

1 cup canned corn (or, if fresh or frozen, blanched)

1 pound shrimp, cooked and peeled (optional)

3 large cloves garlic, finely minced

1 tablespoon olive oil

1 large or 2 small tomatoes, diced

½ cup mushrooms, sliced

½ cup shredded carrots

¼ cup finely minced parsley

½ teaspoon freshly ground black pepper

2 teaspoons butter or margarine

1 tablespoon flour

1 cup skim or low-fat milk

½ cup chicken stock

½ cup grated Parmesan cheese

¼ cup finely minced fresh basil, or 1 teaspoon dried basil

12 ounces spaghetti or linguine

Combine broccoli, asparagus, peas, zucchini, and corn; keep warm. Sauté shrimp 3 to 4 minutes until they turn pink; keep warm. In a skillet, sauté the garlic in the oil for 1 minute, but do not brown. Add the tomatoes, mushrooms, carrot, parsley, and pepper; cook for 4 minutes. Add reserved broccoli mixture, tossing the ingredients gently to combine them well.

In a small, heavy saucepan, melt the butter, and then add the flour, whisking the roux over medium-low heat for 1 minute. Gradually add milk and chicken stock, stirring constantly until sauce thickens slightly. Stir in Parmesan cheese and basil, and heat sauce over medium heat, stirring until cheese melts. Pour sauce over vegetable mixture, and toss the two gently to coat. Add shrimp, if desired, and mix well. Keep warm.

Cook spaghetti or linguine until al dente; drain, and keep warm. Place cooked pasta in a large heated serving bowl or platter. Spread the vegetable and sauce mixture over the pasta; toss gently once or twice, and serve. Yield: 4 to 6 servings.

Cheese Grits

1 cup quick-cooking grits (not instant)
3 cups water
1 teaspoon salt
1 stick margarine
2 eggs, beaten, plus milk to equal 1 cup

8 ounces sharp Cheddar cheese, grated
Garlic powder to taste (optional)
2 to 3 drops hot pepper sauce
Paprika

Preheat oven to 350° F. Grease a 2-quart casserole dish. In a large saucepan, cook grits in salted water. Remove from heat. Stir in margarine, eggs, cheese, garlic powder, and hot pepper sauce. Pour into casserole. Sprinkle top with paprika. Bake for 20 to 30 minutes, or until puffed and nicely browned. Yield: 8 to 10 servings.

Spinach Cheese Grits

4 cups water
½ teaspoon salt
1½ teaspoons garlic powder
1 cup grits

2 cups grated Cheddar cheese
1 (10-ounce) package frozen spinach, thawed
4 eggs, well beaten

Preheat oven to 350° F. Grease a 3-quart casserole dish; set aside. In a saucepan, combine water, salt, and garlic powder. Bring water to a boil, and add grits. Cook for about 2 to 3 minutes at medium-low heat; then add cheese, spinach, and eggs, and stir until cheese melts. Place mixture in prepared dish, and bake for 40 to 50 minutes or until puffy and brown. Yield: 4 servings.

Curried Rice

1⅓ cups white rice
½ tablespoon curry powder
3 tablespoons finely chopped onion
2 tablespoons butter
1 teaspoon salt
1 tablespoon red wine vinegar

⅓ cup slivered almonds, toasted
1 cup finely chopped celery
⅓ cup raisins, chopped
1 cup frozen green peas, thawed
¼ cup mayonnaise

Prepare rice according to package directions. Cook curry powder and onion in butter until onion is soft, but not brown. Add to hot rice along with salt, vinegar, almonds, celery, and raisins. Chill 3 hours. Add peas and mayonnaise. Lightly oil 8 individual (⅓-cup) molds. Pack mixture in molds, and unmold to serve. Yield: 8 servings.

Orange Cashew Rice

1 (11-ounce) can mandarin oranges
Orange juice
3 tablespoons unsalted butter
⅔ cup diced celery
¼ cup finely chopped onion
1½ cups water

2 tablespoons orange zest
1½ teaspoons salt
1 cup uncooked rice
1 cup roasted cashew nuts
Parsley

Drain mandarin oranges, reserving juice. Add enough orange juice to make 1 cup liquid. Melt butter. Add celery, onion, water, mandarin orange juice, orange zest, and salt. Bring to boil. Add rice, stir, and cover. Reduce heat. Cook for 25 to 30 minutes. Gently stir in orange sections and cashew nuts. Garnish with parsley. Yield: 6 servings.

Southern Pecan Pilaf

4 tablespoons unsalted butter,
    divided
1 cup chopped pecans
½ cup chopped onion
2 cups uncooked rice
2 cups chicken stock

2 cups water
½ teaspoon thyme
Black pepper to taste
3 tablespoons chopped parsley,
    divided

Melt 2 tablespoons butter in skillet over medium-high heat. Add pecans and sauté until lightly browned, for about 2 to 3 minutes. Transfer pecans to a small bowl, and set aside. Melt butter in the same skillet. Add onion, and sauté until tender. Stir in rice, coating well with butter. In a saucepan, bring stock, water, thyme, pepper, and 2 tablespoons parsley to a boil. Add rice to mixture. Cover and simmer until liquid is absorbed, for approximately 20 minutes. Add pecans and remaining parsley. Fluff with a fork. Yield: 6 to 8 servings.

Alternatively, place 1 cup sautéed fresh mushrooms in a 6-cup mold. Add pilaf, invert mold, and serve.

Scallion Rice

6 quarts water
4 teaspoons salt
1⅓ cups unconverted long-grain
    rice
⅔ cup finely chopped white part of
    scallion

2 tablespoons unsalted butter
½ cup thinly sliced scallion greens
Salt and freshly ground black
    pepper to taste

In a large saucepan, boil 6 quarts of water and salt. Sprinkle in rice, stirring until water returns to a boil; boil for 10 minutes. Drain rice in a large colander, and rinse. Set colander over a large saucepan of boiling water, cover with a kitchen towel and the lid, and steam rice for 15 minutes, or until fluffy and dry. In a small skillet, cook white part of scallion in butter over moderately low heat, stirring occasionally, until scallion is softened. In a bowl, toss rice with scallion mixture, scallion greens, and salt and black pepper to taste. Yield: 4 servings.

Olive Rice Casserole

Casserole may be prepared earlier in the day and refrigerated until baking time.

1 cup rice
½ cup oil
1 cup tomatoes, with juice
1 cup shredded Cheddar cheese

1 (3-ounce) jar sliced olives
½ cup chopped onions
1 cup water
Salt and black pepper, to taste

Preheat oven to 350° F. Grease a 9x11-inch glass baking dish. Mix all ingredients together, and place in prepared dish. Bake, uncovered, for 1 hour. Stir every 20 minutes so rice cooks evenly. Yield: 8 servings.

Wild Rice and Cream Cheese Bake

1 (6-ounce) box wild rice
½ cup margarine or butter
2 tablespoons flour
1 cup milk

1 (3-ounce) package cream cheese
1 teaspoon salt
1 cup sliced button mushrooms

Preheat oven to 325° F. Grease a 1½-quart casserole dish. Cook wild rice according to directions on box. Pour into colander, and drain well. Melt margarine in top of double boiler; add flour, and stir well until mixture forms a thick paste. Begin to add milk very slowly. Stir constantly. Add cream cheese, and stir until melted and sauce is smooth; add salt. In prepared dish, alternate layers of rice, mushrooms, and cream sauce. Repeat until dish is filled. Be sure to put generous amount of sauce on top. Bake for 20 to 30 minutes or until mixture is hot throughout and golden brown on top. Yield: 12 servings.

Variation: Substitute 1 (6-ounce) box long-grain and wild rice mix (cooked by package directions) for the wild rice. Use 3 (3-ounce) packages of cream cheese instead of 1.

Wild Rice Medley

This dish can be prepared ahead of time, refrigerated,
and baked just before serving.

1 (6-ounce) package long-grain and
   wild rice mix
¼ cup butter or margarine
1 or 2 (4-ounce) cans chopped
   mushrooms
½ cup chopped onion
⅓ cup chopped parsley
1 cup chopped celery

⅛ cup chopped red bell pepper
⅛ cup chopped green bell pepper
¼ cup chicken broth
Salt
Black pepper
8 pieces bacon, cooked and
   crumbled (optional)

Preheat oven to 350° F. Grease an 8x8-inch glass baking dish. Cook rice according to package directions. Melt butter in skillet. Add mushrooms, onion, parsley, celery, and peppers. Sauté until onions are clear and celery and peppers barely tender. Combine with cooked rice; add sautéed vegetables and just enough chicken broth to moisten mixture. Add salt and black pepper to taste. Place into dish, and spread bacon over top. Cover dish with aluminum foil, punch a few holes in the foil, and bake for about 30 minutes. Yield: 4 servings.

Chinese Fried Rice

Fried rice keeps well in refrigerator for several days.
Reheat in microwave oven.

¼ cup butter
1 large onion, chopped
1 large green bell pepper, chopped
1 cup slivered almonds
½ teaspoon garlic salt

¼ teaspoon black pepper
½ cup soy sauce (may use light soy
   sauce)
4 cups cooked long-grain white rice
¼ cup chopped pimiento

In large skillet, melt butter, and brown onion, green bell pepper, and almonds. Add garlic salt, black pepper, and soy sauce; turn off heat. Add 4 cups cooked rice, and mix sauce and vegetables. Keep hot until ready to serve. Add ¼ cup pimiento just before serving. Yield: 4 large servings or 8 smaller servings.

Scrambled Eggs with Cream Cheese and Chives

16 large eggs
4 ounces cold cream cheese, cut
   into bits and softened
2 tablespoons minced fresh chives

Salt and black pepper to taste
2 tablespoons unsalted butter
Chives for garnish

In a bowl, whisk together eggs, cream cheese, minced chives, salt, and black pepper to taste. In a large heavy skillet, melt butter over medium heat. Add egg mixture, cooking and stirring for 6 to 8 minutes, or until eggs are cooked through. Serve eggs sprinkled with additional chives. Yield: 8 servings.

Sausage and Egg Casserole

8 ounces sharp cheese, grated
½ teaspoon dry mustard
½ teaspoon paprika
1 teaspoon salt

1 cup sour cream
1 pound plain sausage, cooked,
   drained, cooled, and crumbled
10 eggs

Preheat oven to 325° F. Grease a 10x6- or 7x11-inch baking dish. Spread 4 ounces of cheese in dish. Mix all seasonings with sour cream, and pour half over cheese. Add crumbled sausage. Beat eggs, and pour over mixture. Spoon remaining sour cream mixture over eggs, and top with remainder of the grated cheese. Bake for 20 to 25 minutes. Yield: 10 to 12 servings.

Ham Frittata

1 (8-ounce) carton cholesterol-free
   egg product
½ cup chopped lean ham
1 tablespoon Dijon mustard
1 teaspoon parsley flakes

¼ teaspoon ground black pepper
1 cup cubed, cooked potato
¼ cup sliced mushrooms
2 tablespoons chopped green bell
   pepper

Preheat broiler. In mixing bowl, combine egg product, ham, mustard, parsley, and black pepper; set aside. Preheat nonstick oven-safe skillet, sprayed with nonstick vegetable spray, over medium heat. Sauté potatoes, mushrooms, and green bell pepper until tender, stirring occasionally. Pour egg product mixture over vegetables. Cook 4 to 5 minutes or until bottom is set. Place skillet in broiler 6 inches from heat. Broil 4 to 5 minutes or until lightly browned. Yield: 4 servings.

Crab Quiche

2 eggs, beaten
½ cup milk
½ cup mayonnaise
2 teaspoons flour
1 (8-ounce) package Swiss cheese,
   shredded

2 (6-ounce) cans crabmeat, drained
1 small onion, chopped
1 deep-dish pie shell, unbaked
Salt and black pepper to taste

Preheat oven to 350° F. Beat eggs and milk together; combine mayonnaise and flour, and stir together with egg mixture. Add Swiss cheese, crab, and onion. Mix together. Add salt and black pepper. Pour mixture into unbaked pie crust. Bake for 45 minutes. Cool for 10 minutes. Yield: 8 servings.

Shrimp, Crab, or Lobster Quiche

2 tablespoons shallots or scallions

3 tablespoons unsalted butter

1 cup cooked and cleaned shrimp, crab, or lobster

¼ teaspoon salt

Pinch of black pepper

2 tablespoons Madeira or dry white vermouth (optional)

3 eggs

1 cup whipping cream

1 tablespoon tomato paste

¼ teaspoon salt

Pinch of black pepper

8- to 9-inch deep-dish pastry shell, baked according to package directions for 5 minutes

¼ cup shredded Swiss cheese

Preheat oven to 375° F. Cook the shallots in butter for about 2 minutes or until tender, but not browned. Add shellfish, and stir gently over moderate heat for 2 minutes. Sprinkle with salt and black pepper. If desired, add wine; increase heat, and boil for 1 minute. Allow to cool slightly. In mixing bowl, beat 3 eggs with the cream, tomato paste, and seasonings. Gradually blend in shellfish, and taste for seasoning. Pour mixture into pie shell, and sprinkle Swiss cheese on top. Bake in upper third of oven for 25 to 30 minutes, or until quiche has puffed and browned. Yield: 4 to 6 servings.

Spinach and Sausage Quiche

1 (8-ounce) package cream cheese, softened

4 eggs

1 (12-ounce) can evaporated milk

1 (10-ounce) package chopped spinach, thawed and well drained

1 pound sausage, cooked and drained

¼ teaspoon red pepper flakes (optional)

1 deep-dish pie crust, baked 5 minutes according to package directions

Preheat oven to 350° F. Beat cream cheese until smooth; beat in eggs and milk. Stir in spinach, sausage, and red pepper. Pour into pie shell, and bake for 50 to 60 minutes. Yield: 6 servings.

Quiche Lorraine

1 stick butter
½ (8-ounce) package cream cheese
1 cup flour
1½ cups half-and-half
3 eggs
1 to 2 teaspoons minced scallion

¼ teaspoon salt
⅛ teaspoon black pepper
1 cup cooked meat (bacon, ham, or sausage)
6 to 8 ounces Swiss or Gruyère cheese, cut into long, 1-inch-wide slices

Cream butter and cream cheese. Add flour to form dough. Roll out crust between waxed paper, and refrigerate 1 to 2 hours. (For shorter preparation time, push crust into pie plate with fingers.) Preheat oven to 450° F. Mix half-and-half, eggs, scallion, salt, and black pepper. Layer meat and cheese in a pie plate. Pour cream mixture over all. Bake for 10 minutes. Reduce heat to 325° F.; bake for 30 minutes. Yield: 6 servings.

Variation: Add steamed vegetables, with or without meat.

Entrees

*Nearly a century old and located in the heart of Pinehurst,
the gracious Holly Inn offers beautiful accommodations
and a lovely Victorian dining room.*

*Whether professional or amateur, many golfing careers
have started at Pinehurst, North Carolina's golfing mecca.*

Flounder Stuffed with Crabmeat

8 long flounder fillets
¼ teaspoon salt
½ pound crabmeat
1 egg, lightly beaten
1 tablespoon Worcestershire sauce
½ teaspoon mustard

¼ cup milk
½ cup crushed buttery crackers
Melted butter
Paprika
Sour Cream Dill Sauce

Preheat oven to 375° F. Lightly salt flounder fillets; set aside. Mix crabmeat, egg, Worcestershire sauce, and mustard, and spread on fillets. Roll fillet into a tight roll. Dip flounder rolls in milk and then in dry cracker crumbs to coat well. Place seam side down in a well greased 13x9x2-inch baking dish. Sprinkle with melted butter and paprika. Bake uncovered for 20 minutes or until nicely browned. Serve with Sour Cream Dill Sauce.

Sour Cream Dill Sauce:
¼ cup egg substitute or 1 egg
1 teaspoon salt
Pinch of sugar
Pinch of ground black pepper
4 teaspoons lemon juice

1 teaspoon grated onion
2 teaspoons finely chopped fresh
  dill or 1 teaspoon dried dillweed
1½ cups sour cream

Beat the egg until fluffy and lemon-colored. Add remaining ingredients. Stir until blended and chill. Yield: 8 servings.

Red Snapper in Parchment Paper

2 tablespoons margarine
6 (4-ounce) red snapper fillets
¼ teaspoon salt
White pepper to taste
2 shallots, minced
½ cup julienned celery

½ cup julienned carrots
½ cup julienned zucchini
½ cup julienned red bell pepper
½ cup yellow squash
Chablis or other dry white wine
6 thin lemon slices

Preheat oven to 400° F. Cut six 12x9-inch pieces of parchment paper or aluminum foil; fold in half lengthwise, creasing firmly. Trim each piece into a heart shape. Place parchment hearts on 3 baking sheets. Place 1 teaspoon margarine on each parchment heart. Place fillets, skin side down, on top of margarine near crease. Sprinkle with salt and white pepper. Top evenly with vegetables. Drizzle 1 tablespoon wine over each fillet; top with lemon slice. Fold over remaining halves of parchment hearts. Starting with rounded edge of heart, crimp and fold edges together to seal. Bake for 20 to 25 minutes or until bags are puffed and lightly browned, and fish flakes easily with a fork. Immediately transfer bags to dinner plates. Cut a cross in top of each bag with scissors, and fold back the bag. Yield: 6 servings.

Poached Salmon with Garlic Mayonnaise

4 (½-pound) salmon fillets
1 cup dry white wine
1 cup water
1 teaspoon dillweed
2 cloves garlic, crushed

¼ cup mayonnaise
1 teaspoon fresh lemon juice
¼ teaspoon white pepper
½ teaspoon Dijon mustard

Preheat oven to 350° F. Place salmon fillets in a 13x9x2-inch baking dish, and cover with wine and water. Sprinkle with dillweed, and cover dish with aluminum foil. Bake for 20 minutes.

Combine garlic and remaining ingredients, and blend until smooth. Remove salmon from oven; discard liquid, and allow to cool. Serve salmon, topped with garlic mayonnaise, at room temperature. Yield: 4 servings.

Sea Bass with Shrimp

1 pound sea bass steaks
1 tablespoon olive oil, divided
2 medium ripe tomatoes, diced
1 (8-ounce) can mushroom stems and pieces, drained
3 cloves garlic, thinly sliced

½ pound cooked shrimp
¼ bunch fresh parsley
1 lemon, cut in wedges, for garnish
2 medium tomatoes, cut in wedges, for garnish

Preheat oven to 400° F. In a 11x7x2-inch baking pan, arrange sea bass in a single layer. Brush with 1 teaspoon of the olive oil. Combine remaining olive oil, diced tomatoes, mushrooms, and garlic, and pour mixture over sea bass. Bake, uncovered, for 10 minutes per inch of thickness of fish. Three to four minutes before fish is done, sprinkle shrimp over top. When sea bass turns white and flakes readily when touched with a fork, transfer it, the shrimp, and the vegetables to a platter lined with parsley. Garnish with lemon and tomato wedges. Yield: 5 servings.

Grilled Ginger Tuna

¾ cup light soy sauce
1½ cups orange juice
½ tablespoon minced garlic

½ tablespoon minced ginger
¼ cup olive oil
6 (1-inch-thick) tuna steaks

Prepare grill. Combine soy sauce, orange juice, garlic, ginger, and oil. Pour over tuna steaks, and marinate, covered, in refrigerator for 4 to 6 hours. Grill tuna over hot coals for approximately 6 to 8 minutes per side. Yield: 6 servings.

Tilapia with Tarragon Sauce

*Lake trout, catfish, rockfish, or Nile perch may be
substituted for the tilapia.*

1 pound tilapia fillets	1 tablespoon fresh lemon juice
Olive oil or canola oil	Tarragon Sauce
Salt to taste	

Rinse fillets, and pat dry. If large, cut into serving pieces. Coat nonstick skillet
with a few drops of oil. After oil is heated, place fillets in pan in one layer,
and sprinkle with salt. Sauté fillets for 10 minutes per inch of thickness
measured at thickest part. Turn halfway through cooking time; sprinkle with
additional salt and lemon juice. Continue to cook until flesh turns opaque in
center of thickest part, and surfaces are golden brown. Serve with Tarragon
Sauce. Yield: 4 servings.

Tarragon Sauce:

½ cup nonfat yogurt	1 teaspoon chopped fresh tarragon
1 tablespoon reduced-calorie	Pinch of salt
mayonnaise	

Prepare tarragon sauce by combining all ingredients, covering, and refrigerating for ½ hour.

Trout Grilled with Tomatoes

4 cleaned trout	8 cherry tomatoes, halved
1 teaspoon salt, divided	¼ cup oil, divided
¼ teaspoon black pepper, divided	1 teaspoon oregano, divided

Prepare grill. Pat trout dry. Sprinkle cavity of each with ¼ teaspoon salt and a
dash of black pepper. Place each trout in a square of aluminum foil large
enough to fold it around the fish. Arrange 4 tomato halves on each trout.
Drizzle 1 tablespoon oil over each trout and dust it with ¼ teaspoon oregano.
Fold each square securely, sealing with a double fold. Grill over medium hot
coals, turning once, for 15 minutes. Serve in foil. Yield: 4 servings.

Tuna (or Salmon) with Ginger Sauce

*Serve fish with additional vegetables, such as whole
steamed green beans with a little lemon juice and
waffle cut sweet potatoes, deep-fried and sprinkled
with cinnamon sugar.*

4 cloves garlic
1 pound organic young spinach
8 (8- to 10-ounce) tuna steaks or
   salmon fillets
½ cup teriyaki sauce
4 (1x1-inch) pieces ginger root,
   peeled
3 medium carrots
8 stalks celery
12 green onions

4 leeks
1 pound mushrooms
½ cup olive oil, divided
¾ cup dry sherry or vermouth
1 lemon
1 pint heavy cream
2 sticks sweet butter, cold
Salt and freshly ground black
   pepper to taste

Crush garlic; set aside. Remove stems and wash spinach; set aside. Marinate tuna steaks in teriyaki sauce for about 30 minutes; remove tuna steaks from marinade and place on broiler pan.

Preheat broiler. Julienne the ginger into ⅛x½-inch pieces. Julienne the carrots, celery, onions, and leeks into ¼x3-inch pieces. Slice the mushrooms thin. Heat a large pan or wok. Add half the olive oil, and sauté garlic quickly but do not brown. Add the spinach, and sauté until wilted. Divide mixture onto 8 plates, making a thin bed of spinach on each plate. Put tuna into broiler, and broil for approximately 10 minutes per inch of thickness, turning once.

As fish is cooking, heat a 12- to 14-inch sauté pan until very hot. Stir-fry ginger quickly; then add vegetables and remaining olive oil. Stir-fry for 2 to 3 minutes; add sherry, and reduce by half. Add juice of the lemon and then the cream. Reduce slightly. Add butter, one slice at a time. Stir until melted. Add salt and black pepper to taste. Place one steak or fillet on each bed of spinach and apportion vegetables and sauce over each steak. Yield: 8 servings.

Tuna with Tomato Basil Sauce

2 tablespoons olive oil
2 cloves garlic
3 tomatoes, diced
¼ cup finely chopped fresh basil
½ teaspoon salt

¼ teaspoon black pepper
4 (4-ounce) fresh tuna steaks (about ½ inch thick)
1 bunch red lettuce or arugula (optional)

Prepare coals, and cover grill with foil. In a blender or food processor, combine olive oil, garlic, tomatoes, basil, salt, and black pepper, and purée until smooth.

Grill tuna over hot coals for about 5 minutes until done, turning only once. Line individual plates with red leaf lettuce leaves. Arrange tuna on top. Grind black pepper over tuna if desired. Serve with sauce. Yield: 4 servings.

Crab Cakes

2 slices bread, crust removed
Small amount of milk
1 pound lump crabmeat
1 teaspoon Old Bay Seasoning
¼ teaspoon salt
1 tablespoon mayonnaise

1 tablespoon Worcestershire sauce
1 tablespoon chopped parsley
1 tablespoon baking powder
1 egg, beaten
Vegetable oil for frying

Break bread into small pieces and moisten with milk. Mix all ingredients and shape into patties. Fry quickly in vegetable oil until brown. Yield: 4 servings.

Scalloped Oysters

1 quart oysters
Black pepper to taste
1 cup toasted breadcrumbs, divided
3 tablespoons flour
6 tablespoons butter

1 cup milk
2 egg yolks
2 teaspoons lemon juice
2 teaspoons Worcestershire sauce
1 teaspoon celery salt

Preheat oven to 350° F. Put oysters in saucepan with black pepper, and cook until edges curl. Make sauce from flour, butter, milk, egg yolks, lemon juice, Worcestershire sauce, and celery salt. Sauce should be consistency of medium white sauce. Fold sauce into oysters. Add ¾ cup breadcrumbs to this mixture. Put in casserole, and sprinkle ¼ cup breadcrumbs on top. Bake for 15 minutes. Yield: 4 servings.

Pan-Seared Scallops with Citrus Sauce

2 tablespoons olive oil
1 pound sea scallops
Juice of 1 orange
Juice of 1 lemon
2 teaspoons cornstarch, mixed with
    2 tablespoons water
Salt and freshly ground black
    pepper to taste

¼ teaspoon dried dill
½ pound angel hair pasta, cooked al dente
½ bunch scallions, chopped
3 tablespoons freshly chopped parsley

Heat pan, and add oil. Heat oil so that scallops sizzle when added. Cook scallops until firm, for 3 to 4 minutes, being careful not to overcook. Add orange juice, lemon juice, and cornstarch, and stir until mixture thickens. Add salt, black pepper, and dill, and stir until blended. Serve scallops and sauce over pasta, and garnish with scallions and parsley. Yield: 2 to 3 servings.

Grilled Scallop, Bacon, and Cherry Tomato Kebabs

24 sea scallops
2 large cloves garlic, minced
4 teaspoons fresh lemon juice
4 teaspoons olive oil

16 slices bacon
24 vine-ripened cherry tomatoes
Lemon wedges as an
   accompaniment

Prepare grill. In a shallow dish, toss scallops with garlic, lemon juice, and oil to coat. Marinate scallops, covered, for 20 minutes in refrigerator.

In a skillet, cook bacon over moderate heat until pale golden but still soft. Transfer scallops to paper towels to drain, reserving grease. Thread scallops, bacon, and tomatoes onto 8 (10-inch) skewers. Brush kebabs with some of reserved grease. On an oiled rack, set about 6 inches over glowing coals, grill kebabs for 3 to 4 minutes. Turn kebabs and grill for 3 to 4 minutes more, or until scallops are just cooked through. Serve kebabs with lemon wedges. Yield: 4 servings.

Grilled Shrimp

Using an outdoor grill adds flavor.

2 cloves garlic, minced
2 tablespoons fresh cilantro,
   chopped
Juice of 3 lemons, or 6 tablespoons
   lemon juice

¼ cup olive oil
1½ pounds fresh, uncooked shrimp,
   peeled and deveined

Prepare grill. Mix garlic, cilantro, lemons, and olive oil together; add shrimp. Marinate for 30 minutes. Thread shrimp on skewers. Grill each side for 2 minutes. Yield: 4 servings.

Shrimp Creole

6 tablespoons oil
6 tablespoons flour
3 pounds shrimp, cooked, peeled, and deveined
2 cups onion, chopped
1 cup celery, chopped
1 cup green pepper, chopped
1 cup scallions, sliced

3 cloves garlic, minced
1 (16-ounce) can tomato sauce
1 (16-ounce) can tomatoes
2 bay leaves
1 cup water
1 tablespoon Worcestershire sauce
1 teaspoon each black pepper, salt, basil, and cayenne pepper

In large stockpot, make a roux with oil and flour by cooking them together, stirring constantly, over very low heat until the mixture browns. Add remaining ingredients, and stir well. Cook, uncovered, stirring periodically, over low heat until thickened. Then, at a slow simmer, cook, covered, for 1½ to 2 hours. Serve over rice. Yield: 8 servings.

Curried Shrimp with Almond Rice

2 tablespoons butter
¼ cup chopped onion
1 minced clove garlic
1 teaspoon curry powder
1 (10¾-ounce) can condensed cream of mushroom soup
½ cup milk

1 pound (or more, to taste) cooked shrimp, peeled and deveined
1 cup uncooked rice
¼ cup slivered almonds, toasted
1 tablespoon parsley
1 tablespoon butter

In 2-quart saucepan, melt butter; sauté onion and garlic until tender, but not brown. Stir in curry powder and soup. Gradually add milk and shrimp; keep warm. Cook rice according to directions; add almonds, parsley, and butter to rice after cooking. Serve shrimp mixture over rice. Yield: 4 servings.

Feta Cheese and Shrimp

2 onions, chopped
Olive oil
3 (16-ounce) cans Italian stewed
  tomatoes
½ teaspoon oregano
3 tablespoons chopped parsley
1 tablespoon Greek seasoning

2 pounds cooked shrimp, peeled
  and deveined
8 ounces Feta cheese, crumbled
1 (16-ounce) package angel hair
  noodles
4 tablespoons butter
½ cup heavy cream or milk
Parmesan cheese

Preheat oven to 350° F. In a saucepan, sauté onions until tender in a small amount of olive oil. Stir in tomatoes and seasonings, and heat mixture thoroughly. Layer tomato mixture, shrimp, and Feta cheese in 13x9x2-inch baking dish. Bake until hot and bubbly, for approximately 10 minutes.

Cook angel hair pasta as directed on package. Drain. Return pasta to pot, and add butter and cream. Stir constantly. Sprinkle in Parmesan cheese. Continue to stir until well mixed. Serve tomato mixture over pasta. Yield: 8 to 10 servings.

Carolina Shrimp in Wine Sauce

1 pound cooked shrimp, peeled and
  deveined
¾ cup chopped onion
¼ cup butter or margarine, melted
3 tablespoons flour
1 cup chicken bouillon

¾ cup sliced mushrooms
½ cup sour cream
¼ cup dry white wine
Cooked rice for 6 people
Parsley or pimiento for garnish

Thaw shrimp, if frozen. In a large saucepan, cook onion in butter until tender. Blend in flour. Add chicken bouillon gradually, and cook until thick, stirring constantly. Add mushrooms, sour cream, wine, and shrimp. Heat, stirring occasionally. Serve over hot, fluffy rice. Garnish with parsley or pimiento. Yield: 6 servings.

Eye of Round with Brown Devil Sauce

A whole 5- to 6-pound eye of round   **Brown Devil Sauce**

Prepare grill. Brown beef over charcoal grill, then roast slowly, covered, until desired doneness. Slice and serve with brown devil sauce. If desired, remove the onions before serving.

Brown Devil Sauce:

4 tablespoons margarine   **¼ teaspoon black pepper**
2 thin slices onion   **2 teaspoons Worcestershire sauce**
4 tablespoons flour   **2 teaspoons vinegar**
2 cups beef broth   **2 tablespoons parsley**
¼ teaspoon salt

Melt margarine. Add onion and sauté lightly. Stir in flour. Add broth and remaining ingredients. Cook for 2 to 3 minutes. Yield: 8 to 10 servings.

Marinated Beef Tenderloin

A 6 to 8 pound beef tenderloin   **1¾ cups soy sauce**
Ground black pepper or cracked   **¾ cup bourbon**
  pepper   **4 strips bacon**
2 cloves garlic, crushed   **1 sliced medium onion**

Place beef in a plastic bag. Sprinkle beef with pepper. Mix garlic, soy sauce, and bourbon; pour mixture over beef. Marinate for at least 2 hours at room temperature or overnight in the refrigerator. Bring beef to room temperature before cooking. Preheat oven to 450° F. Put meat on a rack. Place bacon strips on top of beef. Pour remaining marinade over all, and place onions on top. Place beef in oven, and immediately reduce heat to 400° F. Roast, uncovered, for 35 minutes to 1 hour. Baste frequently. Yield: 10 or 12 entrée servings, or 25 to 35 cocktail servings.

Barbecued Beef Brisket

A 3 pound beef brisket
1 (10¾-ounce) can cream of
   mushroom soup

1 envelope onion soup mix
Barbecue Sauce, or 1 cup
   commercial sauce

Preheat oven to 300° F. Place double thickness of heavy-duty aluminum foil in a 13x9x2-inch baking dish. Foil should be large enough to wrap beef while leaving 1-inch clearance. Mix mushroom soup, onion soup mix, and barbecue sauce. Pour over beef. Seal foil tightly, leaving about 1-inch clearance between the beef and the foil. Bake for 2½ to 3 hours or until meat is almost falling apart. Let stand for 10 minutes. Slice thin; serve with sauce.

Barbecue Sauce:
1 cup ketchup
2 tablespoons prepared yellow
   mustard
¼ cup white vinegar

⅓ cup dark brown sugar
2 teaspoons Worcestershire sauce
½ teaspoon salt
¼ teaspoon hot pepper sauce

Combine all ingredients in a small saucepan, and heat slowly to combine flavors. Stir while heating. Yield: 4 to 6 servings of beef; 8 servings of sauce.

Baked Spicy Corned Beef

A 4 to 6 pound corned beef brisket
2 tablespoons pickling spice
1 orange, sliced
1 stalk celery with leaves, sliced

1 onion, sliced
⅓ cup brown sugar
1 tablespoon prepared mustard

Soak corned beef in water to cover for ½ hour, or longer if beef is deeply corned. Preheat oven to 300° F. Place a large sheet of heavy-duty aluminum foil on a shallow pan. Remove corned beef from water, and pat dry, removing any surface salt. Place beef in center of foil, and pour ¼ cup fresh water over top. Sprinkle with pickling spice, and arrange orange slices and vegetables over and around meat. Bring long ends of foil up over meat, and seal with a double fold. Seal other ends, turning them up so liquid cannot run out. Bake for 4 hours. Unwrap beef and place in shallow pan. Spread with brown sugar and mustard. Bake for 15 to 20 minutes at 375° F. or until glazed. Yield: 8 to 10 servings.

Marinated Chuck Roast

A 3½ pound chuck roast
⅓ cup wine vinegar
¼ cup ketchup
2 tablespoons salad oil
2 tablespoons soy sauce

2 tablespoons Worcestershire sauce
1 teaspoon prepared mustard
1 teaspoon salt
¼ teaspoon black pepper
¼ teaspoon garlic powder

Combine ingredients, and marinate overnight. Turn once or twice. Drain marinade. Grill or broil beef in oven until desired doneness, or cook in crock-pot on high setting for 4 to 6 hours. Yield: 6 to 8 servings.

Barbecue Beef Spareribs

16 to 24 large beef spareribs
1 stick margarine
½ cup white vinegar
½ cup catsup
½ cup lemon juice

½ cup Worcestershire sauce
2 teaspoons prepared mustard
1 cup brown sugar
Hot pepper sauce or cayenne
 pepper to taste, if desired

Preheat oven to 325° F. Trim fat from ribs and arrange them in shallow baking pans. Mix margarine and remaining ingredients in a saucepan; cook on low heat until thoroughly blended. Taste for sweetness, and add sugar, if desired. Baste all ribs very lightly, and roast for 30 minutes. Baste ribs again, and roast for 30 more minutes. Baste one more time, and roast for 30 more minutes. (Total cooking time: 1½ hours). Ribs will look almost charcoaled, but not burned. Yield: 4 servings.

Filet Dijon

2 tablespoons butter
2 tablespoons oil
Salt, pepper, and seasoned salt
  flavor enhancer, to taste
8 filets mignon
½ cup brandy
1 cup heavy cream

1½ tablespoons Worcestershire
  sauce
1½ tablespoons Dijon mustard
¼ teaspoon garlic powder
1 teaspoon parsley, chopped
Cornstarch, as needed

Heat butter and oil in large skillet. Season steaks, and sauté about 5 or 6 minutes per side for rare doneness; transfer to heated platter. Pour off fat in pan, add brandy, and warm. Ignite and shake until flames go out. Combine cream, Worcestershire sauce, mustard, garlic powder, and parsley; add to pan. Cook until hot but not boiling. Add cornstarch to thicken sauce. Spoon sauce over steaks, and serve. Yield: 8 servings.

Steak Diane

1 tablespoon reduced-calorie
  margarine, melted
2 tablespoons low-sodium
  Worcestershire sauce
¾ pound fresh mushrooms, sliced

1 cup chopped onion
4 (4-ounce) beef tenderloin steaks
  (1-inch thick)
¼ cup Dijon mustard, divided
¼ cup brandy

Combine margarine and Worcestershire sauce in a large nonstick skillet; cook over medium heat until hot. Add mushrooms and onion, and sauté them until tender. Place steaks between 2 sheets of heavy-duty plastic wrap, and flatten to ¼-inch thickness, using a meat mallet or rolling pin. Spread 1½ teaspoons mustard on one side of each steak.

Move mushroom mixture to one side of skillet; add steaks, mustard side down. Cook steaks for 3 to 4 minutes over medium heat. Stir mushroom mixture occasionally. Spread 1½ teaspoons mustard on top side of each steak, turn, and cook for 3 to 4 minutes on other side of steak or to desired degree of doneness. Lightly pierce steaks in several places with a fork. Pour brandy over steaks; cover, reduce heat, and simmer for 1 minute. Remove steaks to heated platter; spoon mushroom mixture over steaks. Yield: 4 servings.

Medallions of Veal with Apple Brandy Mushroom Sauce

A ½ pound round of veal (³/₈-inch thick)
Flour for dredging veal
6 tablespoons salted butter
½ pound fresh mushrooms, sliced

¼ cup apple brandy
¼ teaspoon salt
⅛ teaspoon white pepper
1 cup heavy cream

Preheat oven to 200° F. Trim all fat and gristle from veal, and cut it into 2x4-inch pieces. Dredge pieces in flour. In skillet, melt butter, and sauté veal and mushrooms for about 8 minutes until they are golden brown. Remove veal, leaving butter in skillet; keep veal warm in oven.

Add brandy to mushrooms and butter. Mix thoroughly. Add salt and white pepper. Gradually add cream, stirring constantly until sauce thickens. Cook until reduced by one-third, continuing to stir frequently. To serve, remove veal from oven, and spoon the sauce evenly over portions. Yield: 2 servings.

Nectarine Veal Steaks

*Four large ripe peaches can be
substituted for nectarines.*

1 stick unsalted butter
4 veal steaks, pounded
Salt and black pepper to taste
¼ teaspoon ground ginger

6 fresh nectarines, peeled, pitted, and thickly sliced
⅔ cup dry sherry
2 cups sour cream

Melt butter in large skillet. Add steaks, and sauté until browned. Remove from heat, and season with salt, pepper, and ginger. Using a slotted spoon, remove steaks from pan, and sauté nectarines in butter remaining in skillet. Remove nectarines and keep warm with steaks. Add sherry to pan; cook over low heat until liquid is reduced by half. Add sour cream slowly, and heat. Return steaks to pan; warm. To serve, spoon sauce over steaks, and top with browned nectarines. Yield: 4 servings.

Grilled London Broil

A 4- to 6-pound London broil
½ cup olive oil
Juice of 2 lemons
½ cup dry red wine
½ cup dry sherry
2 tablespoons oregano

1 tablespoon soy sauce
1 tablespoon honey
1 tablespoon Worcestershire sauce
3 cloves garlic, finely chopped
2 large onions, thinly sliced
Horseradish Sauce

Trim any excess fat from meat. For the marinade, combine all other ingredients. At least 24 hours before serving, pour marinade over beef, and press it in with the back of a spoon. Refrigerate, and turn often. Remove beef from the refrigerator 2 hours before grilling, and continue to turn. Prepare grill. In a grilling basket, layer half the sliced onions, the beef, and the remaining onions. Grill beef until medium rare. Slice the meat on an angle against the grain. Serve with Horseradish Sauce.

Horseradish Sauce:
1 (8-ounce) package cream cheese
Raw horseradish, grated, to taste

Parsley, to taste

Soften cream cheese in microwave. Add horseradish and parsley. Serve warm.
Yield: 8 to 10 servings.

Flank Steak with Mushroom Sauce

*Mushroom Sauce can be made ahead
and reheated before serving.*

A 2 pound prime flank steak	1 teaspoon salt
1 tablespoon salad oil	2 teaspoons parsley, chopped
1 teaspoon lemon juice	1/8 teaspoon black pepper
1 clove garlic, crushed	Mushroom Sauce

Preheat broiler. Wipe steak with damp paper towel. Combine oil and remaining ingredients. Use half the mixture to brush top of steak. Arrange on lightly greased rack in broiler pan. Broil 4 inches from heat for 5 minutes. Turn; baste with remaining liquid. Broil for 3 to 5 minutes longer. Slice meat in thin slices across grain, and serve with Mushroom Sauce. Yield: 4 to 6 servings.

Mushroom Sauce:	1 bay leaf
3 tablespoons butter	2 tablespoons flour
1 shallot, chopped	1 cup canned beef bouillon
1 clove garlic, chopped	1 cup mushrooms, sliced thick
1 slice onion	1/4 teaspoon salt
2 carrot slices	1/8 teaspoon black pepper
Parsley sprig	1/3 cup Burgundy wine
6 whole peppercorns	2 tablespoons finely chopped fresh
1 whole clove	parsley

Heat butter. Add shallot, garlic, onion, carrots, parsley, peppercorns, clove, and bay leaf. Sauté about 3 minutes. Remove from heat. Add flour and stir until smooth. Cook, stirring until flour is lightly browned, for about 5 minutes. Remove from heat; gradually stir in bouillon. Over medium heat, bring to boiling point, stirring constantly. Reduce heat. Simmer for 10 minutes. Sauté mushrooms in separate skillet for about 5 minutes. Strain bouillon mixture, discarding vegetables. Add salt, black pepper, burgundy, parsley, and mushroom mixture. Yield: 1 1/3 cups.

Marinated Flank Steak Italiano

Leftovers make great sandwiches.

2 to 3 tablespoons soy sauce
1 tablespoon tomato paste
1 tablespoon olive oil
¼ to ½ tablespoon black pepper
½ teaspoon oregano
1 large clove garlic, sliced
A 1½ pound flank steak

1 teaspoon dry basil
1 (6-ounce) package sliced dry salami
1 small mild white onion, thinly sliced
1 (6-ounce) package sliced Provolone cheese

Make a paste with soy sauce, tomato paste, olive oil, black pepper, oregano, and garlic. Score flank steak; spread paste on both sides of meat. Refrigerate for at least 24 hours.

Prepare grill. Lay steak flat. With a sharp knife, cut a deep long slit in the center of a long edge, making a pocket almost as big as the steak. Be careful not to cut through steak at sides or back. Open pocket; sprinkle basil inside. Arrange half the salami over the bottom of the pocket, then add onion, cheese, and remaining salami in even layers. Close with metal skewers. Place steak on a lightly greased grill for 4 to 6 inches above a solid bed of medium coals. Cook, turning once, until steak is done to desired doneness (about 14 minutes for medium-rare). To serve, cut across the grain into ½-inch-thick slices. Yield: 4 to 6 servings.

Oriental Beef with Broccoli

4 servings white rice
1 or 2 large bunches fresh broccoli,
 separated into flowerets
1 pound flank steak
2½ teaspoons cornstarch, divided
2 teaspoons sugar, divided
½ teaspoon ginger

2 tablespoons soy sauce
Dash of garlic powder
5 tablespoons water, divided
5 tablespoons oil, divided
1 can bamboo shoots, drained
1 cup sliced fresh mushrooms
1 teaspoon salt

Prepare rice according to instructions. Cut broccoli flowerets. Slice steak in thin bite-size strips across grain. In small bowl, mix 1½ teaspoons cornstarch, 1 teaspoon sugar, ginger, soy sauce, garlic powder, and 1 tablespoon water. Stir in beef, and set aside. Preheat 2 tablespoons oil in wok. Add beef, and stir-fry for 1 minute. Remove beef. Heat remaining 3 tablespoons oil. Stir in broccoli, bamboo shoots, and mushrooms. Stir-fry 2 minutes. Add salt, 1 teaspoon sugar, and 3 tablespoons water; mix. Cook for 1 minute. Add beef and marinade. Cook and stir for 1 minute. Blend 1 teaspoon cornstarch and 1 tablespoon water. Add cornstarch mixture to wok, stirring until slightly thickened. Serve with white rice. Yield: 4 servings.

Sukiyaki

Sukiyaki is a delicious way to use leftover roast beef.

4 large mushrooms, sliced
4 scallions, sliced
1 medium onion, sliced
3 (5-inch) pieces celery, sliced thin
3 tablespoons salad oil
½ pound rare roast beef, sliced in
 thin strips

½ can beef consommé
Sugar to taste (1 to 2 tablespoons)
4 tablespoons soy sauce
¼ pound fresh spinach, cleaned and
 torn into large pieces
Rice or Chinese noodles

In skillet over medium heat, lightly sauté mushrooms, onions, and celery in oil. Add beef, and heat. Add consommé, sugar, and soy sauce; cook for 5 to 10 minutes. Add spinach. Cook two to three minutes until just hot and limp. Serve over rice or Chinese noodles. Yield: 3 or 4 servings.

Beef and Pork Loaf with Mushrooms

Recipe doubles easily and freezes well.

1½ cups finely chopped onion
½ cup finely chopped celery
2 garlic cloves, minced
1½ teaspoons dried thyme, crumbled
2 tablespoons unsalted butter
2 teaspoons salt
1½ teaspoons freshly ground black pepper
2 cups finely chopped mushrooms (preferably chopped in a food processor)

1½ pounds ground chuck
¾ pound ground pork
1 cup fresh breadcrumbs
2 large eggs, beaten lightly
⅔ cup bottled chili sauce or ketchup, divided
1 (14- to 16-ounce) can stewed tomatoes, drained and chopped
⅓ cup minced fresh parsley leaves
3 slices of lean bacon, halved crosswise

Place rack in middle of oven, and preheat to 350° F. In a skillet, cook onion, celery, garlic, and thyme in butter over moderately low heat, stirring, until onion is tender. Add salt, black pepper, and mushrooms, and cook mixture over moderate heat, stirring, for 5 to 10 minutes. Mushrooms should be tender, and the liquid they give off should have evaporated. Transfer mixture to a large bowl, and let it cool. To the bowl, add the chuck, pork, breadcrumbs, eggs, ⅓ cup chili sauce, tomatoes, and parsley; stir mixture until it is combined well. Form mixture into a 10x7-inch oval loaf in a shallow baking pan, and spread remaining ⅓ cup chili sauce over it, draping bacon pieces across the loaf. Bake meat loaf for 1 hour, or until a meat thermometer inserted in center registers 155° F. Yield: 6 to 8 servings.

Roast Leg of Lamb with Scallion Sauce

¾ cup lemon juice
3 tablespoons Dijon mustard
3 tablespoons olive oil
1 teaspoon fresh rosemary, chopped
  (optional)

3 large cloves of garlic, slivered
1 (6-pound) fresh leg of lamb,
  boned
Flour
Scallion Sauce

For marinade, mix lemon juice, mustard, olive oil, and rosemary. Randomly insert the slivers of garlic into entire leg of lamb. Pour marinade over lamb, and marinate lamb for 24 hours. Preheat oven to 375° F. Remove lamb from marinade. Add enough flour to marinade to make a paste. Coat the lamb with the paste. Place lamb in oven, and roast, uncovered, on a rack for 20 minutes per pound or until a meat thermometer inserted in center registers 165° F. Remove lamb from oven. Serve, sliced, with Scallion Sauce.

Scallion Sauce:
18 scallions
1 tablespoon butter
1½ cups chicken stock
3 tablespoons sugar

¼ teaspoon salt
½ cup heavy cream
2 tablespoons Dijon mustard

Wash the scallions, and trim off tops, leaving ½ inch of the green portion. Melt butter in a skillet, and add chicken stock and sugar. Bring mixture to a boil. Add scallions and salt, and simmer until scallions are tender. Remove scallions from pan. Raise heat, and reduce liquid slightly. Add cream and mustard. Stir until sauce is smooth. Return scallions to pan. Yield: 6 servings.

Orange Glazed Pork Loin Roast

A 4- to 5-pound boneless pork loin, rolled and tied
½ teaspoon salt
½ teaspoon dried thyme

½ teaspoon ground ginger
¼ teaspoon black pepper
3 large cloves garlic, quartered
Orange Glaze

Preheat oven to 350° F. Cut 12 slits in top of pork. Mix together salt, thyme, ginger, and black pepper. Press some of the herb mixture onto the pork. Then place pork on rack in baking pan, and place 1 slice of garlic into each slit. Rub rest of herb mixture over pork. Roast 2 to 2½ hours. Glaze roast, and bake for 45 minutes to 1 hour; glazing again after 30 minutes.

Orange Glaze:
1 cup sugar
2 tablespoons cornstarch
1 tablespoon flour
2 teaspoons grated orange zest
1¼ cup orange juice

½ cup water
¼ cup lemon juice
2 tablespoons prepared mustard
1 tablespoon soy sauce

Mix sugar, cornstarch, and flour in saucepan. Stir in grated orange zest and orange juice. Add remaining ingredients, and stir over medium heat until thick, smooth, and boiling. Simmer for 1 to 2 minutes. Yield: 8 servings.

Ginger Pork Roast

A 3½ pound boneless pork loin, rolled and tied
Salt and freshly ground black pepper to taste

2 teaspoons rosemary leaves
2 tablespoons minced fresh ginger
1 cup dry white wine
¾ cup lemon marmalade

Preheat oven to 350° F. Place pork in shallow roasting pan. Sprinkle with salt, pepper, ginger, and rosemary. Pour wine in bottom of pan. Roast for 1 hour, basting often. More wine may be added, if necessary. Remove from oven. Add 3 tablespoons from pan drippings to lemon marmalade. Spoon marmalade mixture over pork, return to oven, and roast for another 30 to 45 minutes. Slice pork, spoon with pan sauce, and serve. Yield: 10 servings.

Cherry Glazed Pork Loin

A 4-pound boneless pork loin, rolled and tied
Salt and black pepper, to taste

Glaze
¼ cup slivered almonds, toasted

Preheat oven to 325° F. Rub pork with salt and black pepper. Roast, uncovered, for 2 to 2½ hours, or until meat thermometer inserted in center registers 180° F. Glaze roast, and add almonds. Return to oven for about 15 to 20 minutes. Serve sliced, with remaining glaze.

Glaze:
1 (12-ounce) jar cherry preserves
2 tablespoons light corn syrup
¼ cup red wine vinegar
¼ teaspoon salt

¼ teaspoon ground cinnamon
¼ teaspoon ground nutmeg
¼ teaspoon ground cloves

Combine ingredients in a saucepan. Stir over low heat until boiling. Reduce heat, and simmer for 2 minutes. Yield: 8 to 10 servings.

Pork Loin Stuffed with Dried Cherries

A 4-pound boneless pork loin roast, prepared for stuffing
1½ cups dried cherries
2 cloves garlic
Salt and freshly ground black pepper, to taste

4 tablespoons unsalted butter, softened
1½ cups Madeira wine
2 tablespoons molasses

Place rack in middle of oven, and preheat oven to 350° F. Using the handle of a wooden spoon, push the dried cherries into the pocket in the pork. Cut the garlic into thin slivers. Make deep slits in the roast with the tip of a knife, and push the garlic into the slits. Tie pork with butcher twine, and rub its surface with salt and pepper. Set the roast in a shallow baking pan, and smear butter over the roast.

Stir Madeira and molasses together in a small bowl, and pour over the roast. Bake for approximately 20 minutes per pound. Baste frequently. When the roast is done, remove from oven and let stand, loosely covered with foil, for 15 to 20 minutes. Cut into thin slices, and arrange on serving platter. Spoon pan juices over the slices. Serve immediately. Yield: 8 to 10 servings.

Pork Tenderloins with Blackberry Mustard Sauce

1½ teaspoons minced fresh thyme, divided
½ teaspoon freshly ground black pepper
¼ teaspoon salt
¼ teaspoon ground allspice
¼ teaspoon ground cinnamon
2 cloves garlic, minced
2 (¾-pound) pork tenderloins
Vegetable cooking spray
1 tablespoon olive oil

1¼ cups unsalted chicken broth, divided
2 tablespoons balsamic vinegar
1 tablespoon brown sugar
½ teaspoon cornstarch
2 tablespoons water
¼ cup Blackberry Mustard
¾ cup fresh blackberries
Fresh thyme sprigs (optional for garnish)

Combine ½ teaspoon minced thyme, black pepper, salt, allspice, and cinnamon. Trim fat from pork, and rub with thyme mixture. Cover and chill for 2 hours. Coat a large nonstick skillet with cooking spray. Add oil, and place over medium heat until hot. Add pork. Cook for 4 minutes or until browned on all sides. Add ¼ cup chicken broth and 2 tablespoons vinegar to skillet. Bring to a boil. Cover and reduce heat. Simmer for approximately 25 minutes. Remove pork from skillet, and set aside. Keep warm. Add remaining 1 cup of chicken broth and brown sugar to skillet. Bring to a boil, and cook for 5 minutes or until broth mixture is reduced to ½ cup. Strain mixture, and discard solids.

Place cornstarch in a small saucepan; gradually add water. Blend with a wire whisk. Stir in strained broth mixture and ¼ cup Blackberry Mustard. Bring to boil over medium heat. Cook for 1 minute, stirring constantly. Remove from heat. Stir in remaining teaspoon minced thyme. Cut pork into ½-inch-thick slices. Spoon 2 tablespoons sauce onto each of 6 serving plates. Arrange pork on sauce, and top with fresh blackberries and thyme sprigs. Yield: 6 servings.

Blackberry Mustard:
1 cup fresh blackberries
¼ cup, plus 3 tablespoons, hot Dijon mustard

3 tablespoons honey
1 tablespoon balsamic vinegar
1 teaspoon dry mustard

Position knife blade in processor; add blackberries. Process about 1 minute or until smooth; strain and discard seeds. Combine blackberry purée, Dijon mustard, and remaining ingredients in a bowl. Stir well. Store mustard in an airtight container for up to 2 weeks in refrigerator. Yield: 1 cup.

Korean Barbecue Ribs

3 tablespoons sesame seeds, toasted and crushed
1 cup light soy sauce
¼ cup sugar
2 tablespoons corn, or canola, oil
1 scallion, thinly sliced

Garlic powder to taste
1 teaspoon seasoned salt flavor enhancer
½ teaspoon coarse black pepper
3 pounds country-cut pork ribs

Mix all ingredients, and marinate ribs for least 2 hours, turning occasionally. Prepare charcoal grill. Grill ribs until desired doneness. Ribs reheat well the next day. Yield: 6 to 8 servings.

Orange Barbecue Ribs

4 pounds country-style pork ribs
1 (6-ounce) can tomato paste
½ cup packed brown sugar
¼ cup frozen orange juice concentrate, thawed

2 tablespoons red wine vinegar
1 tablespoon prepared mustard
2 tablespoons Worcestershire sauce
½ teaspoon black pepper
¼ teaspoon hot pepper sauce

Cut ribs into 1-rib portions. Combine tomato paste and remaining ingredients. Mix well. Place large piece of foil over coals beneath grill to catch drippings. Place ribs on grill about 6 inches over slow coals. Close hood of grill, and cook for 20 minutes. Turn ribs, close hood, and cook for another 20 minutes. Brush ribs with sauce, and cook covered with hood for 25 to 30 minutes. Continue to brush ribs often with sauce. Yield: 8 to 10 servings.

Corn-stuffed Pork Chops

6 pork chops, 1½-inches thick
1 (7-ounce) can whole kernel corn,
   undrained
1 cup soft bread cubes
¼ cup finely chopped onion

1 teaspoon salt
½ teaspoon ground sage
2 tablespoons shortening
Celery leaves and crabapples for
   garnish

Preheat oven to 350° F. Trim excess fat from pork chops, and cut pockets in each chop from the boneless side. Combine the corn, corn liquid, bread cubes, onion, salt, and sage. Stuff this mixture into the pork chop pockets, and sew pocket openings closed with needle and thread.

Melt shorting in a large iron skillet, and brown pork chops on each side and around the edges. Place browned pork chops in a large 13x9x2-inch baking pan, cover tightly with foil, and bake for 1¼ to 1½ hours. Remove chops to a warmed platter, and garnish with celery leaves and crabapples. Yield: 6 servings.

Pork Chops in Eggplant Sauce

Eggplant thickens sauce as it cooks.

4 pork chops
1 small eggplant
2 tablespoons oil
⅓ onion
½ green bell pepper
Garlic to taste

1 teaspoon salt
¼ teaspoon basil
1 (8-ounce) can tomato sauce
1 cup water
Hot cooked rice

Cut pork chops into cubes. Peel and cut eggplant into cubes. Chop onion, green bell pepper, and garlic into tiny pieces. In a large frying pan, heat oil. Brown pork chops, and then add onion, bell pepper, garlic, salt, and basil. Stir-fry, and add tomato sauce. Simmer for 5 minutes, and add eggplant and water. Cover and simmer on medium low 40 minutes, stirring about every 15 minutes. Serve over rice. Yield: 4 servings.

Lebanese Green Bean Goulash

*This dish can be prepared a day or two ahead of time
and reheated (broth will thicken). It may also be
cooked in crock pot on low setting for 8 to 10 hours.*

**4 to 6 pork chops (may use
    boneless)**
**2 pounds fresh green beans,
    snapped, washed, and drained**
6 to 8 small potatoes, peeled

4 small onions, peeled
1 (6-ounce) can tomato paste
Salt and black pepper to taste
Hot cooked rice

Cut pork away from bones, and line bottom of Dutch oven with meat and
bones. To reduce fat, trim fat from chops. Cover chops with green beans. Add
potatoes and onions, pushing them down into bean layer. Mix tomato paste
with enough water to bring water level to top of beans and potatoes. Add salt
and black pepper. Cook, covered, until beans are tender and potatoes are
done. Serve over rice. Yield: 4 to 6 servings.

Grilled Link Sausages

8 link sausages   **3 tablespoons butter**

With a fork, prick the sausages on all sides, and arrange in a large skillet. Add
enough water to cover halfway up the sausages. Bring water to a boil, reduce
heat, and simmer the sausages for 15 to 20 minutes, turning often. Drain
liquid, add butter, and grill the sausages over moderate heat, turning until
evenly browned on all sides. Yield: 4 servings.

Grilled Chutney Chicken

6 boneless chicken breast halves,
  boned
½ cup lime juice
3 tablespoons soy sauce

1 teaspoon chili powder
1 tablespoon olive oil
Chutney

Marinate chicken breasts for at least 2 hours, or overnight, in mixture of lime juice, soy sauce, chili powder, and olive oil. Grill chicken over low to medium heat, turning often and basting with marinade. When almost done, glaze chicken with chutney. Serve chicken with remaining chutney. Yield: 6 servings.

Chutney:
2 pears
1 apple
Pineapple chunks

2 tablespoons orange juice
½ teaspoon soy sauce

Chop fruit, and sprinkle it with orange juice and soy sauce. If mixture is not at room temperature, heat it to room temperature before adding to chicken.

Grilled Marinated Chicken Breasts

12 chicken breast halves, skinned
  and boned
3 medium garlic cloves, crushed
1½ teaspoons salt
½ cup packed brown sugar
3 tablespoons grainy mustard

¼ cup cider vinegar
Juice of 1 lime
Juice of ½ large lemon
6 tablespoons olive oil
Black pepper to taste

Put chicken in shallow plastic marinating container. In small bowl, mix the garlic, salt, brown sugar, mustard, vinegar, lime juice, and lemon juice. Blend well. Whisk in olive oil, and add black pepper. Pour over chicken, and refrigerate, covered, overnight. Turn once.

Remove chicken from refrigerator 1 hour before you want to cook it, and let it come to room temperature. Prepare grill or preheat broiler. Grill or broil breasts for approximately 6 minutes per side or until done. Be careful not to overcook. Yield: 8 to 10 servings.

Baked Chicken Amandine

This dish may be prepared ahead,
refrigerated, and baked later.

4 whole chicken breasts, skinned,
  boned, and halved
1 stick melted butter
1 cup breadcrumbs
1 cup grated Parmesan cheese
¼ cup parsley

¼ teaspoon garlic powder
1 teaspoon salt
¼ teaspoon black pepper
Slivered almonds
Additional melted butter, if desired

Preheat oven to 350° F. Dip each chicken breast half in melted butter. Combine breadcrumbs, Parmesan cheese, parsley, garlic powder, salt, and black pepper. Coat buttered chicken pieces on both sides in crumb mixture, and roll up tightly. Arrange rolls, seam side down, in 13x9x2-inch baking dish so that they touch. Sprinkle rolls with almonds and more melted butter. Bake, uncovered, for 1 hour. Yield: 4 to 6 servings (2 chicken rolls per serving).

Oven Barbecued Chicken

Chicken may be cooked ahead and later
reheated in a 325° F. oven.

Salt and black pepper to taste
1 chicken, cleaned and cut up
  (skinned, if desired)
1 tablespoon prepared mustard
1 clove garlic, minced
1 green bell pepper, sliced

1 tablespoon Worcestershire sauce
½ cup ketchup
1 cup vinegar
¼ cup sugar
1 large onion, sliced and separated
  into rings

Preheat oven to 375° F. Salt and pepper chicken, cover in baking dish, and bake for 20 minutes. While chicken is cooking, mix mustard and remaining ingredients in saucepan, and simmer for 10 minutes. Remove chicken; pour off grease and juices. Pour sauce over chicken, cover, and return to oven. Reduce oven temperature to 350° F., and cook chicken for 25 to 30 minutes or until tender. Yield: 4 to 6 servings.

Chicken Florentine

1 stick butter
½ cup flour
2 cups milk
1 chicken bouillon cube
1 (10-ounce) package frozen
  spinach, thawed and drained
¼ cup Parmesan cheese

½ teaspoon salt
¼ teaspoon black pepper
4 whole chicken breasts, skinned,
  boned, and flattened
2 tablespoons butter
1 cup combined Swiss cheese and
  Cheddar cheese

Melt butter. Add flour; blend, and cook for 1 minute. Add milk and bouillon cube. Simmer 10 minutes. Add spinach, Parmesan cheese, and salt and pepper. In skillet, sauté chicken breasts with butter until cooked, for approximately 5 to 10 minutes. Place spinach sauce on ovenproof platter. Place chicken breasts on sauce. Sprinkle with Swiss and Cheddar cheese. Place under broiler until cheese bubbles and browns. Serve immediately. Yield: 8 servings.

Sweet-and-Sour Baked Chicken

4 tablespoons margarine
½ cup chopped onion
½ cup coarsely chopped green bell
  pepper
½ cup coarsely chopped carrots
¾ cup ketchup
1 (20-ounce) can pineapple chunks,
  drained and juice reserved
2 tablespoons white vinegar

¼ cup firmly packed brown sugar
Dash garlic salt
½ teaspoon salt
¼ teaspoon black pepper
12 pieces of chicken (breast, legs, or
  thighs), or boneless chicken breast
  halves
Cooked Rice

Preheat oven to 375° F. In medium skillet, heat margarine until melted. Add onion, green pepper, and carrot; sauté for 5 minutes, stirring constantly. Stir in ketchup, 1 cup pineapple juice, vinegar, brown sugar, garlic salt, salt, and black pepper. Cook, stirring constantly, until mixture boils. Add pineapple chunks. Arrange chicken pieces, skin side up, in a 13x9x2-inch ovenproof pan. Pour sweet-and-sour sauce over chicken. Bake, covered, for 45 minutes. Uncover, and bake for about 30 minutes longer. Serve with rice. Yield: 6 to 8 servings.

Tarragon Chicken

Seasoned rice enhances this quick-and-easy dish.

6 tablespoons butter, melted
3 tablespoons lemon juice
3 tablespoons Dijon mustard

1 teaspoon chopped tarragon
6 chicken breast halves, skinned and boned

Preheat oven to 350° F. Mix butter, lemon juice, Dijon mustard, and tarragon; pour over chicken pieces in a casserole dish. Bake, covered, for 45 minutes. Yield: 6 servings.

Chicken Breasts with Whipping Cream Sauce

4 chicken breast halves, boned
½ teaspoon lemon juice
¼ teaspoon salt
Pinch of white pepper
4 tablespoons butter
¼ cup white or brown stock, or chicken bouillon

¼ cup port, Madeira, or dry white vermouth
1 cup whipping cream
Salt and black pepper
Lemon juice, as needed
2 tablespoons fresh minced parsley

Preheat oven to 400° F. Rub chicken with lemon juice, and sprinkle with salt and white pepper. In skillet, heat butter until foaming. Quickly roll chicken in butter, and place in casserole dish. Place buttered wax paper over chicken. Cover casserole, and place in hot oven. After 20 minutes, press top of breasts. If still soft, return to oven. When chicken is springy, it is done. Remove chicken from casserole, and keep on warm platter. Pour stock and wine into casserole with cooking butter, and boil down quickly over high heat until liquid is "syrupy." Stir in cream, and boil down quickly until cream has thickened slightly. Remove from heat and season with salt, black pepper, and lemon juice. Pour sauce over breasts, and sprinkle them with parsley. Serve immediately. Yield: 4 servings.

Chicken with Artichoke Hearts and Capers

Recipe doubles easily.

1 tablespoon butter
2 (6-ounce) chicken breasts halves, skinned, boned, and pounded
Flour
½ medium clove garlic, peeled and chopped
2 artichoke hearts, quartered

¼ cup dry white wine
Juice of 1 lemon
1 tablespoon capers, with juice
1 tablespoon fresh parsley, chopped
4 tablespoons butter, divided into 4 pats

Heat butter in sauté pan. Dredge chicken breasts in flour. Add chicken to butter, and sauté until brown. Turn chicken over; add garlic and artichoke hearts. When garlic just starts to brown, add wine, lemon juice, capers, and parsley. Reduce liquid by half. Remove chicken to serving platter. Bring liquid to a simmer. Fold in whole butter pats, and immediately remove from heat. Spoon artichoke hearts and capers onto chicken. Add enough sauce to cover. Yield: 2 servings.

Kung Pao Chicken

2 tablespoons wine vinegar
2 tablespoons soy sauce
2 teaspoons sugar
1 pound skinned and boned chicken breasts, cut into bite-sized pieces
1 tablespoon cornstarch
2 teaspoons oil

3 tablespoons chopped scallions
2 cloves garlic, minced
½ to 1 teaspoon crushed red pepper
¼ to ½ teaspoon ground ginger, or 1 teaspoon freshly grated ginger
⅓ cup dry roasted peanuts
4 cups hot cooked rice

Mix together wine vinegar, soy sauce, and sugar; set aside. Coat chicken with cornstarch. Heat oil in large skillet or wok. Add chicken, and stir-fry for 5 to 7 minutes, or until cooked. Remove chicken from pan, and add scallions, garlic, red pepper, and ginger. Stir-fry for 15 seconds; then add wine vinegar mixture and chicken, stirring to coat chicken. Mix in peanuts, and serve over rice. Yield: 4 servings.

Sautéed Chicken Breast in a Cajun Potato Crust

Chef Grant Gilbert of Holly Inn in Pinehurst, North Carolina, contributed this recipe.

1 potato, grated
2 tablespoons cornstarch
1 tablespoon lemon juice
1 pinch dried parsley
1 pinch cayenne pepper
1 pinch paprika
1 pinch thyme

1 pinch salt
1 pinch black pepper
4 to 8 ounces light olive oil
1 (4-ounce) whole chicken breast, skinned and boned
2 ounces sour cream
1 pinch tarragon

To make crust, mix potato, cornstarch, lemon juice, parsley, cayenne pepper, paprika, thyme, salt, and black pepper. In skillet, heat oil until almost at smoking point. Test a small portion of potato crust in hot oil. If crust breaks apart, add more cornstarch until it holds well. Coat chicken with potato mixture. Gently fry until golden brown. Place in 350° F. oven for approximately 10 minutes.

Mix sour cream and tarragon, and set side. Remove chicken from oven, and place in center of dinner plate. Cover with herbed sour cream. Around chicken, place your favorite vegetable. Yield: 1 serving.

Chicken and Wild Rice Casserole

Casserole may be prepared ahead and cooked later.

Black pepper to taste
4 chicken breast halves, skinned
1 (6-ounce) package long grain and wild rice (with seasoning packet included), uncooked

2 cups hot water
1 (10¾-ounce) can cream of mushroom soup
½ cup milk or dry sherry
¼ cup slivered almonds (optional)

Preheat oven to 350° F. Sprinkle chicken with pepper, and place it in a 1½- to 2-quart casserole dish. Pour rice and seasoning packet over chicken. Add hot water. Cover dish and bake for 1 hour and 15 minutes. Dilute soup with milk. Pour soup mixture over chicken, and sprinkle with almonds. Return uncovered casserole to oven until soup mixture is bubbly. Yield: 4 servings.

Chicken Stir-Fry

*This quick one-dish meal is low
in fat and cholesterol.*

2 tablespoons cornstarch
1 1/4 cups water
1/3 cup soy sauce
1/3 cup light or dark corn syrup
1/4 to 1/2 teaspoon crushed dried red pepper
4 tablespoons corn oil

1 pound skinned and boned chicken, cut into bite-size pieces
2 cups broccoli flowerets and sliced stems
2 medium onions, cut into thin wedges
1 carrot, cut into 2-inch strips
Hot cooked rice

In bowl, mix cornstarch and water until smooth. Stir in soy sauce, corn syrup, and red pepper; set aside. In large skillet or wok, heat 2 tablespoons corn oil over medium-high heat. Add chicken pieces, and stir-fry for 3 to 10 minutes or until tender. Remove from skillet. Heat remaining oil, and add 2 cups broccoli, onion, and carrot strips. Stir-fry for 2 minutes, or until crisp but tender. Return chicken to skillet. Stir sauce mixture, and add to skillet with chicken and vegetables. Stir, and cook, uncovered, to a boil over medium heat. Simmer for 1 minute. Serve over rice. Yield: 4 to 6 servings.

Twenty-Minute Chicken Parmesan with Spaghetti

4 chicken breast halves, skinned and boned (about 1 pound)
1 egg, slightly beaten
1/2 cup seasoned dry breadcrumbs
2 tablespoons margarine
2 cups tomato sauce

1/2 cup (2 ounces) shredded mozzarella cheese
1 tablespoon grated Parmesan cheese
1 teaspoon dried parsley flakes
3 1/2 cups hot cooked spaghetti (8 ounces dry)

Flatten chicken to an even thickness using palm of hand or meat mallet. Dip chicken in egg, and coat with breadcrumbs. In a 10-inch skillet over medium heat, in hot margarine, cook chicken on both sides. Add tomato sauce. Reduce heat to low. Cover and simmer for 10 minutes. Sprinkle with cheeses and parsley. Cover, and simmer for 5 minutes or until cheese melts. Serve over hot spaghetti. Yield: 4 servings.

Chicken with Tomatoes and Herbs

This dish features a light, yet sweet, taste.
Serve in pasta bowls.

1 medium onion, chopped
2 cloves garlic, minced
1 teaspoon dried rosemary
½ teaspoon thyme
½ teaspoon basil
1 tablespoon olive oil
1½ (14-ounce) cans Italian stewed
  tomatoes

¾ cup ketchup
¼ cup white vinegar
1 tablespoon brown sugar
½ teaspoon salt
½ teaspoon black pepper
2½ to 3 pounds chicken, skinned,
  boned, cooked, and chopped
Cooked spaghetti or angel hair pasta

In a large skillet, sauté onion, garlic, and herbs in olive oil until tender. Stir in tomatoes. Add ketchup, white vinegar, brown sugar, salt, black pepper, and chicken; bring mixture to a boil. Reduce heat, and simmer, covered, for 45 to 50 minutes. Serve over cooked spaghetti. Yield: 4 to 6 servings.

Sautéed Chicken Livers

Serve this dish with rice or noodles.

3 to 4 tablespoons olive oil
4 pinches of fresh garlic
1½ pounds chicken livers, cleaned
1 green bell pepper, chopped
2 small onions, sliced thick

1 (8-ounce) package fresh
  mushrooms
Salt and black pepper to taste
2 tablespoons red wine vinegar

Warm olive oil to cooking temperature in deep 10-inch frying pan. Add garlic when medium temperature is reached. Add livers and sauté them with frying pan lid ajar for approximately 2 minutes. Add green bell pepper, and turn livers. Cook for approximately 2 more minutes with lid ajar. Remove lid, increase heat to medium-high, and add onion, mushrooms, salt, black pepper, and red wine vinegar. Turn all ingredients slowly for at least 1½ minutes, or until sautéed to your taste. Yield: 2 to 4 servings.

Chicken and Artichokes

1 (2½- to 3-pound) chicken, cooked, skinned, boned, and shredded
1 (8½-ounce) can artichoke hearts, sliced
½ cup flour
1 pint half-and-half
1½ cups skim milk
¼ teaspoon cayenne pepper

2 sticks butter
5 ounces Gruyère cheese, coarsely grated
⅓ pound low-fat Cheddar cheese, coarsely grated
1 cup button mushrooms
2 cups Pepperidge Farm stuffing
3 tablespoons butter

Preheat oven to 350° F. Grease a 13x9x2-inch baking dish. Layer shredded chicken. Arrange artichokes on top. Beat together flour, half-and-half, and milk. Add seasoning. In a saucepan, melt butter, and whisk in the flour mixture until cream sauce thickens. Add grated cheeses; whisk to make cheese sauce. Add mushrooms, and pour sauce over chicken and artichoke hearts. Top with stuffing dotted with butter. Bake, uncovered, for 30 minutes. Yield: 8 to 10 servings.

Chicken Breasts with Coronation Sauce

This dish may be prepared ahead of time.

6 chicken breast halves, cooked, skinned, boned, and chilled
¼ cup egg substitute or 1 egg
4 tablespoons lemon juice
2 (16-ounce) cans peeled apricots, ¼ cup juice reserved

1 teaspoon honey
½ teaspoon salt
1 tablespoon curry powder, fried in a little butter
½ teaspoon Dijon mustard
Parsley, to garnish

In saucepan, cover chicken breasts with water, and simmer until done. Place chicken in refrigerator to cool. In a blender, blend egg, lemon juice, apricot juice, honey and all spices and seasonings. Slowly add oil. When thoroughly blended, add apricots, a few at a time, and liquefy. Place chilled chicken breasts in serving dish, and pour the sauce over the chicken. Garnish with parsley, and serve. Yield: 6 servings.

Southwest Chicken Casserole

3 cups cooked rice
8 chicken breast halves, cooked, skinned, boned, and diced
1 pint sour cream
¾ cup mayonnaise
1 to 3 (4-ounce) cans chopped green chiles, drained, depending on taste

1 pound shredded Monterey Jack cheese
1 to 3 teaspoons minced garlic, depending on taste
8 ounces shredded Cheddar cheese

Preheat oven to 350° F. Grease a 13x9x2-inch casserole dish. In a large bowl, mix all ingredients, except the Cheddar cheese. Place mixture in prepared casserole dish, and top it with Cheddar cheese. Bake for 30 minutes. Yield: 6 to 8 servings.

Grandmother's Turkey Hash

Serve hash over waffles or patty shells. May be prepared in advance.

4 tablespoons butter
½ cup flour
1 quart turkey or chicken stock
½ tablespoon salt
¼ teaspoon black pepper
½ teaspoon paprika

8 cups diced cooked turkey
¼ cup chopped pimiento
¼ pound mushrooms, fresh or canned
1½ tablespoons chopped parsley

In a double boiler, melt butter, and slowly add flour to make a thick paste. Add turkey stock, stirring constantly to prevent lumping, and cook until smooth. Season with salt, black pepper, and paprika. Add remaining ingredients. (If fresh mushrooms are used, prepare by sautéing until brown in additional melted butter.) Heat thoroughly over boiling water, and keep hot until ready to serve. Yield: 15 servings.

Turkey Tetrazzini

½ (8-ounce) package medium
  noodles
6 tablespoons margarine
6 tablespoons flour
1 to 1½ teaspoons salt to taste
¼ teaspoon black pepper
½ teaspoon celery salt
2 cups broth

1 cup heavy cream, or half-and-half,
  scalded
⅛ teaspoon sherry
1 (6-ounce) can mushrooms
3 tablespoon minced parsley
⅓ cup toasted slivered almonds
2 cups diced cooked turkey
½ cup grated Parmesan cheese

Preheat oven to 350° F. Grease a 2-quart casserole dish. Cook noodles; drain.
Melt margarine; add flour, and blend well. Add seasonings and broth. Cook
over low heat until thick, stirring frequently. Remove from heat, add cream,
sherry, mushrooms, parsley, and almonds. Alternate layers of noodles, turkey,
and mushroom sauce in prepared dish. Top sauce with Parmesan cheese.
Bake, uncovered, for 45 minutes. Yield: 8 servings.

Turkey and Stuffing Loaves

1 egg, beaten
½ cup milk
¾ cup herb-seasoned stuffing mix
3 tablespoons chopped onion
1 tablespoon dried parsley flakes
½ teaspoon salt

⅛ teaspoon black pepper
1 pound ground turkey
8 ounces bulk pork sausage
¾ can whole cranberry sauce
¼ cup ketchup

Preheat oven to 350° F. Spray broiler pan with nonstick cooking spray. In
bowl, combine egg, milk, stuffing mix, onion, parsley flakes, salt, and black
pepper. Add ground turkey and sausage; mix well. Divide mixture in half, and
shape into loaves. Place both loaves on rack in broiler pan. Bake, uncovered,
for 45 minutes. In saucepan, combine cranberry sauce and ketchup, and cook
until heated through. Spoon some of the sauce over loaves. Bake 15 minutes
more. Serve loaves with remaining heated sauce. Yield: 6 servings.

To microwave: Cook on High, uncovered, for 5 minutes. Reduce power to
Medium, and cook for 10 minutes, giving dish ½ turn after 5 minutes. Remove
meat. Drain off fat. Spoon sauce over loaves. Bake (at 350° F.), uncovered, for
10 to 12 minutes.

Oyster Stuffing

6 tablespoons margarine
6 tablespoons oil or shortening
1½ cups chopped onion
1½ cups chopped celery
6 to 8 slices bread
Water
3 tablespoons minced parsley

Salt and black pepper to taste
¾ teaspoon thyme
¾ teaspoon sage
¾ teaspoon marjoram
¾ teaspoon oregano
½ to 1 cup chopped oysters
2 eggs, slightly beaten

Preheat oven to 400° F. Grease an 8x8-inch casserole dish. Melt margarine in skillet; add oil, onion, and celery. Cook, covered, until onions are tender, but not brown. Crumble bread in large bowl; add enough water to just moisten bread. Stir in onion mixture, parsley, seasonings, oysters, and eggs. Mix well. Place in prepared dish. Bake until brown, for approximately 35 minutes. Yield: 6 servings.

Old-Fashioned Bread Stuffing

This light, fluffy stuffing may be used as a basic recipe for variations with mushrooms, apples, chestnuts, or other nuts and fruits. Stuffing recipe may be doubled.

1 medium onion, minced
1 cup chopped tender celery
2 tablespoons butter or margarine
6 cups breadcrumbs
½ cup finely ground salt pork

1 teaspoon salt
½ teaspoon black pepper
¼ teaspoon each, thyme, marjoram, sage
½ cup chicken broth

Simmer onion and celery in butter until onion is tender. Add breadcrumbs until butter is absorbed. Add remaining ingredients. Blend thoroughly; then stuff turkey and bake according to its weight. Yield: 6 servings.

Variation: Instead of using ground pork, cook the turkey neck and giblets, then cut up and mix with the broth.

$\mathcal{S}$ide Dishes

*New Bern's All Saints Chapel exemplifies Gothic Revival
architecture. It features a steep gable roof,
lancet windows, and stick-style ornamentation.*

*Dressed in their Sunday best, a most proper young lady
and her gentleman friend enjoy a church gathering.*

Asparagus with Sesame Mayonnaise

3 pounds asparagus
2 cloves garlic, minced
1½ teaspoons fresh ginger, chopped
⅓ cup soy sauce
2 tablespoons rice vinegar
2 tablespoons brown sugar
¼ cup egg substitute, or 1 egg

2 tablespoons egg substitute, or 1 large egg yolk
1 tablespoon fresh lemon juice
1½ tablespoons Dijon mustard
1¼ cups vegetable oil
¼ cup sesame oil
⅓ cup sesame seeds, toasted

Trim tough stalks from the asparagus, and cut remainder into 2- to 3-inch diagonal pieces, separating tips and stalks. Steam tips and stalks separately until just crisp-tender. Remove asparagus from heat; set aside.

Place garlic, ginger, soy sauce, vinegar, and brown sugar in a small saucepan. Heat to boiling. Reduce heat, and simmer until reduced by half. Place egg substitutes, lemon juice, and mustard in a processor. With machine running, process; then add the oils in a steady stream, processing until thick. Add reduced soy mixture, and process until well blended. Toss asparagus with dressing, and transfer to a serving bowl. Chill, and sprinkle with sesame seeds before serving. Yield: 8 servings.

Baked Beans

1 (31-ounce) can pork and beans, pork removed
½ cup ketchup
1 tablespoon prepared mustard
1 tablespoon Worcestershire sauce
1 cup firmly packed brown sugar

1 cup finely chopped onions
½ cup finely chopped green bell pepper
6 strips of bacon, sliced into ¼-inch strips

Preheat oven to 350° F. and grease a 2-quart casserole dish. In prepared dish, combine all ingredients, except bacon; mix well. Top mixture with the bacon. Bake for 1 to 1½ hours. Yield: 6 to 8 servings.

Black Bean Pâté with Scallion Sauce

4 cups dried black beans
1 large onion, chopped
6 cloves garlic, minced
1 teaspoon cumin
3 tablespoons butter
1 cup sour cream

6 eggs
2 teaspoons salt
1 tablespoon black pepper
Scallion Sauce
1 red bell pepper, cut into thin strips
16 ounces Feta cheese, cubed

Preheat oven to 350° F., and butter a 9x5-inch loaf pan. Cook beans in rapidly boiling water until soft, for approximately 45 minutes. Drain and let cool. Sauté onion, garlic, and cumin in butter until soft and transparent. Set aside to cool. Transfer black beans to food processor, and pulse briefly until beans are coarsely chopped. Place beans in a large bowl with onion mixture. Add sour cream, eggs, salt, and black pepper. Mix until combined. Place mixture in prepared pan, and cover with buttered foil. Place loaf pan in a larger baking pan, and fill larger pan with enough hot water to come halfway up the sides of the loaf pan. Bake for approximately 1 hour and 20 minutes, or until firm. Cool completely. Remove from pan and cut pâté into ¼- to ½-inch thick slices.

To serve, fan 2 slices of pâté on individual plates. Top with Scallion Sauce. Garnish each serving with red bell pepper slices and about 1 ounce of Feta cheese.

Scallion Sauce:

2 tablespoons egg substitute or 1 egg yolk
½ cup red wine vinegar
2 tablespoons Dijon mustard
2 scallions with tops

3 cloves garlic
1 teaspoon sugar
1½ cups olive oil
Salt and black pepper to taste

In food processor, combine egg yolk, vinegar, mustard, scallions, garlic, and sugar. Process until well blended. With machine running, add olive oil in a steady stream through feeder tube. Season with salt and pepper. Yield: 16 to 18 servings.

Green Beans and Sunflower Seeds

*Frozen green beans may be substituted
for fresh green beans.*

1 small onion, chopped
1 clove garlic, minced
1 pound fresh green beans, washed
  and snapped
¼ cup butter
¼ cup sunflower seeds
½ teaspoon marjoram

½ teaspoon basil
½ teaspoon chervil
1 teaspoon parsley
1 teaspoon chives
⅛ teaspoon savory
⅛ teaspoon thyme
Salt and black pepper

Cover bottom of saucepan with water, add chopped onion and garlic. Add green beans, and simmer, covered, on low heat for 15 minutes or until crisp-tender. Melt butter, and stir in sunflower seeds, herbs, salt, and black pepper. Drain beans, and mix with herb mixture. Serve immediately. Yield: 4 servings.

Better Beans

3 (10-ounce) packages frozen
  French-style green beans, or 2
  (10-ounce) packages baby lima
  beans
6 to 8 slices of bacon

1 large onion, chopped
4 medium tomatoes
2 to 3 tablespoons sugar
Salt and black pepper to taste
¼ cup Parmesan cheese

Cook the beans until crisp-tender; then drain. Fry the bacon, and remove with slotted spoon to paper towels to drain. Crumble. In the bacon grease in the pan, sauté the onion. Add tomatoes, sugar, salt, and pepper. Cover and simmer for 15 minutes. Add the beans and the crumbled bacon. Stir together, and cook for an additional 5 minutes. Remove to serving dish. Sprinkle Parmesan cheese over mixture. Yield: 8 servings.

French-Style Green Bean Casserole

*Cooking the beans with a little bacon fat adds
to the flavor. Casserole may be prepared ahead;
add topping before baking.*

½ (10-ounce) package frozen Silver
    Queen corn
2 (10-ounce) packages frozen
    French-style green beans
2 tablespoons butter
2 tablespoons flour
½ teaspoon black pepper
1 teaspoon salt

1 tablespoon sugar
Dash red pepper flakes
3 tablespoons grated onion
1 cup sour cream
1 cup sharp Cheddar cheese, grated
2 small packages cornflakes,
    crushed (optional)
2 tablespoons melted butter
    (optional)

Preheat oven to 375° F. Cook corn and beans; drain thoroughly. In a saucepan, combine butter, flour, black pepper, salt, sugar, red pepper flakes, onion,
and sour cream. Cook mixture over low heat, stirring constantly until
thickened. Add this mixture to the beans and corn, and pour into a 2-quart
oblong casserole dish. Cover mixture with grated Cheddar cheese. For
topping, if desired, sprinkle crushed cornflakes over cheese, and pour melted
butter over top. Bake for 20 minutes. Yield: 6 to 8 servings.

Three-Bean Baked Dish

½ pound hamburger
½ pound bacon
1 onion, minced
⅓ cup brown sugar
¼ cup ketchup
½ cup barbecue sauce
2 tablespoons mustard
2 tablespoons molasses

½ teaspoon chili powder
1 tablespoon salt
½ teaspoon black pepper
1 (16-ounce) can kidney beans,
    drained
1 (16-ounce) can butter beans,
    drained
2 (16-ounce) cans pork and beans

Preheat oven to 350° F. Brown and drain hamburger and bacon. Brown
onion, and drain. Mix all ingredients together in a large bowl. Put into
13x9x2-inch baking dish. Refrigerate for several hours before baking. Bake,
uncovered, for 1 hour. Yield: 8 to 12 servings.

Sweet-and-Sour Green Beans

*To reduce fat content, use turkey bacon and cooking
spray instead of pork bacon and drippings.*

1½ pounds fresh green beans, or 18
  ounces frozen beans
1 quart water
Salt to taste
4 slices bacon
2 onions, thinly sliced

1 tablespoon dry mustard
1 teaspoon salt
2 tablespoons brown sugar
2 tablespoons white sugar
¼ cup white vinegar

Wash beans, and cut into 1½-inch pieces. In a saucepan, combine green
beans, water, and salt; cover and simmer for 10 minutes. Drain, reserving 1
cup liquid. Cook bacon until crisp. Remove from pan, drain, and crumble.
Sauté onion in bacon drippings. Stir in mustard, salt, sugars, vinegar, and bean
liquid. Bring to boil. Add beans and bacon. Simmer for about 15 minutes.
Yield: 6 servings.

Broccoli Corn Casserole

1 (10-ounce) package frozen
  chopped broccoli
1 (10-ounce) package frozen cream-
  style corn
1¼ cups herb-seasoned stuffing mix,
  divided
1 (10¾-ounce) can cream of
  mushroom soup

1 egg, beaten
3 tablespoons butter or margarine,
  melted
1 small onion, finely chopped
½ cup (2 ounces) sharp Cheddar
  cheese, shredded

Preheat oven to 350° F. and lightly grease a 1½-quart baking dish. Cook
broccoli according to package directions, omitting salt. Drain well. Cook corn
according to package directions. Combine broccoli, corn, 1 cup stuffing mix,
mushroom soup, egg, butter, and onion. (You can sauté onions in margarine
or cook with broccoli to eliminate strong taste.) Mix well. Spoon mixture into
prepared dish. Sprinkle with Cheddar cheese and remaining ¼ cup stuffing
mix. Bake for 30 minutes. Yield: 6 to 8 servings.

Broccoli Timbales with Ginger Orange Carrots

1½ pounds broccoli, trimmed into flowerets that fit ramekins
1½ cups heavy cream
½ teaspoon salt
¼ teaspoon white pepper

Freshly ground nutmeg to taste
⅛ teaspoon cayenne pepper
7 eggs, well beaten
Ginger Orange Carrots
Fresh cilantro to garnish

Preheat oven to 350° F. Place a 13x9x2-inch pan with 1 inch of boiling water in oven. Generously butter 8 ramekins or custard cups. Blanch broccoli in boiling salted water for 2 minutes; drain, and set aside. Combine cream, salt, pepper, nutmeg, and cayenne. Add eggs. Beat well. Arrange broccoli in ramekins, stem side up. Pour egg mixture into ramekins. Set molds in pan of hot water in the oven. Bake for 40 minutes or until knife inserted in the middle of the ramekin comes out clean. Invert timbales onto a heated serving platter or individual plates. Prepare Ginger Orange Carrots, and place around the timbales. Garnish with cilantro leaves.

Ginger Orange Carrots:
36 baby carrots
1¾ cups fresh orange juice

1 tablespoon fresh ginger, grated

Combine carrots, orange juice, and ginger in a saucepan. Simmer over medium-low heat until tender, for about 10 to 12 minutes. Drain before serving. Yield: 8 servings.

Celery Amandine

4 cups sliced celery
4 tablespoons butter
1 teaspoon salt
½ to 1 tablespoon black pepper
1 tablespoon chopped chives
1 tablespoon grated onion

1½ tablespoons all-purpose flour
1 chicken bouillon cube
½ cup water
1 cup light cream
1 cup blanched, slivered almonds

Place celery and butter in a saucepan. Cover and cook slowly until celery is tender. Stir frequently. Add salt and pepper, chopped chives, and onion. Cook 5 more minutes. Sprinkle with flour, and stir well. Dissolve bouillon in water. Gradually add light cream and bouillon to celery. Cook, stirring constantly, until thick. Toast almonds until lightly browned. Sprinkle almonds over celery just before serving. Yield: 6 to 8 servings.

Cabbage au Gratin

A deliciously different way to serve cabbage!

1 stick margarine, melted
2 cups cornflakes, crushed slightly
6 cups shredded cabbage
½ cup chopped onion

1 (10¾-ounce) can cream of celery
  soup
½ cup mayonnaise
1 cup milk
1 cup grated sharp Cheddar cheese

Preheat oven to 350° F. Mix margarine and cornflakes together. Spread half of mixture in 13x9x2-inch Pyrex dish. Reserve other half for topping. Mix cabbage, onion, celery soup, mayonnaise, and milk. Stir mixture together well, and pour over cornflake crust. Sprinkle remaining cornflakes over cabbage mixture. Sprinkle grated Cheddar cheese over cornflakes. Bake for 30 minutes. Yield: 8 to 10 servings.

Corn on the Cob with Basil Butter

The basil butter may be made up to 3 days in advance, kept covered and chilled, and softened before serving.

½ cup loosely packed fresh basil
  leaves
1½ sticks (¾ cup) unsalted butter,
  softened

Salt and freshly ground black
  pepper to taste
12 ears corn, shucked
Fresh basil sprigs for garnish, if
  desired

In a food processor, mince the basil leaves; add butter, salt, and black pepper to taste. Blend the mixture until it is well combined. Transfer the butter to a small serving dish. In a kettle of boiling water, cook the corn, covered, for 3 to 5 minutes, or until just tender; drain. Garnish corn with basil sprigs, if desired, and serve with basil butter. Yield: 6 servings.

Corn and Zucchini with Jack Cheese

2 tablespoons olive oil
1 medium zucchini, cut into ⅓-inch
  cubes
Salt to taste
1 (10-ounce) package frozen corn,
  thawed, or 2 cups fresh corn

1 cup finely chopped red onion
1 cup coarsely grated Monterey
  Jack cheese with hot peppers
2 tablespoons finely crushed corn
  tortilla chips

Preheat oven to 375° F., and butter a 2-quart casserole dish. In a large heavy skillet, heat oil over moderately high heat, and sauté zucchini, stirring occasionally, until lightly browned and just tender, for 2 to 3 minutes. With a slotted spoon, transfer zucchini to a bowl, and season with salt. In oil remaining in skillet, sauté corn and onion over moderately high heat, stirring, for 4 minutes; add salt to taste. Cook, covered, over low heat until corn is crisp-tender, for 2 to 3 minutes. Add corn mixture to zucchini, and season with salt. Allow mixture to cool to room temperature. Stir in Monterey Jack cheese. Place mixture in prepared dish, and sprinkle with tortilla chips. Bake for 20 minutes, or until mixture is completely heated. After addition of cheese, dish may be covered and refrigerated for 1 day before baking. Yield: 4 servings.

Onions Stuffed with Rice

1 cup heavy cream
½ cup sour cream
6 very large onions
4 tablespoons butter
⅓ cup regular white rice
⅓ cup grated Parmesan cheese
¼ cup crème fraîche

2 tablespoons white breadcrumbs
¼ cup minced parsley
½ tablespoon each dried basil, oregano, and tarragon
Salt and black pepper to taste
½ cup white wine or vermouth
2 to 3 cups beef stock or bouillon

Make crème fraîche by mixing heavy cream and sour cream. Let thicken at room temperature 5 to 6 hours. Refrigerate. Preheat oven to 375° F. Peel onions, and cut ends. Scoop out and reserve centers, leaving ½-inch sides and bottoms. Drop into a large pot of boiling salted water. Cook for 10 to 15 minutes or until onions are just tender. Remove carefully from water, and drain upside down. Reserve water. Mince onion centers, and slowly cook in butter in a covered pan until tender; uncover. Raise heat, and brown onions lightly, stirring constantly. Measure 1 cup browned onion into a mixing bowl. Stir rice into water in which onions were blanched. Boil slowly for 10 to 12 minutes or until rice is almost tender. Drain and add to mixing bowl. Add Parmesan cheese and ¼ cup crème fraîche. Mix thoroughly. Add breadcrumbs. (More may be necessary to help mixture hold its shape.) Add herbs, salt, and pepper.

Butter the outside of the onion cups, and place them in a baking dish. Sprinkle inside with salt and pepper. Fill with stuffing, heaping it into a dome. Sprinkle with breadcrumbs and melted butter. Pour wine and enough stock around onions to immerse lowest third of onions. On top of range, simmer mixture; then put the casserole dish into preheated oven. Bake, uncovered, for 1 to 1¼ hours. Maintain oven temperature so liquid remains at a slow simmer. Baste outsides of onions several times. Onions are done when a knife pierces them easily and top is slightly brown. Yield: 6 servings.

Aunt Maggie's Baked Eggplant

1 eggplant
Tomato juice
1 pint tomatoes
2 tablespoons chopped green bell
    pepper
Salt to taste

1 teaspoon sugar, to taste
1 teaspoon basil
½ cup breadcrumbs
1 medium onion
1 tablespoon butter

Preheat oven to 350° F., and grease a 9x9-inch baking dish. Cut eggplant in half lengthwise. Remove flesh carefully, leaving shells intact. Dice flesh, and cook until tender in a small amount of the tomato juice; then strain eggplant well. Stew together tomatoes, green bell pepper, salt, sugar and basil; add enough breadcrumbs to thicken. Sauté onion in ½ tablespoon butter, but do not brown. Combine all vegetables, stir well, and adjust seasonings if needed. Let mixture stand until slightly cooled. Fill eggplant shells, and place them in prepared pan. Bake for 20 minutes or until filling is completely heated. Remove from oven, sprinkle filling with remaining breadcrumbs and ½ tablespoon butter, and return to oven briefly to brown. Yield: 4 to 6 servings.

Potato Cabbage Bake

4 tablespoons butter
1 small cabbage, chopped
2 large onions, chopped
6 red potatoes, cooked, cooled,
    thinly sliced

¼ cup flour
1 (14.5-ounce) can chicken broth
2 cups shredded sharp Cheddar or
    bonbel cheese

Preheat oven to 350° F. Heat butter in large skillet, and sauté cabbage and onions until wilted. Layer cabbage, onions, and potatoes in a 3-quart casserole dish. Stir flour into butter and pan juices, and slowly stir in chicken broth. Stir over low heat until sauce thickens. Pour sauce over vegetables. Top casserole with cheese. Bake for 45 minutes. Yield: 4 to 6 servings.

Sliced Baked Potatoes

This potato dish is attractive, and it is delicious with any kind of meat, fish, or poultry. It may even be used as the main course.

4 medium potatoes
1 teaspoon salt
2 to 3 tablespoons melted butter
3 tablespoons chopped fresh herbs (such as parsley, chives, thyme, or sage)

4 tablespoons grated Cheddar cheese
1½ tablespoons Parmesan cheese

Preheat oven to 425° F. Peel potatoes if the skin is tough; otherwise, just scrub and rinse them. Cut potatoes into thin slices but not all the way through. (Before slicing potato, place a spoon handle next to potato to prevent knife from cutting through potatoes.) Put potatoes in a baking dish; fan them slightly. Sprinkle with salt and drizzle with butter. Then, sprinkle with herbs. Bake for 50 minutes to 1 hour. Remove from oven, and sprinkle with Cheddar and Parmesan cheeses. Bake potatoes for another 10 to 15 minutes until slightly browned, cheeses are melted, and potatoes are soft inside. Yield: 6 to 8 servings.

Microwave Directions: Peel and cut potatoes as indicated above. Place potatoes in a microwave-safe dish or pan. Sprinkle with melted butter and herbs. Microwave on High power for 10 minutes, rearranging potatoes after 5 minutes. Let rest for 5 minutes. Sprinkle with grated cheese and Parmesan. Microwave for another 4 to 6 minutes on high power until cheeses are melted. Sprinkle with salt.

Roasted Rosemary Potatoes

Parsley may be substituted for rosemary.

2 pounds small red new potatoes, unpeeled
4 tablespoons butter
¼ cup olive oil
1 small onion, minced

1 large garlic clove, minced
2 large sprigs fresh rosemary, stems removed
Salt and freshly ground black pepper to taste

Scrub the potatoes lightly under running water and place them in a large saucepan with enough salted water to cover. Bring to a boil, reduce heat, cover, and let cook for 5 minutes. Drain the potatoes and cut into quarters. Dry with paper towels. Heat the butter and oil in a large cast-iron skillet, add the onion and garlic, and sauté mixture over medium heat for 1 minute. Add the potatoes, rosemary, salt, and pepper. Increase heat and cook, for about 20 minutes, or until the potatoes are evenly browned, turning the potatoes frequently. Yield: 4 servings.

Garlic Mashed Potatoes

Jimmy Noble of J. Basul Noble's Restaurant in High Point, North Carolina, contributed this recipe.

2 pounds red potatoes, peeled
7 to 10 cloves garlic
1 stick unsalted butter
1¾ cups heavy cream, heated

1 tablespoon salt
½ teaspoon freshly ground black pepper

Cover potatoes and garlic with water in a large pot, and boil until the potatoes are fork-tender. Drain and return contents to pot or to the mixing bowl of an electric mixer. Add the butter and break up potatoes with the mixer's whisk attachment or with a potato masher. Add hot cream gradually, and season. Beat briefly, and serve. Yield: 4 to 6 servings.

Make-Ahead Mashed Potatoes

**12 to 14 medium potatoes, peeled,
  if desired**
½ to 1 cup milk
**1 stick plus 2 tablespoons margarine
  or butter**

Salt and black pepper to taste
**1 (8-ounce) package cream cheese,
  softened**
6 scallions, chopped

Grease a 9x13-inch casserole dish. In a large saucepan, wash and cut potatoes into small cubes. Cook potatoes in water to cover by 1 inch. Warm milk,
and melt butter. Mix milk and butter together, and set aside. When potatoes
are done, do not drain water. Add the warm milk and butter mixture gradually
to the potatoes while beating the mixture with an electric mixer. Add salt and
pepper, if desired, and add cream cheese in chunks. Continue beating until
chunks are blended and potatoes are of a thinner than average consistency.
Add more liquid, if necessary, to achieve thin consistency. Stir in chopped
scallions. Put potatoes in prepared casserole. Cover and refrigerate. The next
day, dot potatoes with remaining butter. Bake, uncovered, at 350° F. for 30
minutes or until thoroughly warmed. Yield: 6 to 8 servings.

Cranberry-Apple Sweet Potatoes

**5 to 6 medium sweet potatoes,
  peeled, or 2 (18-ounce) cans cut
  sweet potatoes, drained**
1 (21-ounce) can apple pie filling

**1 (8-ounce) can whole cranberry
  sauce**
2 tablespoons apricot preserves
2 tablespoons orange marmalade

Preheat oven to 350° F. Cut fresh potatoes into bite-size pieces, and cook in a
large saucepan with enough water to boil. Drain when fork easily pierces
potato. Spread pie filling in 8x8x2-inch dish, spread potatoes over pie filling.
In a small mixing bowl, stir together cranberry sauce, apricot preserves, and
orange marmalade. Spoon over sweet potatoes. Bake, uncovered, for 20 to 25
minutes. Yield: 8 servings.

Spinach and Cheese Pie

3 leeks, white part only, washed and finely diced

2 tablespoons olive oil

1 pound fresh spinach, cleaned, steamed, chopped, and drained

2 cloves garlic, crushed

1½ cups grated mozzarella cheese

15 ounces ricotta cheese

1 egg

1 tablespoon dried parsley

Ground black pepper

12 sheets of phyllo dough, thawed and handled according to package directions

½ to 1 stick melted butter

Preheat oven to 350° F., and lightly grease a jellyroll pan. Lightly sauté leeks in olive oil until limp and transparent. Increase heat to medium-high, and add the cooked spinach and garlic. Cook, covered, until most of the liquid is evaporated. Remove from heat, and cool.

Meanwhile, combine mozzarella and ricotta cheeses, egg, parsley, and black pepper in a large bowl. Stir in spinach mixture, and set aside. Place one phyllo sheet on prepared pan, and lightly brush with a little melted butter. The phyllo sheet may hang over the edge of the cookie sheet; it will be rolled up later. Place another sheet of phyllo on the first, brush with melted butter, and continue until 6 sheets are stacked. Place the spinach mixture onto the center of the phyllo, and pat it into a rectangular shape. Top with the remaining 6 sheets of phyllo, again brushing each lightly with melted butter. Roll in the sides of the pie first lengthwise, and then widthwise. Seal with a little water, and brush top and sides with melted butter. Bake for 35 to 40 minutes. Cut into squares to serve. Yield: 6 to 8 servings.

Spinach Artichoke Bake

2 (10-ounce) packages frozen
  chopped spinach
4 tablespoons melted butter
1 (8-ounce) package cream cheese,
  softened

1 teaspoon lemon juice
1 (13¾-ounce) can artichoke hearts
Italian breadcrumbs

Preheat oven to 350° F. Cook spinach in saucepan, and drain well. Add butter and cream cheese; then add lemon juice. Mix well. Chop artichoke hearts, and add to spinach mixture. Place in an 8x8-inch casserole dish, and bake for 20 to 25 minutes, uncovered, until bubbly. Yield: 8 servings.

Variation: Divide mixture evenly among 8 medium tomatoes that have been cored and flesh removed. Bake according to above directions.

Posh Squash

This casserole may be made a day ahead.

2 pounds yellow squash, sliced
¼ cup green bell pepper, chopped
1 small onion, chopped
Salt and black pepper to taste
2 eggs, beaten

1 cup mayonnaise
1 cup Parmesan cheese
Butter pieces
Bread or cracker crumbs

Preheat oven to 350° F., and butter a 2½-quart casserole dish. Cook squash, green pepper, and onion in a saucepan with a little water until squash is tender; drain well. Add salt and pepper, eggs, mayonnaise, and Parmesan cheese. Pour into prepared dish. Dot with butter, and top with crumbs. Bake for 30 minutes. Yield: 8 to 10 servings.

Cajun Squash and Zucchini Casserole

You may freeze this dish. Omit croutons
until ready to cook.

1 medium onion, diced
4 ounces butter or margarine
1 pound yellow squash, cooked and mashed
1 pound zucchini, cooked and mashed
1 can (10½-ounce) tomatoes, drained and chopped

4 ounces grated sharp Cheddar cheese
1½ teaspoons salt
Dash of black pepper
1 cup Cheddar cheese croutons, or Cheddar cheese-flavored crackers

Preheat oven to 350° F., and butter a 2½-quart casserole dish. Sauté onion in butter; place mixture in large bowl. Add all ingredients except croutons; mix well. Pour into prepared dish, and top with croutons. Bake, uncovered, for 45 minutes. Yield: 8 to 10 servings.

Stuffed Zucchini

Stuffed Zucchini may be cut into bite-size
pieces and used as an appetizer.

4 medium zucchini, halved lengthwise
3 tablespoons butter or margarine
¾ cup finely chopped onion
3 small cloves garlic, crushed
Salt and black pepper to taste
1½ tablespoons flour

½ cup crumbled Feta cheese
¾ cup grated Swiss cheese
2 tablespoons chopped parsley
1 tablespoon fresh chopped dill
4 egg whites, beaten
Paprika

Preheat oven to 375° F. Scoop out the zucchini pulp, leaving a ½-inch rim. Chop the pulp into little bits, and cook in butter with onion, garlic, salt, and black pepper until onions are tender. Combine with flour, Feta and Swiss cheeses, herbs, and egg whites. Fill the zucchini cavities with mixture, and dust with paprika. Place filled shells on jellyroll pan. Bake for 30 minutes, or until filling solidifies. Yield: 8 servings.

Tomato-Vidalia Onion Pie

1 (9-inch) deep-dish pie crust
2 medium tomatoes, peeled
1 small Vidalia onion, peeled and
  chopped
1½ teaspoons dried basil

4 slices bacon, fried until crisp and
  crumbled
¾ cup sharp Cheddar cheese, grated
¾ cup mozzarella cheese, grated
2 tablespoons light mayonnaise

Preheat oven to 350° F. Bake pie crust until lightly browned. Slice tomatoes, and drain on paper towels. Place drained tomatoes into the pie shell. Top with chopped onion. Sprinkle with basil. Combine crumbled bacon, Cheddar and mozzarella cheeses, and mayonnaise. Spread evenly over top of pie. Bake for 25 minutes or until bubbly and golden brown. Cool slightly before slicing. Yield: 8 servings.

Tomatoes Stuffed with Artichoke Hearts

2 (16-ounce) cans whole peeled
  tomatoes, drained
1 teaspoon salt
¼ teaspoon freshly ground black
  pepper
½ teaspoon sugar

1 teaspoon dried basil
1 (14-ounce) can artichoke hearts,
  drained and rinsed
Butter
1 cup seasoned Italian breadcrumbs
¾ cup grated Parmesan cheese

Preheat oven to 400° F. Butter a 10x6½x2-inch casserole dish. Cut a cross in each tomato so that it can hold an artichoke heart. Place tomatoes in prepared dish. Blend salt, black pepper, sugar, and basil. Sprinkle mixture over tops and sides of tomatoes. Allow tomatoes to stand for 15 minutes. Place 1 artichoke heart in the center of each tomato, and top with a generous pat of butter. Combine breadcrumbs and Parmesan cheese. Sprinkle half of the crumb-cheese mixture over tops and sides of tomatoes. Bake for 10 minutes; then sprinkle remaining crumb mixture over tomato tops. Preheat broiler. Broil tomatoes for 2 to 3 minutes or until golden brown. Serve hot. Yield: 6 to 8 servings.

Vegetables Tossed in Olive Butter

*This dish is great for guests. Prepare raw vegetables
ahead; steam just before serving.*

4 small red potatoes, unpeeled and
  sliced
1 pound fresh asparagus, cut into
  2-inch pieces
1 small red bell pepper, cut into
  2-inch julienne strips
1 zucchini, sliced

½ pound fresh mushrooms, sliced
1 (7-ounce) jar baby corn ears
⅓ cup butter, melted
3 tablespoons lemon juice
⅓ cup sliced ripe olives
1 tablespoon lemon zest

Place potatoes on steaming rack in a large Dutch oven; add water to depth of
1 inch. Bring to a boil; cover, and steam for 5 minutes. Add asparagus and red
bell pepper; cover, and steam for 5 minutes. Add zucchini and mushrooms;
cover, and steam for 5 minutes. Add corn; cover, and steam for 1 minute.
Transfer vegetables to a bowl. Mix butter, lemon juice, olives, and lemon zest.
Toss vegetables with olive butter. Yield: 6 servings.

*Variation: One (10-ounce) package frozen asparagus can be substituted for 1
pound fresh asparagus. To cook, add thawed asparagus with red pepper,
zucchini, and mushrooms.*

Vegetable Shish Kebab

1¼ cups oil
1¼ cups vinegar
2 tablespoons red wine
2 cloves crushed garlic
Dash each of basil, oregano, salt, and pepper
24 large mushrooms
1 small eggplant, cut in 1½-inch chunks
2 medium bell peppers (green, red, or yellow)
6 medium tomatoes, quartered
2 medium onions, cut in 1-inch chunks
Hot cooked rice
Parmesan cheese (optional)

Combine oil, vinegar, wine, garlic, and herbs; put marinade in a large container or mixing bowl.

Clean the mushrooms, and marinate them whole. Broil the eggplant chunks until soft, but not mushy. Add them, still hot, to marinade. Stir well, and let stand at least 3 hours.

Cut the peppers in wide strips. Skewer the vegetables in alternating sequence, and baste them with extra marinade as they barbecue, roast, or broil. Serve on a bed of rice, sprinkled with Parmesan cheese. Yield: 6 servings of 2 skewers each.

Baked Apples with Cream Cheese

6 tart apples, cored and peeled
Juice of ½ lemon
Butter
1 (8-ounce) package cream cheese, softened
½ cup granola
Cinnamon, to taste

Preheat oven to 350 ° F., and butter a 7x11-inch baking pan. Peel and core apples, and slice them in half horizontally. Sprinkle generously with lemon juice. For filling, combine cream cheese and granola. Stuff each apple half with one teaspoon of filling. Sprinkle the apple tops lightly with cinnamon. Bake for approximately 30 minutes or until apples are tender when pierced with a fork. Yield: 12 servings.

Cranberry-Apple Casserole

3 cups tart, peeled apples, diced	½ cup brown sugar
2 cups fresh, whole cranberries	⅓ cup all-purpose flour
1 cup granulated sugar	1½ cups rolled oats
1 cup chopped pecans	½ cup melted butter

Preheat oven to 325° F. Mix apples, cranberries, and sugar, and place in a 13x9x2-inch pan.

For topping, mix together pecans and remaining ingredients; sprinkle over fruit. Bake for 1 hour. Yield: 8 servings.

Poached Pear Halves in Cream Sherry Sauce

1 cup cream sherry	2 tablespoons fresh lemon juice
½ cup sugar	⅛ teaspoon ground nutmeg
½ (3-inch) cinnamon stick	2 firm Bosc pears
3 whole cloves	Mint sprigs, for garnish

Bring sherry, sugar, cinnamon, cloves, lemon juice, and nutmeg to a boil in a 3-quart saucepan. Peel, halve, and core pears just before placing in boiling sherry mixture. Reduce heat and cook pears, covered, until tender, for approximately 30 minutes. Remove pears onto platter. Boil sherry mixture until it becomes the consistency of thin syrup. Boil about 15 minutes longer, stirring often, so syrup does not burn. Pour syrup over pears. Garnish with mint sprigs. Yield: 2 servings.

Pineapple au Gratin

2 (20-ounce) cans pineapple
chunks, drained
1 cup sugar
6 tablespoons self-rising flour

1 to 2 cups sharp Cheddar cheese,
grated
1 sleeve round buttery crackers,
crumbled
1 stick melted margarine or butter

Preheat oven to 350° F., and grease a 13x9x2-inch Pyrex dish. Mix pineapple, sugar, flour, and Cheddar cheese, and pour into dish. Top mixture with cracker crumbs. Pour melted butter over crumbs, and bake, uncovered, for 20 to 25 minutes. Let stand at least 10 minutes before serving. Serve warm. Yield: 6 to 8 servings.

Fresh Fruit Compote

1 red Delicious apple, unpeeled, cut
into ½-inch cubes
1 pear, cut in ½-inch cubes
2 seedless oranges, peeled, sliced,
and quartered
1 banana, peeled and sliced

½ fresh pineapple, cut in chunks
(about 2 cups)
¼ cup orange liqueur
3 tablespoons lemon juice
2 tablespoons sugar

Place all fruit in large serving bowl. Combine liqueur, lemon juice, and sugar. Stir until sugar is dissolved. Sprinkle over fruit, and toss gently. Cover and refrigerate until well chilled. Toss again before serving. Yield: 8 servings.

Curried Fruit

6 tablespoons butter or margarine
1 cup firmly packed light brown
sugar
1 teaspoon curry powder
1 (20-ounce) can peach slices, cut
in bite-size pieces

1 (20-ounce) can pear halves, cut in
bite-size pieces
1 (20-ounce) can pineapple chunks
1 (15-ounce) jar spiced apple rings,
cut in pieces (optional)
Maraschino cherries, for garnish

Preheat oven to 325° F. In a saucepan, combine butter, brown sugar, and curry powder. Bring to a boil. Drain fruit; arrange in shallow 2-quart baking dish, and pour hot sauce over it. Garnish with cherries. Bake for 30 to 40 minutes or until bubbly. Serve hot. Yield: 8 to 10 servings.

Crusty Baked Fruit

6 to 8 tart apples, peeled and sliced
½ fresh pineapple, cut and sliced
½ cup brown sugar
½ cup sugar
1 teaspoon nutmeg
½ cup apple juice, or apple cider
2 tablespoons apple juice, or
   pineapple juice

½ dozen stale glazed doughnuts, or
   croissants
½ cup oats, not quick-cooking
1 cup chopped pecans
1 stick butter, melted
2 to 3 tablespoons butter, very cold

Preheat oven to 350° F., and butter an 8x8-inch baking dish. In a mixing bowl, stir together apples and pineapple with sugars, nutmeg, and juices. In a processor or blender, process doughnuts into crumbs. Add oats and chopped pecans to the crumbs. Pour the melted butter into the crumb mixture, and mix well. Put one-third of the crumbs into baking dish; then layer with half the fruit. Top fruit with half of the remaining crumbs; then add remaining half of fruit. Place the remaining crumbs on fruit. Dot crumbs with 2 to 3 tablespoons butter. Bake until hot and bubbly throughout, for approximately 1 hour. Yield: 4 to 6 servings.

Rainbow Row Baked Fruit

⅓ cup butter
¾ cup brown sugar
1 tablespoon curry powder
Dash of apple pie spice
Splash of sherry or applejack brandy
3 (30-ounce) cans pear halves
1 (30-ounce) can sliced peaches

1 (16-ounce) can pineapple chunks
1 (30-ounce) can plums
1 (16-ounce) can blueberries
1 (8-ounce) can mandarin oranges
1 (16-ounce) can apricot halves
¾ cup whole walnuts

In a small saucepan, combine butter, brown sugar, curry powder, apple pie spice, and sherry or brandy. Heat until sugar dissolves.

Preheat oven to 350° F. Drain fruits well. Arrange them decoratively in a 13x9x2-inch casserole dish. Pour sauce over fruit. Bake for 1 hour, or microwave on medium high for 30 minutes. Yield: 10 servings.

Fresh Cranberry Orange Relish

Relish freezes well.

1½ (12-ounce) bags cranberries, frozen

2 quartered oranges, with top rind, bottom rind, and seeds removed

2 medium to large apples, cored, unpeeled, and quartered

2 cups sugar

¼ cup orange liqueur, or to taste

Chop cranberries, orange pieces, and apples in a food processor. Once processed, place in large bowl; add sugar and liqueur, and stir by hand. Chill relish in refrigerator for several hours before serving. Yield: 6 to 8 servings.

Cranberry Relish

1 (16-ounce) can whole berry cranberry sauce

½ cup raisins

½ cup peeled, chopped apple

6 tablespoons sugar

6 tablespoons white vinegar

⅛ teaspoon allspice

⅛ teaspoon ginger

⅛ teaspoon cinnamon

Combine all ingredients in 2-quart saucepan. Cook on medium heat, stirring occasionally until sauce thickens, about 30 minutes. Serve warm or chilled. Yield: 15 to 20 servings.

Pepper Relish

Red peppers may be substituted for other hot peppers for color and more flavor.

12 green bell peppers

12 hot peppers

12 onions

1 quart cider vinegar

2 cups sugar

1 tablespoon salt

Process green bell peppers, hot peppers, and onions in food processor. Put in a large bowl, and cover with boiling water; set aside for 15 minutes. Strain and put in large sauce pot. Add vinegar, sugar, and salt, and simmer, uncovered, for 25 minutes. When cool, put in clean jars and refrigerate. Refrigerated, relish will keep for 1 year. Yield: 4 cups.

Pineapple Salsa

*This salsa has a Caribbean flavor and is very good
served over pork chops, Mahi Mahi, and chicken.*

*Jim Cason of Providence Café in Charlotte, North
Carolina, contributed this recipe.*

2 fresh pineapples, cored and
  coarsely diced
1 red pepper, seeds removed and
  finely diced
1 jalapeño, seeded and finely diced
½ red onion, finely diced
½ bunch of cilantro, chopped and
  stems removed

1 teaspoon curry powder
1 teaspoon chili powder
½ teaspoon white pepper
1 teaspoon salt
Juice and zest of 2 limes
1 (6-ounce) can pineapple juice

Combine all ingredients, and chill overnight. Serve cold. Yield: 3 cups.

Spinach Pesto

This pesto freezes well.

1 (10-ounce) box frozen chopped
  spinach
½ cup chopped parsley
½ cup grated Parmesan cheese
¼ cup pine nut or walnut pieces

2 to 3 garlic cloves, minced
1 teaspoon salt
½ teaspoon freshly ground black
  pepper
⅔ cup olive oil

Thaw and squeeze as much water as possible out of spinach. In food processor, mix spinach, parsley, Parmesan cheese, nuts, garlic, salt, and black
pepper. Blend until smooth. With food processor motor running, slowly add
olive oil. Yield: 1½ cups.

Seafood Cocktail Sauce

This sauce enhances crab,
shrimp, and oyster cocktails.

⅔ cup ketchup
3 tablespoons chili sauce
2 tablespoons horseradish, grated
3 tablespoons fresh lemon juice

Dash of cayenne pepper
⅛ teaspoon onion powder
2 teaspoons Worcestershire sauce

Mix all ingredients well and chill. Yield: 1 cup.

Tomato Coulis

2 slices bacon
3 shallots
3 cloves garlic
1½ cups tomato purée
2 tablespoons tomato paste

2 cups chicken stock
1 bay leaf
4 sprigs thyme
Salt and black pepper to taste

In a large saucepan, cook bacon until crisp. Add shallots and garlic, and sauté briefly. Add tomato purée, tomato paste, and chicken stock. Add herbs, salt, and black pepper. Cook slowly until reduced by one-third. Press through strainer, and correct seasoning to taste. Serve with crab cakes or other seafood. Yield: 3½ cups.

Basil Tartar Sauce

1 cup fresh basil
½ cup mayonnaise
1 tablespoon sour cream

1 teaspoon lemon juice
1 teaspoon minced garlic
Salt, black pepper, and hot pepper
   sauce to taste

Combine all ingredients. Mix well. Serve with crab cakes. Yield: 2 cups.

Horseradish Pecan Sauce

2 egg yolks
2 tablespoons prepared horseradish
1 tablespoon water
1 tablespoon butter

½ teaspoon sugar
Pinch of salt
1 cup heavy cream, whipped
½ cup finely chopped pecans

In the top of a double broiler, combine egg yolks, horseradish, water, butter, sugar, and salt. Blend well. Cook over low heat, stirring constantly until thick. Cool completely. Fold cream into cooled mixture. Chill overnight. Before serving, add pecans. Yield: 1½ cups.

Jazzy Jezebel Sauce

*Serve sauce with ham or cream cheese and crackers.
Sauce keeps for several months in refrigerator.*

1 (18-ounce) jar pineapple
  preserves
1 (18-ounce) jar apple jelly
1 (1.5-ounce) container dry mustard

¾ (5-ounce) jar prepared
  horseradish
1 tablespoon cracked pepper

Blend all ingredients in food processor. Refrigerate. Yield: 2 pints.

Tsatsiki (Yogurt Dip)

*Serve with grilled chicken, chicken kebabs, or grilled
chicken sandwiches.*

1 clove garlic
1 teaspoon olive oil
1 cup yogurt

1 diced cucumber
Salt and black pepper to taste
Dash of white vinegar

Mash or press garlic, and mix with olive oil. Add to yogurt, stirring well. Mix with remaining ingredients, and chill. Yield: 1 cup.

Faith Mary's Mustard

1 cup spicy hot dry mustard
1 cup apple cider vinegar

1 cup sugar
2 eggs, beaten

Soak mustard and vinegar overnight in top of double boiler. The next day, add sugar and eggs. Slowly cook, uncovered, in double boiler for 1 hour, stirring often. Pour through strainer and into jar. Do not freeze. Mustard keeps in refrigerator for several months. Yield: 1 pint.

Hot Dog Chili Sauce

1½ pounds ground chuck (85% to 90% fat-free works well)
3 tablespoons chili powder
1 tablespoon cumin

1 (8-ounce) can tomato sauce
Salt, black pepper, and sugar to taste

Cover ingredients with water, and simmer, uncovered, for 1½ to 2 hours. Add water as necessary as sauce cooks, but sauce must be thick enough to spoon over hot dogs. Sauce freezes well. Yield: 12 to 15 servings.

Desserts

*In a remarkable contrast of old and new, Old Salem
retained its eighteenth-century village characteristics even
as the modern city of Winston-Salem developed around it.*

*Fulfilling its mission, The Children's Home Society brings
the blessings of permanent, safe, and loving homes to
children across North Carolina.*

Apricot Nectar Cake

1 (6-ounce) box lemon-flavored
   instant pudding
1 (18¼-ounce) box yellow cake mix
1¾ cups vegetable oil

6 ounces apricot nectar
1 teaspoon lemon extract
4 eggs, well beaten
Glaze

Preheat oven to 325° F. Lightly oil and flour tube pan. In a large bowl with an electric mixer, combine pudding mix with cake mix. Add vegetable oil, apricot nectar, and lemon extract. Blend well; add eggs. Blend well. Put cake mixture in prepared pan, and bake for 1 hour. Pull rack out, and let cake cool partly out of oven for 15 minutes. Then remove warm cake completely from oven, turn cake out of pan, and drizzle glaze over cake. Yield: 12 to 14 servings.

Glaze:

¾ cup confectioners' sugar   ½ cup orange juice

Combine sugar with orange juice. Drizzle over warm cake.

Apple Cake

1 cup oil
2 cups sugar
3 eggs
3 cups all-purpose flour
1 teaspoon salt

1 teaspoon baking soda
2 teaspoons vanilla extract
1 cup chopped nuts
1 (21-ounce) can pie-sliced apples;
   diced, if desired

Preheat oven to 350° F. Grease and flour a 13x9x2-inch baking pan. Cream oil with sugar. Add eggs, one at a time, alternating with flour. Sift salt and baking soda into mixture, and mix well. Add vanilla extract, nuts, and apples. Bake 50 to 60 minutes, or until brown and toothpick inserted into center of cake comes out clean.

Icing:

1 stick margarine
1½ cups brown sugar

6 tablespoons evaporated milk

Melt margarine with brown sugar. Boil, stirring for 3 minutes. Add evaporated milk, and cook for 1 minute more. Bring to a boil, stirring constantly. Cook icing. With a mixer, beat icing until it loses its sheen. Spread on cake. Yield: 18 servings.

Apple Dapple Cake

2 cups granulated sugar
3 cups sifted all-purpose flour
1 teaspoon baking soda
1 teaspoon salt
1 teaspoon cinnamon
½ teaspoon cloves

3 eggs, lightly beaten
1½ cups vegetable oil
2 teaspoons vanilla extract
1 cup chopped nuts
3 cups chopped apples

Preheat oven to 350° F. Grease and flour a 13x9x2-inch baking pan. Combine sugar, flour, baking soda, salt, cinnamon, and cloves; mix well. Stir in eggs, oil, and vanilla extract. Mix until all ingredients are moist. Then stir in nuts and apples. Pour batter into prepared pan. Bake for about 1 hour, or until toothpick inserted in middle comes out clean. Cool slightly, and add topping while cake is warm. Yield: 24 servings.

Topping:
4 tablespoons butter
¼ cup milk

1 cup brown sugar

Boil butter, milk, and brown sugar for 4 minutes over medium heat. Pour mixture over top of warm cake, and spread to cover.

Alternate Topping: 1 stick margarine, 1 cup brown sugar, ½ cup evaporated milk, 1 cup coconut. Cook ingredients, except coconut, for 3 minutes after mixture comes to a boil. Remove from heat, and stir in coconut. Pour mixture over hot or warm cake, and spread to cover.

Applesauce Cake

½ cup shortening
1 cup sugar
1 egg
1 teaspoon vanilla extract
1¾ cups all-purpose flour
¼ teaspoon salt
1 teaspoon cinnamon

½ teaspoon allspice
½ teaspoon ground cloves
1½ cups applesauce
¾ teaspoon baking soda
1 cup raisins (optional)
1 cup nuts (optional)

Preheat oven to 350° F. Grease and flour a 13x9x2-inch pan. Cream together shortening and sugar until fluffy. Beat in egg and vanilla extract. Sift together flour, salt, cinnamon, allspice, and cloves. Combine applesauce and baking soda. Alternately blend the dry ingredients and the applesauce into the creamed mixture. Add raisins or nuts, if desired. Beat slowly until just blended. Pour batter into prepared pan, and bake for 35 minutes. Sprinkle cooled cake with confectioners' sugar or cinnamon sugar. Yield: 24 servings.

Old-fashioned Caramel Cake

1 stick margarine
1½ cups sugar
2 eggs
2 cups sifted all-purpose flour
1 cup buttermilk

1 teaspoon baking soda
1 tablespoon white vinegar
1 teaspoon vanilla extract
Caramel Icing

Preheat oven to 350° F. Grease and flour two 9-inch round pans. Cream margarine and sugar together until light and fluffy. Add eggs, one at a time, and continue beating. Add sifted flour alternately with buttermilk. Blend well. Stir in baking soda, which has been dissolved in vinegar; add vanilla extract. Pour into prepared pans. Bake for 25 minutes. Cool and spread with Caramel Icing. Yield: 12 servings.

Caramel Icing:
2 cups light brown sugar, firmly
  packed
1 cup sugar
2 tablespoons light corn syrup
¾ cup milk

¼ cup shortening
¼ teaspoon salt
4 tablespoons butter
1¼ teaspoons vanilla extract

Bring all ingredients, except vanilla extract, to a full rolling boil, stirring constantly; boil briskly for 3 minutes. Cool mixture to lukewarm temperature. Add vanilla extract, and beat until creamy.

Carrot Raisin Cake with Irish Cream Frosting

2 cups all-purpose flour
4 eggs
2 cups sugar
1½ cups oil
2 teaspoons baking soda
3 cups grated carrots (use food
  processor or blender to grate)

2 teaspoons cinnamon
1 teaspoon salt
½ cup chopped pecans
½ cup raisins (optional)
Irish Cream Frosting
½ cup chopped pecans (optional)

Preheat oven to 350° F. Grease and flour two 9-inch round pans. Mix sugar and oil. Add sifted dry ingredients and carrots. Add eggs one at a time, beating well after each addition. Add pecans and raisins; blend well. Bake in prepared pans for 40 to 50 minutes. Cool completely. Spread layers, sides, and top with Irish Cream Frosting. Sprinkle frosting with chopped pecans, if desired. Yield: 12 servings.

Irish Cream Frosting:

1 (8-ounce) package cream cheese,
  softened
1 stick butter
1 teaspoon vanilla extract

1 (16-ounce) box confectioners'
  sugar, sifted
½ cup Irish Cream liqueur or heavy
  cream

With electric mixer, blend cream cheese, butter, vanilla extract, and sugar; stir in liqueur.

Quick Carrot Sheet Cake

4 eggs
2 cups sugar
3 (4½-ounce) jars strained baby
  food carrots
1¼ cups Wesson oil
1 teaspoon vanilla extract
2 cups all-purpose flour
1 teaspoon salt

1 teaspoon cinnamon
2 teaspoons baking soda
1 (8¼-ounce) can crushed
  pineapple, drained
1 cup chopped nuts
1 cup golden raisins
Frosting
½ cup crushed nuts (optional)

Preheat oven to 350° F., and grease and flour a 13x9x2-inch pan. Cream together eggs, sugar, carrots, oil, and vanilla extract. Beat well, then add flour, salt, cinnamon, and baking soda. Add pineapple, nuts, and raisins. Pour into prepared pan, and bake for 50 to 55 minutes. When cool, spread with frosting. Sprinkle with nuts, if desired. Yield: 18 servings.

Frosting:

1 (8-ounce) package cream cheese,
  room temperature
1 stick margarine

1 (16-ounce) box confectioners'
  sugar
1 teaspoon vanilla extract

Using electric mixer, blend all ingredients together well.

Black Bottom Cups

1 (8-ounce) package cream cheese, softened
1 egg
⅓ cup sugar
⅛ teaspoon salt
1 (6-ounce) package semi-sweet chocolate chips
1½ cups sifted all-purpose flour
1 cup sugar

¼ cup cocoa
1 teaspoon baking soda
½ teaspoon salt
1 cup water
⅓ cup oil
1 tablespoon white vinegar
1 teaspoon vanilla extract
Sugar and sliced almonds, for garnish

Beat together cream cheese, egg, ⅓ cup sugar, and salt; add chocolate chips, and set aside. Sift together flour, 1 cup sugar, cocoa, baking soda, and salt. Add water, oil, vinegar, and vanilla extract.

Preheat oven to 350° F. Fill 18 paper-lined muffin tins one-third full with batter. Top each with 1 heaping teaspoon cream cheese mixture. Sprinkle each with sugar and sliced almonds. Bake for 30 to 35 minutes. Yield: 18 cupcakes.

Chocolate Cheesecake

1 (12-ounce) box thin chocolate wafers
¼ teaspoon cinnamon
1 stick unsalted butter, melted
4 (8-ounce) packages cream cheese
4 eggs

2 cups sugar
1 tablespoon cocoa
1 tablespoon vanilla extract
1 (12-ounce) package semi-sweet chocolate chips, melted
2 cups sour cream

Preheat oven to 350° F. Butter a 10-inch springform pan. Grind wafers in blender. Mix with cinnamon and butter. Chill in prepared pan. In mixer, beat cream cheese until fluffy. Add 1 egg at a time, alternating with sugar. Add cocoa and vanilla extract. Mix well, and fold in melted chocolate. Stir in sour cream, and pour into chilled crust. Bake 1 hour and 10 minutes. Cool for several hours before serving; then refrigerate. Yield: 12 servings.

Cherry Cheesecake

½ (12-ounce) box vanilla wafers
4 tablespoons soft butter
1 cup plus 2 tablespoons sugar
¼ teaspoon cinnamon
2 (8-ounce) packages cream cheese, softened
1 cup light cream

2 tablespoons all-purpose flour
¼ teaspoon salt
3 eggs
1 teaspoon vanilla extract
¾ teaspoon grated lemon zest
Topping

Preheat oven to 325° F. Grease a 10-inch springform pan; set aside. Roll or grind cookies. Mix with soft butter, 2 tablespoons sugar, and cinnamon. Pat crumb mixture on bottom and sides of pan. Mix cream cheese with cream and remaining sugar that has been mixed with flour and salt. Beat egg yolks until thick and light. Beat egg whites to soft peaks and fold in batter. Pour into crust. Bake for 1 hour. Turn off oven, and leave cake in oven for 1 hour with door closed. Do not open oven door, or cake will fall. Cool thoroughly. Add topping and refrigerate at least 8 hours before serving. Yield: 10 to 12 servings.

Topping:

1 (20-ounce) can red cherries
2 tablespoons cornstarch

⅓ cup sugar
⅛ teaspoon grated lemon zest

Drain cherries; reserve juice. Mix cornstarch with ¾ cup cherry juice, add sugar and lemon zest. Cook mixture 15 minutes over low heat, stirring constantly. Cool; add cherries, and pour on cooled cake, spreading to ½ inch of edge.

Chocolate Amaretto Cheesecake

6 chocolate wafers, finely crushed
1½ cups light cream cheese
1 cup sugar
1 cup 1% low-fat cottage cheese
6 tablespoons unsweetened cocoa
¼ cup all-purpose flour
¼ cup amaretto

1 teaspoon vanilla extract
¼ teaspoon salt
1 egg
2 tablespoons semi-sweet chocolate mini chips
Chocolate curls (optional)

Preheat oven to 300° F. Sprinkle chocolate wafer crumbs in bottom of a 7-inch springform pan. Set aside. Position knife blade in food processor bowl; add cream cheese, sugar, cottage cheese, cocoa, flour, amaretto, vanilla extract, and salt, processing until smooth. Add egg, and process until just blended. Fold in chocolate morsels.

Slowly pour mixture over crumbs in pan. Bake for 1 hour and 5 to 10 minutes until cheesecake sets. Allow cake to cool in pan on wire rack. Cover and chill at least 8 hours. Remove sides of pan, and transfer cheesecake to a serving plate. Garnish with chocolate curls, if desired. Yield: 12 servings.

If an 8-inch springform pan is used, bake 45 to 50 minutes.

For Chocolate-Mint Cheesecake: substitute ¼ cup crème de menthe for amaretto.

Chocolate Cherry Cheese Cake

1½ cups chocolate wafer crumbs
¼ cup melted butter
3 (8-ounce) packages cream cheese
1½ cups sugar
4 eggs
⅓ cup kirsch or cherry liqueur

4 (1-ounce) squares semi-sweet chocolate
½ cup sour cream
Topping
Maraschino cherries with stems, chocolate curls, and toasted almonds for garnish, if desired

Preheat oven to 350° F. Combine wafer crumbs and melted butter, and press mixture into the bottom and 1 inch up the sides of a 10-inch springform pan; set aside. Beat cream cheese until fluffy. Add sugar gradually and then eggs one at a time, beating after each addition. Add the kirsch. Blend well, and pour batter into prepared pan. Bake for 1 hour. Allow cake to cool in pan on wire rack. Melt the chocolate over medium heat, and cool slightly. Stir in sour cream. Mix and pour over cooled cake. Remove cake from pan, and chill while preparing topping. Spread or pipe topping onto top of chocolate layer. Garnish with cherries, chocolate curls, and/or toasted almonds. Yield: 8 servings.

Topping:

1½ tablespoons kirsch or cherry liqueur
1 cup whipping cream, whipped until stiff

1 pound confectioners' sugar
Pinch of salt

Fold kirsch into the whipped cream; then fold in sugar and salt gradually.

Italian Cheese Cake

2 pounds ricotta cheese	1 pint sour cream
2 (8-ounce) packages cream cheese	6 teaspoons all-purpose flour
2 cups sugar	1 teaspoon vanilla extract
6 eggs	

Preheat oven to 350° F. In large bowl with an electric mixer, cream ricotta and cream cheese. Add sugar. Slowly beat in 1 egg at a time. Alternately add in sour cream and flour. Mix in vanilla extract. Pour batter into 1 (10-inch) or 2 (7-inch) springform pans. Place pan into larger pan filled with 1 inch hot water. Bake for 1½ hours. Turn off oven, and leave cake in oven for 1 hour with door closed. Do not open oven door, or cake will fall. Refrigerate for 24 hours before serving. Yield: 10 to 12 servings.

New York Cheesecake

Cake may be frozen after it is refrigerated.

½ (12-ounce) box vanilla wafers	4 eggs
2 teaspoons sugar	2 cups sour cream
4 tablespoons butter, melted	1 cup heavy cream
1½ cup sugar	1 teaspoon vanilla extract
3 (8-ounce) packages cream cheese, softened	

Preheat oven to 350° F. Crush vanilla wafers to make 1½ cups crumbs. Combine with sugar and melted butter. Rub a 10-inch springform pan with butter on bottom and about ¼ inch up sides. Add crumbs to pan, and pat down bottom and sides; set aside.

Cream sugar and cream cheese. Mix in eggs one at a time. Add sour cream, and mix well; add heavy cream and vanilla extract. Pour into pan. Bake for 1 hour. Shut oven off, and leave cake in oven for 1 hour to brown. Remove from oven, and allow to cool to room temperature. Cover with foil, and refrigerate for 2 days. Yield: 10 to 12 servings.

Cherry Cake with Hot Cherry Sauce

1 (16-ounce) can pitted tart cherries
  in water, liquid reserved
10 drops red food coloring
¼ cup shortening
¼ teaspoon almond extract
½ teaspoon vanilla extract
¾ cup sugar

1 egg
1⅓ cups sifted all-purpose flour
2 teaspoons baking powder
½ teaspoon salt
½ cup milk
½ cup chopped nuts
Hot Cherry Sauce

Preheat oven to 350° F. Grease an 8-inch square or 9-inch square baking pan. Drain cherries, reserving liquid. Add water to liquid to make 1 cup. Add red food coloring, and set aside for sauce. Thoroughly cream together shortening, extracts, and sugar. Add egg, and beat well. Sift dry ingredients; add alternately with milk, beating until smooth after each addition. Fold in cherries and nuts. Pour into prepared pan. Bake for 45 to 50 minutes. Cut in squares, and serve warm with Hot Cherry Sauce. Yield: 8 servings.

Hot Cherry Sauce:
½ cup sugar
1½ tablespoons cornstarch

Dash of salt
Reserved liquid (1 cup) from
  cherries

In a small saucepan, combine sugar, cornstarch, and salt. Stir in reserved cherry liquid. Cook, stirring constantly, until thick.

Chocolate Layer Cake and Frosting

Cocoa powder
1 stick butter
1 box brown sugar
3 eggs
3 squares unsweetened chocolate, melted
2¼ cups sifted cake flour

2 teaspoons baking soda
½ teaspoon salt
1 cup sour cream
1 cup hot water
1½ teaspoons vanilla extract
Frosting

Preheat oven to 350° F. Generously grease and dust with cocoa powder two 9-inch round pans. Cream butter; add brown sugar, and beat well. Add eggs, one at a time, and beat well after each addition. Add chocolate, and mix well. Combine flour, baking soda, and salt in a separate bowl. Add to chocolate mixture alternately with sour cream. Beat well. Add water, and mix well. Stir in vanilla extract, and mix well. Batter will be thin. Pour batter into prepared pans, and bake for 45 minutes or until cakes test done. Let the layers cool in the pans for 10 minutes; then turn the layers out onto racks to cool completely. Spread layers, sides, and top with frosting. Yield: 10 to 12 servings.

Frosting:
4 squares unsweetened chocolate
1 stick butter
2 teaspoons vanilla extract

½ cup milk
1 (16-ounce) box confectioners' sugar

Stirring constantly, melt the chocolate and the butter in a large heavy saucepan over low heat. Remove the pan from the heat. Pour other ingredients into the pan. Put the pan in a sink or very large bowl, and surround the pan with ice. With an electric mixer, beat the mixture at high speed until the mixture reaches spreading consistency.

Invert one of the cake layers onto a plate. Spread one-fourth the frosting on top, and top it with the second layer. Spread the remaining frosting on the sides and top.

Easy Chocolate Cake

2 cups sugar	1 cup vegetable oil
2 cups self-rising flour	2 eggs, well beaten
1 stick margarine or butter	1 teaspoon vanilla extract
4 tablespoons cocoa	½ cup buttermilk
1 cup water	Chocolate Frosting or Buttermilk Frosting

Preheat oven to 350° F. Grease and flour a 13x9x2-inch casserole dish or cake pan. Mix together sugar and flour; set aside. In saucepan combine margarine, cocoa, water, and oil. Bring to a boil, and boil for 1 minute, stirring constantly. Pour over sugar and flour mixture, and stir until smooth. Add eggs, vanilla extract, and buttermilk. Stir until well mixed. Pour into prepared dish. Bake about 40 minutes. Remove from oven, and pour chocolate icing over top while cake is still hot. If using buttermilk frosting, allow cake to cool completely before frosting it. Yield: 18 servings.

Chocolate Frosting:

1 stick butter or margarine	Pinch of salt
4 tablespoons cocoa	4 tablespoons milk
1 teaspoon vanilla	1 (16-ounce) box confectioners' sugar

In saucepan mix together all ingredients, except confectioners' sugar, and bring to a boil. Remove from heat and add sugar gradually. If mixture is too thick to pour, add more milk. Pour frosting over hot cake.

Buttermilk Frosting:

1 (16-ounce) box confectioners' sugar, sifted	¼ cup margarine, melted
¼ cup cocoa	1 teaspoon vanilla extract
	⅓ cup buttermilk

Sift together sugar and cocoa. Add margarine, vanilla, and buttermilk; beat well. Spread on cooled cake.

Decadent Fudge Cake

2 sticks butter or margarine, softened
1½ cups sugar
4 eggs
½ teaspoon baking soda
1 cup buttermilk
2½ cups all-purpose flour
1½ cups semi-sweet chocolate mini chips, divided

2 (4-ounce) bars sweet baking chocolate, melted and cooled
⅓ cup chocolate syrup
2 teaspoons vanilla extract
4 ounces white chocolate, chopped
2 tablespoons plus 2 teaspoons shortening, divided

Preheat oven to 300° F. Heavily grease and flour a 10-inch Bundt pan. Cream butter in a large mixing bowl; gradually add sugar, beating well with electric mixer at medium speed. Add eggs, one at a time, beating after each addition. Dissolve baking soda in buttermilk, stirring well. Add to creamed mixture alternately with flour, beginning and ending with flour. Add 1 cup mini chips, melted chocolate, chocolate syrup, and vanilla, stirring until just blended. Do not overbeat. Spoon batter into prepared pan. Bake for 1 hour and 25 to 35 minutes or until cake springs back when touched. Invert onto serving plate immediately, and let cool completely.

Combine 4 ounces chopped white chocolate and 2 tablespoons shortening in top of double boiler; bring water to boil. Reduce to low; cook until mixture is melted and smooth. Remove from heat. Drizzle melted white chocolate mixture over cooled cake. Melt remaining ½ cup mini chips and 2 teaspoons shortening in a small saucepan over low heat, stirring until smooth. Remove from heat, and let cool; drizzle over white chocolate. Yield: 10 to 12 servings.

Chocolate Mousse Cake

7 ounces semi-sweet chocolate
  morsels
1 stick unsalted butter
7 eggs, separated

1 cup sugar, divided
1 teaspoon vanilla extract
⅛ teaspoon cream of tartar
Whipped Cream Frosting

Preheat oven to 325° F. In a small saucepan, melt chocolate and butter over low heat. In large bowl, beat egg yolks and ¾ cup sugar for about 5 minutes, or until very light and fluffy. Gradually beat in warm chocolate mixture and vanilla extract.

In another large bowl, beat egg whites with cream of tartar until soft peaks form. Add remaining ¼ cup sugar, 1 tablespoon at a time. Continue beating until stiff. Fold egg whites carefully into chocolate mixture. Pour three-fourths batter into an ungreased 10-inch springform pan. Cover remaining batter and refrigerate.

Bake cake for 35 minutes. Prepare frosting. Remove cake from oven and cool. Cake will drop as it cools. Remove outside ring of pan. Stir refrigerated batter to soften. Spread on cake. Refrigerate until firm. Spread with frosting over tops and sides. Refrigerate several hours or overnight. Yield: 8 to 10 servings.

Whipped Cream Frosting:
1 cup whipping cream
⅓ cup confectioners' sugar

1 teaspoon vanilla

Whip cream, and add sugar and vanilla. Beat until stiff.

Chocolate Chocolate Russe Cake

4 ounces (4 squares) unsweetened chocolate
¾ cup sugar
⅓ cup milk
6 eggs, separated
3 sticks unsalted butter
1½ cups confectioners' sugar, divided

⅛ teaspoon salt
1½ teaspoons vanilla extract
3 dozen ladyfingers, or Vienna cookies, split
1 cup heavy whipped cream, whipped
Shaved unsweetened chocolate

Melt chocolate squares in top part of double boiler over hot water. Mix sugar, milk, and egg yolks. Add to chocolate, cook until smooth and thickened, stirring constantly; cool. Cream butter well. Add ¾ cup confectioners' sugar, and cream thoroughly. Add chocolate mixture, and beat well. Beat egg whites with salt until stiff; gradually beat in remaining ¾ cup confectioners' sugar. Fold into chocolate mixture. Add vanilla extract. Line 10-inch springform or loose-bottomed pan with split ladyfingers. Put in alternate layers of one-third mixture and remaining ladyfingers. Chill overnight. Remove to cake plate. Garnish with whipped cream and shaved chocolate. Yield: 10 to 12 servings.

Chocolate Torte

1¼ cups sifted all-purpose flour
¾ teaspoon baking soda
½ teaspoon salt
1 (8-ounce) package pitted dates, chopped
¾ cup brown sugar, firmly packed
½ cup water
1 stick butter or margarine

1 (6-ounce) package semi-sweet chocolate chips
2 eggs
½ cup milk
½ cup orange juice
1 cup English walnuts, chopped
Chocolate Cream Whip
Grapes (optional)

Preheat oven to 350° F. Thoroughly grease, then flour, a 15x10x1-inch jellyroll pan. On wax paper, sift together flour, baking soda, and salt. In large saucepan, combine dates, brown sugar, water, and butter; cook, stirring constantly, over low heat until dates soften. Remove from heat, and immediately stir in chocolate chips; stir until chocolate melts. With spoon, beat in eggs. Alternately beat in flour mixture and milk and orange juice. Stir in walnuts. Pour batter into prepared pan; bake for 25 to 30 minutes or until top springs back when lightly touched with finger. Let torte stand in pan 15 minutes; then loosen with spatula, and turn out on wire racks to cool.

When torte is thoroughly cool, cut it crosswise into 3 pieces, each piece 5 inches wide. On oblong tray, place one torte piece, and spread it with about one-third Chocolate Cream Whip. Stack second torte piece on top. Spread with Chocolate Cream Whip. Top with third torte piece. Decoratively frost top with remaining Chocolate Cream Whip. Refrigerate until ready to serve. At serving time, garnish with grapes if desired. Yield: 20 servings.

Chocolate Cream Whip:
½ cup semi-sweet chocolate chips
2 tablespoons honey
1 tablespoon water

½ teaspoon vanilla extract
1 cup heavy cream
⅛ teaspoon salt

In small saucepan, combine chocolate chips, honey, and water. Stir over low heat until chocolate is melted; remove from heat. Stir in vanilla extract; then cool until slightly thickened. In a mixing bowl, combine heavy cream and salt. Beat mixture until thick and soft peaks form; then gently fold in melted chocolate mixture.

Old-Fashioned Gingerbread with Lemon Sauce

½ cup butter or magarine, softened
1 cup sugar
1 egg
1 cup unsulphured molasses
2½ cups all-purpose flour
1½ teaspoons baking soda

½ teaspoon salt
1 teaspoon ground cinnamon
1 teaspoon ground ginger
1 cup water
Lemon sauce

Preheat oven to 350° F., and lightly grease and flour a 13x9x2-inch baking pan. Beat butter at medium speed with electric mixer. Gradually add sugar, and beat well. Add egg and molasses and mix well. Combine flour, baking soda, salt, cinamon, and ginger. Add to creamed mixture alternately with water, beginning and ending with flour. Mix well after each addition. Bake for 35 to 40 minutes. Serve with Lemon Sauce. Yield: 12 to 15 servings.

Lemon Sauce

½ cup butter or margarine
1 cup sugar
¼ cup water

1 egg, beaten
Juice and zest of 1 lemon

Melt butter in saucepan. Add remaining ingredients, stirring constantly. Cook over medium heat until mixture reaches 160° F. on a candy thermometer. Yield: 2 cups.

Amaretto Pound Cake

2 sticks butter
½ cup shortening
3 cups sugar
5 eggs, well beaten
3 cups sifted all-purpose flour

½ teaspoon baking powder
1 cup milk
2 tablespoons amaretto or 1 tablespoon almond extract
¼ to ½ cup slivered almonds

Preheat oven to 325° F. Grease and flour Bundt pan. Cream butter, shortening, and sugar until light and fluffy. Add eggs. Combine flour and baking powder. Add to cream mixture, alternating with milk. Stir in amaretto. Pour batter into prepared pan, and sprinkle almond slivers on top. Bake for 1 hour and 10 minutes, or until toothpick inserted in center comes out clean. Yield: 12 servings.

Apple Cider Pound Cake

2 sticks margarine, softened
½ cup shortening, softened
3 cups sugar
6 eggs
3 cups all-purpose flour
½ teaspoon salt

½ teaspoon baking powder
½ teaspoon ground allspice
1¼ teaspoon ground cinnamon
¼ teaspoon ground cloves
1 cup apple cider
1 teaspoon vanilla extract

Preheat oven to 325° F. Grease and flour a tube pan. Soften margarine and shortening. Add sugar, and beat 10 minutes with mixer at medium speed. Add eggs one at a time. Sift flour, salt, baking powder, allspice, cinnamon, and cloves together, and add to mixture, alternating with apple cider. Add vanilla extract; mix well. Bake for approximately 1½ hours, or until cake tests done. Cover with aluminum foil tent once cake is sufficiently brown. Yield: 10 to 12 servings.

Brown Sugar Pound Cake

1 cup butter-flavored shortening
½ cup butter
1 (16-ounce) box light brown sugar
1 cup white sugar
5 large eggs
3 cups all-purpose flour

1 teaspoon baking powder
1 cup milk
3 teaspoons vanilla extract
1 cup black walnuts, finely chopped
  (optional)

Preheat oven to 325° F. Grease and flour a tube or Bundt pan. Cream shortening and butter. Add sugars. Beat in eggs, 1 at a time. Sift together flour, and baking powder. Add alternately with milk. Add vanilla extract and walnuts. Pour into prepared pan. Bake for 1½ hours. Remove cake from oven, allow to cool in pan for 10 minutes. Remove cake from pan, place on rack, and cool completely. Yield: 12 servings.

Buttermilk Pound Cake

5 eggs, separated
2 sticks butter or margarine,
   softened
2½ cups sugar
2 teaspoons vanilla extract

½ teaspoon baking powder
1 cup buttermilk
½ teaspoon salt
3 cups all-purpose flour

Preheat oven to 300° F. Grease and flour two 8x4x2½-inch loaf pans or a Bundt or tube pan. Beat egg whites until stiff, and set aside. Cream butter, add sugar and vanilla extract gradually. Add egg yolks, 1 at a time, beating well after each addition. Dissolve baking powder in buttermilk. Mix salt with flour. Add flour, 1 cup at a time, to batter, alternating each addition with ½ cup of buttermilk. Carefully fold in egg whites. Pour batter into prepared pans. After baking cake for 15 minutes at 300° F., increase oven temperature to 350° F. Bake for at least 45 minutes or until a toothpick inserted in the center comes out clean. Do not remove cake from oven too soon, or it will fall as it cools. To prevent the cake from becoming too brown, loosely cover it, while it is baking, with a tent of aluminum foil once it is sufficiently brown. After cake cools in pan for 10 minutes, carefully remove it, and allow it to continue cooling. Yield: 12 servings.

Chocolate Sour Cream Pound Cake

3 sticks butter, softened
3 cups sugar
5 eggs, at room temperature
3 cups all-purpose flour
½ cup cocoa
1 teaspoon baking soda

¼ teaspoon salt
1 (8-ounce) carton commercial sour
   cream
1 cup very hot water
2 teaspoons vanilla extract

Preheat oven to 325° F. Grease and flour a 10-inch tube pan. Cream butter; and gradually add sugar, beating well. Add eggs, 1 at a time, beating well after each addition. Combine flour, cocoa, baking soda, and salt; add to creamed mixture alternately with sour cream, beginning and ending with flour mixture. Mix well after each addition. Add hot water, and mix well. Stir in vanilla extract. Pour batter into prepared pan. Bake for 1 hour and 25 minutes or until cake tests done. Cool cake in pan 10 to 15 minutes. Remove from pan, and cool completely. Yield: 12 servings.

Strawberry Kringle Cake

1½ cups sugar
1½ cups sour cream
1½ cups mashed fresh strawberries
2 tablespoons strawberry gelatin

¼ cup boiling water
1 (18¼-ounce) package yellow cake mix
1½ cups frozen whipped topping, thawed

Four days before serving, combine sugar, sour cream, and strawberries. Dissolve dry strawberry gelatin in boiling water; cool and add to sour cream mixture. Store in refrigerator overnight. Prepare and bake layer cake according to package directions. Cool layers; cut each in two horizontally to make a total of 4 layers. Spread sour cream mixture between layers and on top. Store cake for 3 days in refrigerator. Before serving, spread top and sides with whipped topping. Yield: 10 to 12 servings.

Pumpkin Cake Roll

3 eggs
1 cup sugar
⅔ cup canned or fresh cooked pumpkin
¾ cup self-rising flour
2 teaspoons cinnamon

1 teaspoon ginger
½ teaspoon nutmeg
1 teaspoon vanilla extract
Filling
½ cup pecan pieces

Preheat oven to 350° F., and spray a 15x10x1-inch jellyroll pan with nonstick vegetable spray. Beat eggs in a small bowl for 5 minutes. Then add sugar. Gently fold pumpkin into eggs. In second bowl, combine flour, cinnamon, ginger, nutmeg, and vanilla extract. Add this dry mixture to the pumpkin mixture, and pour into prepared pan. Bake for 15 minutes. While warm, remove cake from pan on to a clean dish towel; starting with long end, roll into a roll, and let cool. Unroll cake and spread with filling to edges. Then sprinkle with ½ cup pecan pieces, and reroll. Chill. To serve, dust with additional confectioners' sugar, and slice. Yield: 8 to 10 servings.

Filling:
4 tablespoons unsalted butter
1 teaspoon vanilla extract

1 (8-ounce) package cream cheese
1 cup confectioners' sugar

Combine all ingredients; beat until smooth and spreadable.

Orange Cranberry Torte

2¼ cups sifted all-purpose flour
1 cup sugar
¼ teaspoon baking powder
1 teaspoon baking soda
½ teaspoon salt
1 cup chopped pecans
1 cup diced dates

1 cup chopped fresh cranberries
Grated zest of 2 oranges
2 eggs, beaten
1 cup buttermilk
¾ cup salad oil
1 cup orange juice
1 cup sugar

Preheat oven to 350° F. Grease well and flour a 10-inch tube or Bundt pan. Sift together flour, sugar, baking powder, baking soda, and salt. Stir in pecans, dates, cranberries, and zest. Combine eggs, buttermilk, and salad oil. Add to fruit and flour mixture. Stir by hand until well blended. Pour into prepared pan. Bake 1 hour.

While cake is baking, combine orange juice and sugar in a small saucepan. Bring to a boil, stirring constantly until sugar dissolves. Remove from heat.

When cake is done, remove from oven, and pour hot juice mixture over top. Do not remove cake from pan. Allow cake to cool, then refrigerate for at least 24 hours before serving. To serve, preheat stove burner to high. Place cake pan on burner for 30 seconds. Remove pan, invert, and turn cake out on serving plate. Yield: 18 servings.

Birthday Party Vanilla Cupcakes

These cupcakes are a birthday celebration favorite!

¾ cup shortening
1½ cups sugar
3 eggs
2 cups all-purpose flour
1½ teaspoons baking powder

¼ teaspoon salt
1 cup milk
1½ teaspoons vanilla extract
Vanilla Frosting

Preheat oven to 350° F. Line approximately 30 muffin tins with paper or foil liners. Beat shortening in a large bowl at medium speed with electric mixer; add sugar, and beat well. Add eggs, 1 at a time. Add all other ingredients; blend into creamed mixture. Spoon batter into muffin pans, filling each two-thirds full. Bake for 15 to 18 minutes, or until wooden pick inserted in center of cupcake comes out clean. Allow cupcakes to cool completely before frosting. Decorate cupcakes as desired. Yield: 26 to 35 cupcakes.

Vanilla Frosting:

1½ sticks butter or margarine, softened
¾ cup shortening
1 (16-ounce) package confectioners' sugar

2 teaspoons milk, plus additional, if needed
1 teaspoon vanilla extract
Desired food coloring and decorations

Beat butter and shortening at medium speed with electric mixer; add confectioners' sugar, milk, vanilla extract, and desired food coloring. Beat mixture until light and fluffy. If needed, add additional milk until frosting reaches spreading consistency.

Almond Crunch Cookies

1 cup sugar
1 cup confectioners' sugar
2 sticks margarine, softened
1 cup vegetable oil
1 teaspoon almond extract
2 eggs
3½ cups all-purpose flour
1 cup whole wheat all-purpose flour

1 teaspoon baking soda
1 teaspoon cream of tartar
1 teaspoon salt
2 cups coarsely chopped almonds
1 (6-ounce) package almond brickle baking chips
Sugar

Preheat oven to 350° F. In large bowl with an electric mixer, combine sugar, confectioners' sugar, margarine, and oil until well blended. Add almond extract and eggs; mix well, and set aside. In second bowl, combine all-purpose flour, whole wheat flour, baking soda, cream of tartar, and salt; mix well. Add to sugar mixture; mix at low speed until well blended. By hand, stir in almonds and brickle chips.

Shape large tablespoonfuls of dough into balls. Roll balls in sugar. Place 5 inches apart on ungreased cookie sheets. With fork dipped in sugar, flatten each in a crisscross pattern. Bake for 12 to 18 minutes or until light golden brown around the edges. Cool 1 minute; remove from pan. Yield: 42 (4-inch) cookies.

Butter Cookies

Dough may be refrigerated for up to one day before baking.

2 sticks unsalted butter, softened
1½ cups sugar
2 eggs, well beaten
1 teaspoon vanilla extract

4 scant cups all-purpose flour
2 teaspoons baking powder
¼ teaspoon salt
Colored sugar, cinnamon candies, raisins, or sprinkles

Preheat oven to 350° F. Cream together butter and sugar. Add eggs and vanilla extract. Sift together flour, baking powder, and salt. Add to egg mixture, and blend well to form a stiff dough. Take a quarter of the dough, refrigerating remainder, and roll out thin on floured surface. Cut with floured cookie cutters. Decorate with colored sugar, cinnamon candies, raisins, or sprinkles. Repeat until all dough is used. Bake cookies on ungreased cookie sheets for 6 to 12 minutes or until edges are slightly browned. Yield: 4 to 5 dozen cookies.

Incredible Chocolate Chip Cookies

4 sticks unsalted butter, softened
2 cups sugar
2 cups brown sugar
4 eggs
2 teaspoons vanilla extract
4 cups all-purpose or cake flour
5 cups oatmeal, processed in
  batches in blender until powdered

1 teaspoon salt
2 teaspoons baking powder
2 teaspoons baking soda
2 (12-ounce) packages semi-sweet
  chocolate chips
1 (8-ounce) milk chocolate bar,
  grated
3 cups chopped nuts

Preheat oven to 375° F. Cream together butter, sugar, and brown sugar. Add eggs and vanilla extract. In a separate bowl combine flour, oatmeal, salt, baking powder, and baking soda. Mix together all ingredients and add chocolate chips, grated chocolate, and nuts. On ungreased cookie sheet, place golf ball-sized balls of dough 2 inches apart. Bake 14 minutes or until golden brown. Remove cookies from sheet and cool on racks. Yield: 112 large cookies.

Nutty Chocolate Chip Cookies

1 cup unsalted butter, softened
¾ cup sugar
¾ cup packed light brown sugar
1 tablespoon vanilla extract
1 tablespoon coffee-flavored liqueur
1 tablespoon hazelnut-flavored
  liqueur
2 eggs

2½ cups all-purpose flour
1 teaspoon baking soda
½ teaspoon salt
4 cups milk chocolate chips
1 cup chopped walnut halves
  (optional)
½ cup pecan halves
½ cup macadamia nuts

Preheat oven to 325° F. Cream butter, sugar, vanilla extract, coffee-flavored liqueur, and hazelnut-flavored liqueur until light and fluffy. Add eggs; beat well. Combine flour, baking soda, and salt; gradually beat into creamed mixture. Stir in chocolate chips and nuts. Mix well. Place in storage container and refrigerate overnight. Drop by teaspoonfuls onto ungreased cookie sheet. Bake for approximately 10 to 13 minutes or until golden brown. Cool slightly, remove from cookie sheet, and serve immediately. Yield: 3 to 4 dozen cookies.

Cowboy Cookies

A 1950's Wrigley's chewing gum
wrapper featured this recipe.

2 cups sifted all-purpose flour
½ teaspoon baking powder
1 teaspoon baking soda
½ teaspoon salt
1 cup shortening
1 cup sugar
1 cup brown sugar

2 eggs
2 cups rolled oats (not quick-
cooking)
1 teaspoon vanilla extract
1 (8-ounce) package semi-sweet
chocolate chips
1 cup chopped nuts (if desired)

Preheat oven to 350° F., and grease a cookie sheet. Sift together flour, baking powder, baking soda, and salt; set aside. Blend together shortening and sugars. Add eggs, and beat until fluffy. Add flour mixture, and mix. Add rolled oats, vanilla extract, and chocolate chips. Stir in nuts. Drop by rounded teaspoonfuls on cookie sheet, and bake for 12 to 15 minutes. Remove, and let cool on racks. Cookies freeze well. Yield: 11 dozen cookies.

M & M® Party Cookies

2 sticks unsalted butter, softened
1 cup firmly packed brown sugar
½ cup sugar
2¼ cups sifted all-purpose flour
1 teaspoon baking soda

1 teaspoon salt
2 teaspoons vanilla extract
2 eggs
2 cups (1-pound) M & M® candies,
divided in half

Preheat oven to 375° F. Cream butter and sugars. In separate bowl, sift flour, baking soda, and salt. Add vanilla extract and eggs to first mixture, beat well. Add dry ingredients. Place 1 cup M & M®'s in batter. Mix. Drop by teaspoon-fuls onto ungreased cookie sheet. Decorate top of each cookie with 5 to 7 candies before placing in oven. Bake 8 to 10 minutes. Cool on wire rack. Store in airtight container. Yield: 90 cookies.

Gingersnaps

1 cup vegetable shortening
1 cup sugar
1 egg, beaten
¼ cup unsulphured molasses
2 cups all-purpose flour
¼ teaspoon salt

1 tablespoon baking soda
1½ teaspoons cinnamon
1½ teaspoons ground cloves
1½ teaspoons ginger
Sugar (optional)

Preheat oven to 350° F. Cream together shortening and sugar. Beat in egg and molasses. Sift flour, salt, baking soda, cinnamon, ground cloves, and ginger together in a medium-sized bowl. Add molasses mixture, and blend well. Chill cookie dough for at least 1 hour. Using your hands, roll the dough into 1-inch balls. Bake on ungreased cookie sheets for 7 minutes. Cool on wire racks. If desired, roll dough balls in sugar before baking. Yield: 3 dozen cookies.

Sour Cream Drop Cookies

A 40-year-old family favorite.

1 cup shortening
1½ cups sugar
2 eggs
1 teaspoon vanilla extract
1 teaspoon baking soda
1 cup sour cream

3½ cups all-purpose flour
½ teaspoon salt
1 teaspoon nutmeg
2 teaspoons baking powder
Sugar

Preheat oven to 375° F., and lightly grease a cookie sheet. Cream together shortening, sugar, eggs, and vanilla extract. Mix well, and set aside. Dissolve baking soda in sour cream; set aside. Sift together flour, salt, nutmeg, and baking powder. Alternately blend flour mixture and sour cream with shortening mixture until all ingredients are mixed. Drop dough by teaspoonfuls on cookie sheet. Sprinkle cookies with sugar, and bake for about 10 minutes or until cookies are a very light brown. Yield: About 3½ dozen cookies.

Tea Cakes

2 sticks unsalted butter, softened
3 cups confectioners' sugar, divided
1 teaspoon vanilla extract

¾ cup finely chopped pecans
¾ teaspoon salt
2¼ cups all-purpose flour

In a bowl with an electric mixer, cream the butter with ½ cup confectioners' sugar until the mixture is light and fluffy. Beat in vanilla extract, pecans, and salt until the mixture is combined well. Add the flour, beat the dough until it is combined well, and chill it, covered, for at least 6 hours or overnight.

Preheat oven to 375° F., and lightly butter a cookie sheet. Let the dough stand at room temperature until it is just pliable and form it into balls about ¾-inch in diameter. Arrange the balls of dough about 1 inch apart on prepared baking sheets, and flatten them slightly to form small disks. Bake the cookies for 12 to 15 minutes, or until they are pale golden on the bottom. While the cookies are baking, sift the remaining 2½ cups sugar into a shallow dish. As the cookies come out of the oven, roll them immediately in the sugar to coat them. Transfer the cookies to a rack, let them cool, and roll them in the sugar again. The cookies may be made 3 days in advance and kept in an airtight container. Yield: 6 dozen cookies.

Sour Cream Apple Squares

2 cups all-purpose flour
2 cups firmly packed brown sugar
1 stick margarine, softened
1 cup chopped pecans
2 teaspoons cinnamon
1 teaspoon baking soda

½ teaspoon salt
1 cup sour cream
1 teaspoon vanilla extract
1 egg, beaten
2 cups, peeled, chopped apples

Preheat oven to 350° F. In bowl, with electric mixer, combine flour, brown sugar, and margarine; blend dough at low speed until crumbly, and stir in pecans. Press about 2¾ cups of mixture into bottom of an ungreased 13x9x2-inch baking pan. To the remaining crumb mixture, add cinnamon, soda, salt, sour cream, vanilla extract, and egg. Beat until thoroughly blended. Stir in chopped apples. Spoon evenly over bottom layer. Bake for 35 to 40 minutes. Place pan on a wire rack to cool. Cut into 16 squares. Yield: 16 servings.

Chocolate Chip Cream Cheese Bars

2 (20-ounce) packages refrigerated
   chocolate chip cookie dough,
   frozen for at least 1 hour
2 (8-ounce) packages cream cheese,
   softened

1/2 cup sugar
2 eggs
2 teaspoons vanilla extract

Preheat oven to 375° F. Grease a 13x9x2-inch baking pan. Slice 1 package cookie dough into 1/4-inch slices. Line bottom of pan with slices, pressing dough slices together if needed. Combine cream cheese, sugar, eggs, and vanilla. Mix until smooth; then pour over cookie layer. Slice remaining package of cookie dough into 1/4-inch slices and place in single layer over cream cheese mixture. Do not press these dough slices together. Bake for 35 minutes. Cut into squares when cool. Yield: 24 bars.

Chocolate Oat Bars

2 sticks plus 2 tablespoons butter or
   margarine
2 cups packed brown sugar
2 eggs
4 teaspoons vanilla extract, divided
2 1/2 cups sifted all-purpose flour
1 teaspoon baking soda

1 teaspoon salt
3 cups quick-cooking rolled oats
1 (15-ounce) can sweetened,
   condensed milk
1 (12-ounce) package semi-sweet
   chocolate chips
1/2 teaspoon salt

Preheat oven to 350° F. Grease a 15 1/2x10 1/2x1-inch jellyroll pan. In large mixing bowl, cream 2 sticks butter with 2 cups brown sugar. Beat in eggs and vanilla extract. Sift together flour, soda, and salt. Stir in oats. Stir flour mixture into butter mixture until blended, and set aside. In heavy saucepan over low heat, melt together condensed milk, chocolate chips, remaining butter, and salt, blending until smooth. Stir in remaining 2 teaspoons vanilla. Pat 2/3 of oat mixture in bottom of baking pan. Spread chocolate mixture over dough. Dot with remaining oat mixture. Bake for 25 to 30 minutes. Cool; cut into bars. Yield: 30 bars.

Brownies

Cocoa powder
1 stick unsalted butter
2 (1-ounce) squares unsweetened
   chocolate
2 eggs

1 cup sugar
¾ cup self-rising flour
¾ cup chopped nuts
1 teaspoon vanilla extract

Preheat oven to 350° F. Grease and dust with cocoa powder an 8x8-inch baking pan. Melt butter; add unsweetened chocolate, and stir until melted. In a bowl, beat the eggs; add sugar and flour. Add chocolate and butter mixture, nuts, and vanilla extract. Bake in a prepared pan for 20 to 25 minutes. Spread with frosting. Cool, and cut into squares. Yield: 16 brownies.

Brownie Frosting:
4 tablespoons unsalted butter
2 (1-ounce) squares unsweetened
   chocolate

¾ to 1 (16-ounce) box of
   confectioners' sugar
1 teaspoon vanilla extract
3 to 4 tablespoons milk

Melt butter with chocolate. After it melts, add confectioners' sugar, vanilla extract, and enough milk for spreading consistency.

White Chocolate Macadamia Brownies with Hot Fudge Sauce

2 (6-ounce) bars good quality white chocolate, coarsely chopped

2 large eggs

½ cup sugar

4 tablespoons unsalted butter, melted

1 teaspoon vanilla extract

1 cup all-purpose flour

¼ teaspoon salt

1 (6-ounce) bar white chocolate, coarsely chopped

½ cup macadamia nuts, chopped

Hot Fudge Sauce

Preheat oven to 350° F. Grease and flour a 13x9x2-inch pan. Melt 2 chocolate bars in a heavy saucepan over low heat, stirring constantly. Remove from heat and let stand 10 minutes. With an electric mixer at high speed, beat eggs until foamy. Gradually add sugar, 1 tablespoon at a time, beating 2 to 4 minutes. Stir in melted chocolate and butter. Add vanilla extract (mixture may appear curdled). Add flour and salt, and stir until blended. Stir in remaining chocolate bar and nuts. Spoon into prepared pan and bake for 25 minutes. Cool. Cut into squares. Serve with Hot Fudge Sauce. Yield: 12 servings.

Hot Fudge Sauce:

⅔ cup whipping cream

¼ cup sugar

1 (4-ounce) bar bittersweet chocolate, coarsely chopped

1½ tablespoons unsalted butter

1½ tablespoons light corn syrup

Combine sugar and cream in a small heavy pan. Cook over low heat, stirring constantly until sugar dissolves. Add chocolate, and stir until melted. Stir in butter and syrup until melted.

Microwave Brownies

Do not overcook brownies or cut until cool. If using
a conventional oven, bake for 20 to 25 minutes at
350° F. For 13x9x2-inch pan, double ingredients.

⅓ cup margarine
2 (1-ounce) squares unsweetened
  chocolate
1 cup sugar
2 eggs

¾ cup all-purpose flour
½ teaspoon baking powder
1 teaspoon vanilla extract
½ cup chopped nuts

Place margarine and chocolate in a 2-quart glass bowl. Microwave on high for 1½ minutes, or until chocolate melts. Using a wooden spoon, beat sugar into chocolate mixture. Add eggs to mixture, beat well. Stir in flour and baking powder until well combined. Stir in vanilla extract and nuts.

Using shortening or nonstick vegetable spray, lightly grease an 8x8-inch glass baking dish. Pour batter into dish, and spread it to a uniform thickness. Turning dish halfway around after 3 minutes, microwave on medium-high (or 70%) for 6 to 8 minutes. Yield: 16 (2-inch) brownies.

Southern Chewy Cake

In memory of Allen Wyke Kivett (1967-1992).
Southern Chewy Cake was his favorite dessert.

½ cup butter or margarine
2 cups packed brown sugar
2 eggs, unbeaten
1 teaspoon vanilla extract

1½ cups sifted all-purpose flour
2 teaspoons baking powder
¼ teaspoon salt
1 cup coarsely chopped pecans

Preheat oven to 350° F. Grease a 13x9x2-inch pan. Melt butter or margarine in heavy saucepan. Stir in sugar until it is dissolved and bubbles. Cool until lukewarm. Sift flour, baking powder, and salt together. Stir eggs into sugar mixture one at a time. Add flour mixture and blend well. Add nuts and vanilla extract. Batter will be thick. Spread in pan. Bake for 30 to 35 minutes. Freezes well. Yield: 30 servings.

Dutch Brown Bag Apple Pie

*Serve alone or with whipped cream,
ice cream, or sharp Cheddar cheese.*

1 (9-inch) deep-dish unbaked pie
shell
5 large Granny Smith apples, peeled
and sliced
½ cup plus 2 tablespoons flour,
divided

1¾ cups sugar, divided
2 teaspoons cinnamon
¼ cup heavy cream
1 stick margarine

Preheat oven to 350° F. Toss together apples, 2 tablespoons flour, 1¼ cups sugar, cinnamon, and cream until apples are coated. Place them in prepared crust.

In a small bowl, cut margarine into remaining flour and sugar. Sprinkle topping over pie, covering apples. Place pie in brown paper bag, fold end over and fasten with paper clips. Bake for 1 hour and 15 minutes. Yield: 8 servings.

Sour Cream Apple Pie

1 (8-inch) deep-dish unbaked pie
shell, unbaked
1 cup sour cream, or custard style
vanilla yogurt
¾ cup sugar
2 tablespoons all-purpose flour

1 teaspoon cinnamon
¼ teaspoon salt
1 teaspoon vanilla extract
1 egg
2 cups grated apples, firmly packed
into measuring cup

Preheat oven to 400° F. Mix sour cream, sugar, flour, cinnamon, and egg. Add grated apples. Pour apple mixture into pie shell. Bake for 25 to 30 minutes. Remove pie from oven, and sprinkle the topping mixture over top of pie. Bake 20 to 25 minutes more. Cool before serving. Yield: 8 servings.

Topping:
½ cup brown sugar
⅓ cup all-purpose flour

4 tablespoons margarine
1 cup pecan pieces or slivered
almonds

Mix together all ingredients.

Noble's Tart Tatin

*Jimmy Noble of J. Basul Noble's Restaurant in High
Point, North Carolina, contributed this recipe.*

8 to 9 Granny Smith apples　　　　**6 ounces sugar**
3 ounces butter

Preheat oven to 375° F. Melt butter with sugar in a 9-inch skillet or sauté pan.
Peel and quarter apples, removing the cores. Arrange apple quarters in a
circular pattern in the pan, filling in the center and piling apples in a dome.
Cook the apples, undisturbed, over medium low heat until the sugar syrup
which forms around the edges is golden brown and caramelized. Rotate the
position of the pan on the burner until the sugar is caramelized on all sides,
for 1 to 1½ hours.

While the pan of apples is hot, cover with prepared 9-inch chilled pastry
round, and bake for 20 minutes or until pastry is golden brown. Cool completely. To remove from pan, heat pan again on the burner on high heat. After
20 to 30 seconds, steam puffs from edges and crust puffs. Loosen tart with a
snap of the wrist by jerking it towards you. Invert onto a plate or serving dish.
Yield: 8 servings.

Pastry:
1 stick unsalted butter, cold　　　　**Pinch of salt**
1 cup unbleached all-purpose flour　　**Ice water**
2 tablespoons sugar

Cut butter into bits, and mix with flour, sugar and salt. Rub butter into flour
with fingers, mashing the bits into flakes quickly and lightly tossing, trying not
to warm the butter. Incorporate until mealy. Toss in water, 1 teaspoon at a
time, just until dough comes together in a ball. Flatten into a disk, wrap, and
chill 1 hour. Unwrap dough and roll out on lightly floured surface. Cut dough
to fit pan. Patch tears with excess dough.

Black Forest Pie

1 (8-ounce) container frozen
    whipped topping, thawed and
    divided
1 (8-inch) prepared chocolate pie
    crust

1 cup milk (1% or 2%)
1 (3-ounce) package sugar-free
    instant chocolate pudding mix
1 cup light cherry pie filling

Spread ¾ cup whipped topping in bottom of chocolate pie crust. Combine milk and pudding for 1 minute at low speed. Fold in 1½ cups whipped topping. Spread in pie crust. Spoon remaining whipped topping around outer edge of pie top. Pour cherries in well formed by whipped topping. Chill pie in refrigerator for at least 3 hours. Yield: 6 servings.

Fresh Blueberry Cream Pie

1 cup sour cream
2 tablespoons flour
¾ cup sugar
1 teaspoon vanilla extract
¼ teaspoon salt
1 egg, beaten

2½ cups fresh blueberries
1 (9-inch) unbaked pie shell
3 tablespoons flour
3 tablespoons butter, softened
3 tablespoons chopped pecans or
    walnuts

Preheat oven to 400° F. Combine sour cream, flour, sugar, vanilla extract, salt, and egg. With electric mixer set at medium speed, beat mixture for 5 minutes, or until smooth. Fold in blueberries. Pour filling into pie shell and bake for 25 minutes. Combine flour, butter, and nuts, stirring well. Sprinkle over top of pie. Bake 10 more minutes. Chill pie before serving. Yield: 8 servings.

Buttermilk Pie

1 (9-inch) unbaked pie shell
3 whole eggs
1 cup sugar
1½ rounded tablespoons flour

½ cup unsalted butter, melted
½ cup buttermilk
1 teaspoon vanilla extract or lemon
   extract

Preheat oven to 400° F. Bake shell for 5 minutes, remove, and reduce oven temperature to 300° F. Beat eggs until fluffy. Blend eggs with remaining ingredients, and pour into pie shell. Bake for 1 hour or until the filling is firm. If pie crust becomes too brown during baking, cover it with strips of aluminum foil. Yield: 8 servings.

Cherry Cheese Pie Supreme

If desired, substitute blueberry pie filling.

1 (9-inch) unbaked pie shell
1 can (1 pound, 5-ounce) cherry pie
   filling
4 (3-ounce) packages cream cheese
½ cup sugar

2 eggs
½ teaspoon vanilla extract
1 cup dairy sour cream
1 tablespoon brown sugar (optional)

Preheat oven to 425° F. Prepare pie shell. Spread half of cherry pie filling in bottom of shell; set aside rest of pie filling. Bake shell 15 minutes or just until crust is light golden brown. Remove from oven. Reduce oven temperature to 350° F. Meanwhile, in small bowl with a mixer, beat cream cheese with sugar, eggs and vanilla extract until smooth. Pour over hot cherry pie filling and bake 25 minutes. (Filling will be slightly soft in center.) Cool completely on rack.

If desired, sweeten sour cream with 1 tablespoon brown sugar. To serve, spoon sour cream around edge of pie. Fill center with remaining pie filling. Yield: 8 servings.

Black Bottom Pie

2 (8- or 9-inch) cooked pie shells, or 32 chocolate wafers and 1 stick butter, melted

½ cup sugar

1 tablespoon cornstarch

2 cups scalded milk

4 beaten egg yolks

1 (6-ounce) package semi-sweet chocolate chips

1 teaspoon vanilla extract

1 tablespoon (1 package) unflavored gelatin, softened in ¼ cup cold water

4 egg whites

½ cup sugar

¼ teaspoon cream of tartar

1 cup whipping cream, whipped and sweetened to taste with confectioners' sugar

1 (1-ounce) semi-sweet chocolate square, shaved

If making crust, roll chocolate wafers until fine. Mix with melted butter. Pack firmly into two 9-inch pie pans, covering sides and bottom. Bake at 350° F. for 10 to 12 minutes. Cool.

For filling, combine sugar and cornstarch, set aside. Slowly add scalded milk to egg yolks. Stir sugar mixture into eggs and milk. Cook in top of double boiler until custard coats spoon. To 1 cup of custard, add chocolate pieces. Stir until chocolate melts. Pour chocolate custard into bottom of pie shells. Chill.

Add softened gelatin to remaining hot custard. Stir until dissolved. Chill until slightly thick. Add vanilla extract and rum flavoring.

Beat egg whites and cream of tartar, adding sugar gradually until mixture stands in stiff peaks. Fold in completely cooled custard gelatin mixture. Pour over chocolate layer, and chill until set.

Top pies with whipped cream and chocolate shavings.

Yield: 2 pies, or 12 to 16 servings.

Chocolate Meringue Pie

2 cups milk
1 cup sugar
⅔ cup sifted all-purpose flour
Pinch of salt
2 tablespoons unsalted butter
1½ teaspoons vanilla extract

2 (1-ounce) squares unsweetened
  chocolate
3 eggs, separated
1 (9-inch) pie shell, baked
¼ teaspoon cream of tartar
6 tablespoons sugar

Preheat oven to 400° F. To make chocolate filling, scald milk in a saucepan. In a separate bowl, mix flour, sugar, and salt. Slowly add flour mixture to scalded milk, stirring well until mixture is smooth. Add chocolate, stir until chocolate melts and mixture begins to thicken. Stir a little of the mixture into the egg yolks, and add remaining egg yolk mixture to chocolate mixture. Cook until thickened, about 2 minutes; then add butter. Remove mixture from heat, let cool, and add 1 teaspoon vanilla extract. Pour mixture into baked pie shell. To make meringue, beat egg whites with cream of tartar until frothy. Gradually add 6 tablespoons sugar and ½ teaspoon vanilla extract, beating continuously until mixture is glossy. Cover chocolate filling with meringue, and seal meringue to crust. Bake for 8 to 10 minutes or until meringue is lightly browned. Yield: 8 servings.

Chocolate Chess Pie

3 (1-ounce) squares unsweetened
  chocolate
1 stick butter
2 cups sugar
4 whole eggs

1 teaspoon vanilla extract
½ cup plus 2 tablespoons
  evaporated milk
2 (9-inch) regular pie shells

Preheat oven to 350° F. Melt together chocolate and butter. In a small bowl, beat together sugar, whole eggs, and vanilla extract. Pour egg mixture into melted chocolate and butter. Add evaporated milk, and stir until well blended. Pour into unbaked pie shells. Bake for 25 minutes. Turn oven down to 200° F. and bake for 10 more minutes. Yield: 2 pies or 16 servings.

Chocolate Butterscotch Walnut Pie

*Susan Keever of Sugar Magnolias Restaurant in High
Point, North Carolina, contributed this recipe.*

1½ sticks butter, melted
1¾ cups sugar
8 eggs
½ cup bourbon (optional)

2 (8-inch) deep-dish pie shells,
   unbaked
1 cup semi-sweet chocolate chips
½ cup butterscotch chips
1¼ cups chopped walnuts

Preheat oven to 350° F. Mix melted butter and sugar until well blended. Add
unbeaten eggs all at one time. Mix well. Add bourbon, and blend. Fill 2 pie
shells with layers of chocolate chips, butterscotch chips, and walnuts. Pour
liquid mixture over chips and walnuts. Place pies on a cookie sheet. Bake for
45 minutes or until knife inserted in center comes out clean. Yield: 12 to 16
servings.

Chocolate Pecan Pie

1 stick margarine or butter, melted
3 cups sugar
7 tablespoons cocoa
1 (12-ounce) can evaporated milk
1 tablespoon vanilla extract

4 eggs
2 cups flaked coconut
1 cup chopped pecans
Pinch of salt
3 (8-inch) regular pie shells,
   unbaked

Preheat oven to 350° F. In bowl with electric mixer, mix margarine, sugar,
cocoa, milk, vanilla extract, and eggs. Mix at low speed. Stir coconut and
pecans into mixture. Divide mixture among 3 pie shells. Bake for 45 minutes.
Yield: 3 pies, or 18 servings.

Chocolate Peanut Butter Cream Pie Supreme

1 package refrigerated pie crust (to make 9-inch crust)
1 teaspoon all-purpose flour
1 stick margarine or butter, softened
1½ cups confectioners' sugar, divided
2 eggs
¾ cup semi-sweet chocolate chips, melted

¾ teaspoon vanilla extract
¾ cup finely chopped peanuts, divided
1 (8-ounce) package cream cheese, softened
½ cup creamy peanut butter
1 (12-ounce) container frozen whipped topping
Chocolate curls (if desired)

Heat oven to 450° F. Prepare pie crust according to package directions for a one crust pie, using 9-inch pie pan. Bake for 9 to 11 minutes or until crust is golden brown. Cool.

Cream margarine and ½ cup confectioners' sugar until light and fluffy. Add 1 egg, and beat 2 to 3 minutes. Blend in chocolate and vanilla extract. Mix well. Spread one cup of chocolate filling evenly over cooled baked crust. Reserve remaining chocolate filling for top of pie. Sprinkle with ½ cup peanuts.

In large bowl with an electric mixer, combine cream cheese and peanut butter, and blend at medium speed until well blended. Add confectioners' sugar and 1 egg, beating until smooth and creamy. Fold in whipped topping. Spoon peanut butter filling evenly over chocolate filling. Spread remaining chocolate filling in a circle over top of pie to within 2 inches of edges. Sprinkle ¼ cup peanuts over peanut butter filling. Garnish chocolate filling with curls. Refrigerate at least 3 hours before serving. Yield: 8 to 10 servings.

Heavenly Chocolate Delight Dessert

1 stick margarine, softened
1 cup all-purpose flour
1 cup chopped walnuts
1 (8-ounce) package cream cheese, softened
1 cup confectioners' sugar

1 (12-ounce) container frozen whipped topping
3 cup whole milk
2 (3-ounce) packages chocolate instant pudding
1 chocolate-covered toffee candy bar, crumbled

Preheat oven to 350° F. Stir together margarine, flour, and walnuts to make crust mixture. Press crust mixture into a 13x9x2-inch baking pan. Bake for about 15 minutes. Allow crust to cool completely.

Combine cream cheese, confectioners' sugar, and whipped topping; spread mixture on top of crust. Combine milk and chocolate instant pudding and spread on cream cheese layer. Spread whipped topping on chocolate layer, and sprinkle with crumbled chocolate bar. Keep refrigerated until ready to serve. Yield: 16 servings.

Coconut Pie

1 (9-inch) unbaked pie shell
2 eggs
2 cups sugar
2 cups grated or flaked coconut

1 stick melted butter or margarine
⅓ cup buttermilk
1 teaspoon lemon extract
Pastry for 9-inch pie

Preheat oven to 325° F. Brown pie shell for about 3 minutes. Beat eggs lightly. Add sugar, coconut, butter, buttermilk, and lemon extract. Pour mixture into pie shell, and bake for 45 to 50 minutes or until set. Yield: 8 servings.

Orange Coconut Cream Pie

1 cup sugar	³/₄ cup flaked coconut
3 tablespoons all-purpose flour	1 tablespoon grated orange zest
3 tablespoons cornstarch	1 (9-inch) pastry shell, baked
¼ teaspoon salt	Meringue
3 egg yolks	1 to 2 tablespoons flaked coconut
1½ cups water	(optional)

Preheat oven to 325° F. Combine sugar, flour, cornstarch, and salt in a large heavy saucepan. Set sugar mixture aside. Combine egg yolks, water, orange juice, and lemon juice. Gradually stir egg yolk mixture into sugar mixture. Cook over medium heat, stirring constantly until mixture thickens and boils. Remove from heat. Stir in ³/₄ cup coconut and orange zest. Spoon into pastry shell. Spread meringue over hot filling and seal to edge of pastry. Sprinkle top of pie with 1 to 2 tablespoons coconut, if desired. Bake for 25 to 28 minutes. Yield: 8 servings.

Meringue

4t o 6 egg whites	½ cup sugar
½ to ³/₄ teaspoon cream of tartar	½ teaspoon vanilla extract

Beat egg whites and cream of tartar at high speed with electric mixer until foamy. Gradually add sugar, 1 tablespoon at a time, beating until stiff peaks form and sugar dissolves, for 2 to 4 minutes. Add vanilla extract, and beat well.

Coconut Crunch Torte

1 cup graham cracker crumbs	½ teaspoon salt
½ cup chopped English walnuts	1 teaspoon vanilla extract
½ cup shredded coconut	1 cup sugar
4 egg whites, at room temperature	Butter pecan ice cream

Preheat oven to 350° F., and grease well an 8-inch round pie plate. Combine crumbs, walnuts, and coconut; set aside. Beat egg whites with salt and vanilla until foamy; gradually add sugar. Continue beating until mixture peaks. Fold crumb mixture into stiff egg whites. Spread into prepared pie pan. Bake for 30 minutes. Cool and serve with a scoop of butter pecan ice cream. Yield: 6 servings.

Chocolate Chip Pie

1 cup sugar
½ cup all-purpose flour
½ cup butter (do not substitute)
2 eggs, well beaten
1 teaspoon vanilla extract
2 teaspoons bourbon

1 cup semi-sweet chocolate chips
1 cup chopped walnuts or pecans
1 (9-inch) unbaked pie shell
1 cup whipping cream, whipped, and flavored with 1 teaspoon bourbon, for garnish

Preheat oven to 350° F. Mix sugar with flour. Cream butter. Gradually add the sugar mixture to butter. Add eggs, vanilla extract, and bourbon. Mix thoroughly. Add chocolate chips and chopped nuts. Pour into pie shell. Bake for 40 to 45 minutes. To serve, heat slightly, and garnish with whipping cream flavored with bourbon. Yield: 8 servings.

Luscious Lemon Pie

1 cup sugar
1¼ cups water
1 tablespoon margarine
¼ cup cornstarch
3 tablespoons cold water
6 tablespoons lemon juice
1 teaspoon grated lemon zest

4 egg yolks
2 tablespoons milk
1 deep-dish pie crust, or 2 (8-inch) pie crusts, baked
4 egg whites
6 tablespoons sugar
1 teaspoon lemon juice
1 teaspoon lemon zest

Preheat oven to 350° F. Combine sugar, water, and margarine; heat until dissolved. Add cornstarch with 3 tablespoons cold water; cook slowly until clear for about 8 minutes. Add lemon juice and grated zest. Cook 2 minutes. Slowly add egg yolks that have been beaten with milk; bring to a boil, and stir constantly. Cool and pour into baked pie crust. For meringue, beat egg whites; add sugar, and mix well. Add lemon juice and zest. Spread meringue on filling, and seal to crust. Bake for 12 to 15 minutes until lightly brown. Yield: 10 to 12 servings.

Out-of-This-World Lemon Pie

4 eggs, separated
¾ cup sugar
¼ cup lemon juice
1 teaspoon lemon zest
½ teaspoon gelatin, dissolved in 1
teaspoon cold water

1 (9-inch) pie shell, baked
½ cup whipping cream, whipped,
and sweetened with ½ teaspoon
sugar

In a double boiler, blend egg yolks, sugar, lemon juice, and zest. Cook over hot water, stirring constantly, until thick, about 20 minutes. Stir dissolved gelatin into hot mixture. Cook another 2 minutes. Cool slightly.

Beat egg whites until very stiff, and fold into lemon mixture. Pour into baked pastry shell. Chill in refrigerator. Top with sweetened whipped cream, if desired. Yield: 8 servings.

Key Lime Pie

1 tablespoon unflavored gelatin
1 cup sugar, divided
¼ teaspoon salt
4 eggs, separated
½ cup Key lime juice

¼ cup water
1 cup whipping cream
1 (9-inch) pie shell, baked, or
graham cracker crumb pie shell

Mix gelatin, ½ cup sugar, and salt in saucepan. Beat egg yolks well; add lime juice and water. Stir into gelatin mixture. Cook over low heat, stirring constantly, until mixture just comes to a boil. Remove from heat. Cool, stirring occasionally, until mixture mounds slightly when dropped from a spoon.

Beat egg whites until soft peaks form. Gradually add ½ cup sugar, beating until stiff. Fold into cooled gelatin mixture. Whip cream, and fold into lime mixture. Some whipped cream may be reserved for topping, if desired. Pour into prepared crust. Chill until firm. Yield: 8 servings.

Old-Fashioned Oatmeal Pie

1 (9-inch) deep-dish pie shell
¾ cup honey
2 eggs, beaten
¾ cup quick-cooking oats
¾ cup coconut

¾ cup packed brown sugar
½ cup butter or margarine, softened
½ cup raisins
½ cup chopped walnuts
Whipped cream for garnish

Preheat oven to 350° F. Combine honey, eggs, oats, coconut, brown sugar, butter, raisins, and walnuts; mix well in large bowl. Pour into pie shell. Bake for 40 to 45 minutes or until filling browns and knife blade inserted near center comes out clean. Serve, warm or cold, topped with whipped cream. Yield: 8 servings.

Fresh Peach Polka Dot Pie

4 large, or 8 small, fresh peaches, peeled and halved or quartered
1 (9-inch) pie shell, unbaked
¾ cup sugar
¼ cup all-purpose flour

½ teaspoon cinnamon
⅛ teaspoon salt
1 cup whipping cream
¼ cup slivered almonds

Preheat oven to 400° F. Arrange peaches in pie shell. Mix sugar, flour, cinnamon and salt; stir in cream gradually. Pour over peaches. Sprinkle with almonds. Bake for 45 minutes or until filling is set. Serve warm or cold. Yield: 8 servings.

Pecan Pie

1 cup sugar
4 tablespoons self-rising flour
2 (9-inch) pie shells, unbaked
2 cups pecans, crushed a little

4 tablespoons margarine, melted
4 eggs
2 cups light corn syrup
1 tablespoon vanilla extract

Preheat oven to 350° F. Mix sugar and flour together. Line 2 unbaked pie shells with pecans. Combine rest of ingredients and pour into shells. Place pies on cookie sheet. Bake for 35 to 40 minutes. Yield: 2 pies, or 12 to 16 servings.

Pumpkin Pie with Bourbon and Walnuts

Pie Shell:

2 cups all-purpose flour
¼ teaspoon salt

⅔ cup vegetable shortening
¼ cup ice water

Preheat oven to 400° F. Combine flour and ¼ teaspoon salt in a mixing bowl, and cut in shortening with a pastry cutter until texture is like coarse meal. Stirring with a wooden spoon, gradually add water until a firm ball of dough forms. Wrap dough in plastic, and chill for at least 30 minutes. On a lightly floured surface, roll out dough to a ⅛-inch thickness, and fit the pastry into a 10-inch pie pan.

Filling:

¾ cup crushed walnuts
3 cups pumpkin purée (fresh or canned)
1 cup brown sugar
4 eggs, beaten
¾ cup heavy cream
½ cup milk

¼ cup bourbon
1½ teaspoons ground cinnamon
¼ teaspoon ground cloves
½ teaspoon ground ginger
Pinch of nutmeg
½ teaspoon salt

Sprinkle crushed walnuts over bottom of pie shell. In a large mixing bowl, combine remaining ingredients and stir until well blended. Spoon mixture evenly into pie shell, and bake for 10 minutes. Reduce heat to 350° F., and continue baking for about 25 minutes, or until the pie is slightly firm and a straw inserted into the center comes out clean. Let pie stand for 30 minutes before serving. Yield: 8 servings.

Praline Pumpkin Pie

⅓ cup butter
⅓ cup packed brown sugar
½ cup chopped pecans
1 (9-inch) pie shell, lightly baked
1 (3.5-ounce) package egg custard
  mix

1½ cups canned pumpkin
¼ cup packed brown sugar
1⅔ cups evaporated milk
1 egg yolk
1½ teaspoons pumpkin pie spice
½ cup pecan halves

Preheat oven to 425° F. Combine butter and ⅓ cup brown sugar in saucepan. Cook until sugar melts and bubbles vigorously. Remove from heat, and stir in nuts. Spread mixture evenly over bottom of pie shell. Bake for 5 minutes. Remove from oven, and cool.

In a saucepan, combine custard mix, pumpkin, ¼ cup brown sugar, milk, egg yolk, and spice. Quickly bring to a boil, stirring constantly. Pour into cooled pie shell, and decorate top with pecans. Cool or chill until set (about 3 hours). Yield: 6 servings.

Tipsy Almond Trifle

3 cups milk
9 egg yolks
¼ cup plus 2 tablespoons sugar
Pinch of salt
¾ teaspoon vanilla extract
¾ cup heavy cream

Dry sherry, to taste
1 pint whipping cream, whipped
  and flavored with sugar, almond
  extract, and dry sherry, to taste
2 (10-ounce) angel food cakes,
  broken into pieces
¾ cup sliced almonds, toasted

Heat milk in the top of a double boiler until a film forms on top. In a small bowl, beat the egg yolks with the sugar and salt until light in color, and add mixture, very gradually, to the hot milk. Place over boiling water, and continue to cook, stirring constantly, until the mixture coats a spoon. Cool. Add vanilla extract and dry sherry to taste. Beat the cream until stiff, and fold into cooled custard. Set aside.

In trifle dish, layer pieces of angel food cake, custard sauce to cover the cake, whipped cream, and sliced almonds. Repeat as necessary, ending with almonds. Yield: 12 to 16 servings.

Lemon Tarts

1 cup, plus 1 teaspoon, sugar
2 tablespoons flour
Pinch of salt
3 whole eggs, beaten
Juice of 1½ lemons

Zest of 1 lemon
1 stick unsalted butter
1 (9-inch) pie shell, or 8 individual
   tart shells, baked
1 cup whipping cream

Combine 1 cup sugar, flour, and salt in top of double boiler. Mix well. Add eggs, lemon juice, and zest. Stir constantly until thickened. Add butter. Pour into baked shell. With electric mixer at high speed, beat whipping cream until stiff. Add remaining 1 teaspoon sugar. When filling is cool, top pie or tarts with whipped cream. Yield: 8 servings.

Pineapple Tarts

1 stick butter
1 cup sugar
2 eggs, separated
34 graham crackers
2 teaspoons baking powder
¾ cup milk

1 cup chopped pecans
2 teaspoons vanilla extract
¾ cup sugar
1 (11-ounce) can crushed pineapple
1 cup whipping cream, whipped
   (optional)

Preheat oven to 350° F. Line 18 muffin tins with paper liners. Cream together butter and sugar. Add egg yolks, one at a time. Using a rolling pin, crush graham crackers. Beat egg whites until stiff. Sprinkle baking powder over crumbs. Add to butter mixture, alternating with milk. Stir. Add pecans, vanilla extract, and stiffly beaten egg whites. Stir. Divide mixture among muffin tins. Bake for 25 to 30 minutes. Remove tarts from oven and leave in fluted cups. Bring ¾ cup sugar to a boil; then add crushed pineapple. Top tarts with pineapple mixture. Serve warm. Top with whipped cream, if desired. Do not freeze tarts. Yield: 18 tarts

Easy Apple Dumplings

Serve with ice cream.

1¾ cups sugar, divided
2 cups water
4 tablespoons butter or margarine, plus additional for topping

8 Granny Smith apples (for 13x9x2-inch pan), or 5 Granny Smith apples (for 10x6x2-inch pan)
1 (10-ounce) can refrigerated biscuits
Cinnamon

Preheat oven to 325° F. In a large saucepan, heat ¾ cup sugar, water, and butter. Slice apples, and add to mixture. Place apple mixture in baking pan. Using kitchen shears, clip biscuits into small pieces, and drop evenly on top of apples. Sprinkle 1 cup sugar on top. Then, sprinkle generously with cinnamon. Dot with bits of butter. Bake for about 1 hour, or until golden brown. Stir or push biscuits down into juice 2 or 3 times while baking. Yield: 8 to 10 servings.

Creamy Light Banana Pudding

6 graham crackers (regular or cinnamon)
1 (.9-ounce) box vanilla sugar-free instant pudding
1½ cups skim milk

½ cup light frozen whipped topping
½ cup plain or vanilla yogurt (regular or low-fat)
2 bananas
¼ cup graham cracker crumbs

Line a 9x9-inch pan with graham crackers. Mix instant pudding with milk; whip with a wire beater until smooth. Beat in whipped topping and yogurt until smooth. Pour half of the pudding mixture into pan lined with graham crackers. Slice bananas on top of mixture. Spread remaining pudding mixture over bananas. Sprinkle graham cracker crumbs on top. Refrigerate for 3 to 4 hours before serving. Yield: 9 servings.

Pots-de-Crème

This dessert is delicious and elegant.

1 (12-ounce) bag semi-sweet
  chocolate chips
½ cup egg substitute, or 2 eggs,
  beaten slightly

4 tablespoons sugar
2 teaspoons vanilla extract
1½ cups milk
Whipped cream for garnish

Put chocolate chips, eggs, sugar, and vanilla extract into blender. Heat milk to boiling point, and pour into blender. Blend thoroughly. Pour mixture into demitasse cups or similar small cups, and chill thoroughly. Serve with small dollop of whipped cream on top. Yield: 4 to 6 servings.

Chocolate Cake Pudding

Chocolate Cake Pudding is a wonderful
old-fashioned dessert!

2 cups water
5 tablespoons cocoa
½ cup brown sugar
½ cup white sugar
Pinch of salt
1 tablespoon margarine or butter
¾ cup sugar
1 cup all-purpose flour

½ teaspoon salt
1 teaspoon baking powder
1½ tablespoons cocoa
2 tablespoons vegetable oil
½ cup milk
½ cup chopped pecans
1 teaspoon vanilla extract
¼ teaspoon almond extract

Preheat oven to 350° F., and grease an 8¼x8¼-inch baking dish. In a saucepan, heat water, cocoa, brown sugar, white sugar, salt, and margarine. Do not boil. Set mixture aside. Sift together ¾ cup sugar, flour, salt, baking powder, and cocoa; set aside. Combine vegetable oil and remaining ingredients, and mix with dry ingredients. Pour batter in dish. Pour hot cocoa mixture over batter. Do not stir. Bake for 30 minutes. Cool or chill before serving. Yield: 8 servings.

Chocolate Mousse

2 (6-ounce) packages semi-sweet chocolate chips
1 stick plus 2 tablespoons unsalted butter
1 cup egg substitute, or 8 eggs yolks
¼ cup Cognac
1 cup egg substitute, or 8 egg whites
¾ cup heavy whipping cream, whipped and sweetened to taste
1 (1.55-ounce) bar milk chocolate, grated

Melt chocolate chips and butter over hot water in double boiler. Beat egg substitute or egg yolks into chocolate mixture, one at a time. Cool 10 minutes. Stir in Cognac. Beat egg substitute or egg whites with electric mixer until stiff. Fold chocolate mixture and egg whites together. Pour into a 1-quart dish. Refrigerate. Serve with whipped cream, and sprinkle grated chocolate curls from candy bar on top. Yield: 4 servings.

Champagne Sherbet

1¼ cups sugar
1 cup water
1½ cups champagne
3 tablespoons lemon juice
¼ cup egg substitute, or 2 egg whites
2 tablespoons sugar
Additional champagne (about 1 cup)
Lemon wedges, for garnish

Combine 1¼ cups sugar and water in a small saucepan; boil 4 to 5 minutes without stirring. Remove from heat, and chill. Stir in champagne and lemon juice. Beat egg substitute or egg whites until foamy. Add 2 tablespoons sugar, and continue beating until stiff. Fold into champagne mixture. Turn into a shallow metal bowl and freeze; then beat in food processor fitted with a steel knife. Sherbet will be soft. Spoon into glasses, top each serving with 2 tablespoons champagne, and garnish with lemon wedge. Yield: 6 to 8 servings.

Low Cholesterol Banana Pineapple Ice Cream

1 (3-ounce) box instant vanilla
pudding
2 (12-ounce) cans evaporated skim
milk
3 bananas, sliced

1 (16-ounce) can crushed pineapple
2 teaspoons vanilla extract
2½ cups sugar
Skim milk

Mix vanilla pudding, milk, bananas, pineapple, vanilla extract, and sugar, and pour into container of 1-gallon ice cream freezer. Fill container to ¾ full with skim milk. Freeze according to freezer manufacturer's directions until firm. Yield: 8 to 10 servings.

Sinful Chocolate Ice Cream

12 (2.15-ounce) chocolate-covered
caramel nougat candy bars
1 (14-ounce) can sweetened
condensed milk

½ gallon whole milk, divided, plus
additional, if needed
1 (5.5-ounce) can chocolate syrup

Combine candy and sweetened condensed milk in a large saucepan. Cook over low heat, stirring constantly, until candy is melted. Allow to cool, stirring occasionally. Add 1 quart of whole milk to the candy mixture. Beat with hand mixer until blended. Pour into freezer container of a gallon ice cream freezer; stir in chocolate syrup. Add 1 quart of milk. (Additional milk may be needed to fill container to within 4 inches of the top or to the fill line.) Freeze according to manufacturer's directions. Yield: 8 to 10 servings.

Rich Chocolate Custard Ice Cream

1¾ cups sugar
¼ cup flour
¼ teaspoon salt
2 cups milk
2 eggs, slightly beaten

3½ (1-ounce) squares unsweetened
chocolate, chopped
1 tablespoon vanilla extract
4 cups light cream

Combine sugar, flour, and salt in large saucepan. Stir in milk gradually; blend in eggs, and add chocolate. Cook over medium heat, stirring constantly, until chocolate melts and mixture boils; boil for 1 minute. Cool. Add vanilla extract and cream to cooled custard. Fill chilled ice cream container two-thirds full. Freeze according to manufacturer's directions. Yield: 6 to 8 servings.

Chocolate Sandwich Cookie Freeze

28 chocolate sandwich cookies, crushed
4 tablespoons butter or margarine, melted
½ gallon coffee ice cream, softened
1 cup sugar
1 (12-ounce) can evaporated milk
1 teaspoon vanilla extract
4 (1-ounce) squares semi-sweet chocolate
6 tablespoons margarine
1 (12-ounce) carton frozen whipped topping
1 cup slivered almonds, toasted

Mix crushed chocolate sandwich cookies and melted butter. Pat into 13x9x2-inch pan. Layer coffee ice cream on cookies. Freeze. Mix sugar, evaporated milk, vanilla extract, chocolate, and margarine in a saucepan. Heat and let boil for 1 minute. Cool. Pour over ice cream, and freeze. Spread whipped topping on chocolate layer. Sprinkle topping with almonds. Yield: 8 servings.

Frozen Nutty Buddy Pie

1 (3-ounce) package cream cheese
1 cup confectioners' sugar
½ cup crunchy peanut butter
½ cup milk
1 (8-ounce) carton frozen whipped topping
1 (9-inch) prepared chocolate cookie pie crust
½ cup crushed peanuts
½ cup chocolate syrup

In mixing bowl, combine cream cheese, sugar, peanut butter, and milk. Beat until smooth. Gently fold in whipped topping. Pour filling into prepared pie shell. Garnish with crushed peanuts, and drizzle chocolate syrup over filling in a fine stream. Freeze until firm, and store in freezer. Yield: 6 to 8 servings.

Crunchy Ice Cream Dessert

1 cup all-purpose flour
1 stick butter, melted
¼ cup light brown sugar, packed
1 cup chopped pecans or walnuts

1 (12.25-ounce) jar caramel-
  flavored topping
½ gallon vanilla ice cream, softened

Preheat oven to 350° F. Butter an 11x7x1½-inch shallow baking pan and a 2-quart casserole. Mix together flour, butter, brown sugar, and nuts. Spread in prepared pan, and bake, stirring occasionally, for 20 minutes or until browned. Divide mixture in half. Place half in bottom of prepared 2-quart casserole. Cover with caramel topping. Spread vanilla ice cream over top; sprinkle remaining nut mixture on ice cream. Freeze solid. Cut into squares to serve. Yield: 12 to 14 servings.

Fresh Strawberries with Sherry Crème

6 egg yolks
¾ cup sugar
¾ cup cream sherry
1 teaspoon vanilla extract
¾ cup whipping cream

6 egg whites or ¾ cup egg substitute
2 quarts strawberries, hulled and
  sliced
Lemon balm or mint sprigs, for
  garnish

Mix egg yolks and sugar until creamy. Stir in sherry. Place mixture in double boiler over simmering water. Stir mixture until it is thick and smooth. Remove from heat, and cool completely. Add vanilla extract. Whip cream and fold into cooled mixture. Beat egg substitute or egg whites until stiff, and fold into mixture. Divide strawberries among twelve stemmed glasses. Spoon sherry crème over strawberries. Garnish each dessert with a sprig of lemon balm or mint. Yield: 12 servings.

Melons in Mint Sauce

1 small cantaloupe
1 small honeydew melon
½ cup sugar

1 cup water
6 to 8 fresh mint leaves, coarsely chopped
Mint sprigs, for garnish

Scoop out melons with melon ball cutter; set aside. Combine remaining ingredients in a small saucepan; bring to a boil, stirring constantly. Reduce heat, and simmer 5 minutes. Remove from heat and let cool. Strain. Pour sauce over melon balls; chill 2 to 3 hours. Serve in stemmed glasses with a sprig of mint in each glass. Yield: 6 servings.

Fresh Strawberries in Port

1 quart fresh strawberries
½ cup sugar

1 cup red or white port wine
Whipped cream, unsweetened and softly whipped (optional)

Gently wash strawberries in cold water, and hull. Drain thoroughly. In medium bowl, gently toss strawberries with sugar. Add wine. Refrigerate at least 2 hours, stirring occasionally. If desired, top individual servings with whipped cream. Yield: 6 servings.

Holiday Ambrosia

Holiday Ambrosia freezes well.

1 (8-ounce) package cream cheese, softened
2 tablespoons sugar
½ cup chopped nuts
1 cup coconut
1 (11-ounce) can crushed pineapple

2 cups orange pieces
1 teaspoon vanilla extract
1 (12-ounce) container frozen whipped topping
Juice of 1 lemon
Angel food cake

Mix cream cheese and sugar. Add nuts, coconut, pineapple, oranges, and vanilla extract. Mix well, and fold in whipped topping and lemon juice. Serve on angel food cake. Yield: 2½ cups.

Caramel Corn

To reduce sweetness, double the amount of popcorn.

1 cup packed brown sugar
1 stick butter or margarine
¼ cup light corn syrup
Dash of salt

½ teaspoon vanilla extract
½ teaspoon baking soda
6 quarts popped popping corn, with
  unpopped kernels removed

Preheat oven to 225° F. Combine brown sugar, butter, corn syrup, and salt in heavy saucepan. Bring to boil over medium to medium-high heat. Stir occasionally to mix. When boiling starts, do not stir anymore and reduce heat. Continue the gentle boil for 5 minutes. Do not overcook, or coating will not spread onto popcorn. Remove syrup from heat, and stir in vanilla extract and baking soda. Soda will cause syrup to foam. Stir thoroughly and pour onto popped and sorted corn. Toss gently until popcorn is thoroughly coated. Spread onto jellyroll pans or 2 to 3 (13x9x2-inch) pans, and bake for 90 minutes. Stir 3 times to break up caramel corn and to allow drying. Store in airtight container for 6 to 8 weeks. Yield: 3 to 4 quarts.

French Chocolates

1 (12-ounce) package semi-sweet
  chocolate pieces
1 cup walnuts, ground
¾ cup sweetened condensed milk
1 teaspoon vanilla extract

Dash of salt
Shredded coconut
Chocolate sprinkles
Chopped nuts

Place chocolate pieces in a medium, heat resistant non-metallic mixing bowl. In microwave oven, heat chocolate, uncovered, on full power, for 4 minutes or until melted. Stir in ground walnuts, condensed milk, vanilla extract, and salt. Cool for 5 minutes. Roll mixture into balls and dip into coconut, chocolate sprinkles, or nuts, as desired. Place on greased cookie sheet and refrigerate until set. Yield: 50 chocolate balls.

Norwegian Crunch

Norwegian Crunch freezes well.

2 sticks butter, melted
1 egg yolk
1 cup dark brown sugar
1 cup self-rising flour

1 teaspoon vanilla extract
6 (1.55-ounce) chocolate bars
½ to ¾ cup chopped pecans

Preheat oven to 325° F., and butter a jellyroll pan. Beat butter, egg yolk, brown sugar, flour, and vanilla extract together with a wooden spoon or spatula until smooth and thick, like caramel. Spread on prepared pan. Bake at 325° F. for 25 minutes. Arrange chocolate bars on top of mixture. Let stand for 5 minutes; then spread evenly. Top with pecans while still warm. Slightly press nuts into candy. Cool. Cut into bars and refrigerate. Yield: 36 (1x3-inch) bars.

Peanut Butter Balls

1 (1-pound) box confectioners'
  sugar
1 (18-ounce) jar peanut butter

1 stick butter
12 ounces (any style) chocolate
Paraffin wax

Combine sugar, peanut butter, and butter. Mix well, and roll into 1-inch balls. Using a double boiler, melt chocolate and ⅛ stick of paraffin wax. Dip the balls, using a spoon or toothpick. Place balls on waxed paper, and allow to harden overnight. Yield: Approximately 100 balls.

Holly Wreaths

1 stick butter	**1½ teaspoons green food coloring**
30 large marshmallows	**3½ cups corn flakes**
½ teaspoon vanilla extract	**Red cinnamon candies**

Melt butter and marshmallows over low heat; stirring constantly. Add vanilla extract and food coloring, and stir until blended. Fold in corn flakes. Drop by tablespoonfuls on cookie sheets, and shape balls into wreaths. Decorate with red cinnamon candies. Yield: 20 wreaths.

Spiced Pecans

1 egg white	**½ cup sugar**
1 teaspoon cold water	**Pinch of salt**
1 quart whole pecans	**2 tablespoons cinnamon**

Preheat oven to 325° F. Beat egg white and water until stiff. Stir in pecans until all are coated. In a separate bowl, combine sugar, salt, and cinnamon. Pour mixture over pecans, and stir until coated. Spread pecans in a single layer on jellyroll pan. Bake, uncovered, for 1 hour. Stir every 15 minutes. Yield: 1 quart.

Praline Confection

20 to 24 graham crackers	**1 cup light brown sugar**
2 sticks butter	**1 cup nuts**

Preheat oven to 350° F. Line a 13x9x2-inch pan with whole graham crackers. In a medium saucepan, bring butter and sugar to rolling boil, and boil for 2 minutes. Add nuts, and remove from heat. Pour over crackers, and spread evenly. Bake for 10 minutes. Cool slightly. Cut into squares, and place on cookie sheet. Chill for a few minutes in freezer. Remove and store in covered container. Yield: 24 squares.

Monster Munch

2 cups Crispix® cereal (spider webs)
1 cup chocolate chips (bats' teeth)
1 cup raisins (cats' eyes)

1 cup peanuts (monsters' toes)
1 cup miniature marshmallows (ghosts' toes)

In a black pot, add the appropriate ingredient as you recite the following poem:

Monster munch, monster munch,
A special meal for Halloween lunch.
When you eat this ghoulish treat,
Your spooky look will be complete!
Stir it round, stir it round,
It's the creepiest dish I've found.

Spider webs, so thick and sticky,
Teeth from bats, so sharp and black,
Eyes from cats still glaring, staring,
Monsters' toes with crunchy bones,
Toes from ghosts, a freaky sight!

Stir it round, stir it round,
It's the creepiest dish I've found.
Eat some more on Halloween night,
Go and spread some holiday fright!

CHS Cookbook Committee

Executive Committee

Louise Greaves
Chairperson

Nan Sipe
Finance Chairperson

Bob Holt
Retail Marketing Chairperson

Claudia Pass
Editor

Kay Norris
General Marketing Chairperson

Cindy Turner
Assistant Editor

Kay Warfield
Graphics Chairperson

Suzan Anderson
Recipe Coordinator

Julia Jones
Advisor

Regional Chairpersons

Coastal .... Lois Corder, Lynda Martin
Eastern .... Gloria Cooper, Teresa Farmer
Piedmont I .... Meredith Muse, Gary Ritz
Piedmont II .... Sandy Brubaker
Sandhills .... Ely Aponte
Southern .... Carol Goss
Triangle .... Francis Wilder
Western .... Mary Ann Gough

Regional Marketing Chairpersons

Coastal .... Lois Corder, Lynda Martin
Eastern .... Tracey Bell, Gloria Cooper, Teresa Farmer
Piedmont .... Julia Jones
Sandhills .... Cindy Davis, Judy Harrison, Gladys McCauley
Southern .... Kay Norris
Triangle .... Brenda Martin, Laura Raynor, Carol Wiggs
Western .... Dianne Dill, Jeanne Warner

Recipe Contributors

Apex, NC
Debbie & David Dixon
Nancy Lischwe

Arden, NC
Martha Anderson
Barbara Swinehart
Gladys Warren

Asheboro, NC
Marian Jane Accles
Joy H. Menius
Betty B. Page
Andrea Patterson
Anne Seay Potter
Billy Potter
Kathy Walker

Asheville, NC
Harriet Forbes
Mary Ann Gough
LaDonna McCook
Debi Morgan
Mary Ann Morton
Jane Reynolds
Virginia Wick

Belmont, NC
Norma B. Jones

Bladenboro, NC
Mary S. Buie

Boone, NC
Sandy Brubaker
Louise Denton

Burlington, NC
Larry C. Crawford
Celia Touloupas Sims
Jennifer B. Talley
Carole Workman Walker

Butner, NC
Mary B. Boyette

Canton, NC
Diane Mease

Cary, NC
Henny Dowd
Ann A. Lawhon
Ann & Virgil Steele

Charlotte, NC
Ann Ballenger
Pamela Satterfield Berry
Cindy Bishop
Doug Brown
Carol Caudill

Mabel Andrews Cook
Carol S. Goss
Alice Kerr
Pam Misle
Bryan & Josh Norris
Dorothy Pease
Tom Ponsonby
Clarrisa Porter
Jill Robins
Mary & Jimmy Roupas
Mary B. Saclarides
Joan Shirley
Robert Slotkin
Cate Stadelman
Patricia Todd
Dollye Peay Walters

Claremont, NC
Mrs. Jimmy Bolick

Clemmons, NC
Margaret N. Gidley
Melissa Nifong

Colerain, NC
Tra J. Perry

Connelly Springs, NC
Skip Carson

Creedmoor, NC
Linda Tilley

Davidson, NC
Jean Jackson

Denver, NC
Barbara Lauro

Dobson, NC
Hazel Comer

Dunn, NC
Midge Carpenter
J. E. H. Williams

Durham, NC
Diane Albert
Anne Chappel
Gloris Colvin
Martha DeBerry
Freda Hurwitz
Pattie L. Lewis
Phyllis Vandenburg

Elizabeth City, NC
Alice Ann Morris

Elizabethtown, NC
Faye Womble

Emerald Isle, NC
Erin Rebecca Johnson

Faison, NC
Ester C. Cates

Farmville, NC
Jean Jones

Fayetteville, NC
Ely Aponte
Bonnie Findley
Karen Horton
Patricia Knox
Suzanne Kosarich
Shanda Loftin
Sarah Thomas

Franklin, NC
Elizabeth Hill

Garner, NC
Debra Entwistle
Charlene A. Ratliff
Mary Shulby
Carol H. Tharrington

Garysburg, NC
Lillie Mae Grant

Gastonia, NC
Ellen G. Snider

Graham, NC
Bank, Norma, Ann,
   Jerry, Mike, Robin,
   & Lawren Smith

Greensboro, NC
Joann Anderson
Jane Armfield
Doris Arnold
Doris E. Barbee
Caroline E. Barber
Ann Barnes
Beth Berg
Jean B. Brooks
Martha Brown
Marcella Bryant
Connie Carter
Helen Clark
Louann A. Clarke
Cam Cleaver
Viki Coble
Jo Codispoti
Gayle Cox
Mrs. Nathan Cox
Annette Z. Davis
Betsy Dunn

Anna Elder
Sandy Emerson
Mrs. Thomas Farquhar
Ruth Foster
Louise Greaves
Betty Hankins
Frances Hartmann
Beverly Isaacson
Hilda F. Johnson
Julia Jones
Lynn Jones
Donna M. Kimmel
Vira Kivett
Sheila Lee
Maura McGinn
Nancy Michaud
Mona Miller
Meredith Muse
Jean Navarro
Freddie Neiditz
Pattie S. Newlin
June Payne
Dianne Peebles
Helen A. Poore
Lanita Presson
Ruby Richbourg
Gary Ritz
Nancy Roberts
Nancy Saunders
Mary Ann Seay
Mrs. George Seay
Nan & Richard Sipe
Heather Sisk
Donna Steele
Martha Stewart
Nancy Stiefel
Ann Stroud
Becky Taylor
Mrs. Robert Taylor
Pat Thompson
Stephanie Thompson
Bill Tutterow
Judy Tutterow
Lynn Tutterow
Mary Tutterow
Ruthie Tutterow
Clara Vaughn
Kay Warfield
Sadie Weaver
June Welborn
Sheila Wells
Helen Williams
Peppermint Zealy

Greenville, NC
Patsy Duke
Mary H. Everett
Beatrice Harris
Mary Holland

Susan G. Lewis
Donna Lucas
Melba Howard Stallings
Sarah Sugg
Gracie Mebane Vines

Henderson, NC
Millie Coghill
Sarah Dawson Davis
Tina Pierce

Hendersonville, NC
Lisa Obermiller

Hertford, NC
Candice Eley

Hickory, NC
Melanie P. Cockerham
Mrs. Van C. Elledge
Penny Gaddy
Judy Ingold
Mary Stewart Tarrant

High Point, NC
Anne W. Andrews
Mildred S. Clinard
Catty Gross
Doris Henley
Mrs. F. M. James
Doris Towers

Huntersville, NC
Robyn Turton

Indian Trail, NC
Patsy Turner

Jacksonville, NC
Ann Hines

Jamestown, NC
Ken Murray

Kernersville, NC
Anonymous

Kings Mountain, NC
Lynn P. Murphy

Kinston, NC
B. J. Stanley
Emma Grant Wade

Knightdale, NC
Polly Addison

Leland, NC
Beatrice Sellars

Lenoir, NC
Pastor Leaner Alston
Melanie Anderson
Brenda Dietz
Dianne Dill
Sharon Tutterow Mitchell

Lola Richards
Sharon Blair Tolbert

Lexington, NC
Cathy Koontz

Lincolnton, NC
Gigi Mills Poole

Lumber Bridge, NC
Pamela Dover

Lumberton, NC
Mrs. Fred Mussellwhite

Madison, NC
Janet Bullard
Jacqueline Comer

Marian, NC
Patricia Lerch

Marshville, NC
Sylvia Jenkins

Matthews, NC
Debbie Blum

Mocksville, NC
Sandra Rogers

Monroe, NC
Lorraine P. Belk

Moravian Falls, NC
Katherine Irvin Bentley

Morehead City, NC
Iris R. Odell

Moyock, NC
Diane Horne

Mt. Holly, NC
Sandra Ann Bralley

Mt. Airy, NC
Sally Estes
Mildred E. Jones

Murfreesboro, NC
Deborah Brett Lane

New Bern, NC
Nora Barden
Gloria Cooper
Linda Edwards
Kathy Pate
Henrietta Proudfoot

New London, NC
Iva L. Howington

Newton, NC
Lettice Clapp
Jan Kirkpatrick

Oakboro, NC
Barbara M. Carpenter

Ocean Isle, NC
Betty L. Beall

Pfafftown, NC
Mrs. Eldridge C. Hanes
Alice G. Schwartz

Pilot Mountain, NC
Barbara M. Wilkerson

Pinehurst, NC
Linda McVay

Pittsboro, NC
Marge Matteson

Pleasant Garden, NC
Bellene Caldwell

Raeford, NC
Judy Harrison

Raleigh, NC
Debra Alis
Suzan Bentley Anderson
Nancy Hinton Andrews
Libby Wade Barber
Becky Burmester
Mary Cadwallader
Lee Cahoon
Collins Chalmers
Brenda Chandler
Mary Jane Ethridge Clark
Pam Tollefsen Clark
Margaret Davis
Donna Edwards
Jeannie Ford
Debbie Franke
Ellen H. Gates
Peggy Glass
Deborah Graham
Mrs. Jesse Helms
Patricia Hight
Betty Hubbard
Becky Hutchins
Neville Jones
Jill Lewis Kirby
Mary Long
Brenda Martin
Jim Millen
Betty Munns
Colleen Nicholson
Sharon Nicholson
Judy Nunnenkamp
Claudia White Pass
Mary Patterson
Laura Raynor
Mrs. Jack G. Reed
Karen D. Rosser
Yorke Wooten Sartorio
Janet Black Schreiner
Mary Catherine Sigmon

Dianne J. Slade
Sharon Smart
Ann Smith
Robin M. Smith
Anne K. Stancil
Fabian Thornhill
Ellen Vitek
Marlene Weber
Mary Grier Wheless
Sylvia White
Carol Wiggs
Frances Wilder

Ramseur, NC
Josephine A. Moore

Richfield, NC
Shirley Starnes

Robersonville, NC
Mildred L. Hardison

Rocky Mount, NC
Beverly K. Thompson

Rowland, NC
Mackie Pate

Roxboro, NC
Janie Cameron Wagstaff

Rural Hall, NC
Ivah K. Harris
Maxine Kiger
Darene C. Pendry

Salisbury, NC
Deborah Messinger
Nancy Zimmerman

Saluda, NC
Diane Land

Sanford, NC
Gladys R. McAuley
Mrs. Reid Suggs

Selma, NC
Alice Parker
Lois Jones
Angel Phillips

Shelby, NC
Mary G. Davis
Raye Hedden
Judy Patel
Linda Thompson
Doris Whitaker

Smithfield, NC
Judy Hayes
Deidra Kraft
Ann Wilson
Lynn Wood

Southern Pines, NC
Cindy Davis
Cleon Hayes

Southport, NC
Pat Brunning

Spindale, NC
Pat Hardin

Spring Lake, NC
Armelle Hall

Stanfield, NC
Jane F. Harwood

Statesville, NC
Caroline L. Avery

Swansboro, NC
Mrs. Jean Nassef Ormond

Taylorsville, NC
Sara Goodnight

Thomasville, NC
Anita Silvestri
Vivi Starnes

Troutman, NC
Lucille Suther

Valdese, NC
Tammy M. Black
Sylby P. Martinat

Vanceboro, NC
Evelyn Duzan

Wade, NC
Wanda Matthews

Wake Forest, NC
Lisa McLemore
Elizabeth Toney Melvin
Susan Minner

Warrenton, NC
Mamie King

West Jefferson, NC
Sally Reeves

Whiteville, NC
Genie Carter

Wilkesboro, NC
Jodi D. Swofford

Williamston, NC
Verna Perry

Wilmington, NC
Becky A. Coleman
Faydene Corbett
Lois Corder
Ginny Craft
Kim Edwards

Judy Fulk
Lynda Martin

Wilson, NC
Ann Beddard
Teresa K. Farmer
Susan Forbes
Angela Bogue Hare
Terry Hey
James G. Lamm
Sally Miller
Harriet Forbes Vinson
Sue V. Warren
Wendy Whitley

Winston-Salem, NC
Mrs. J. Glenn Butler
Kathy Davis
Betty Earle
Sheila F. Fox
Lucy Gidley
Bealie Kiger
Krista Kiger
Norris Masten
Pattie Tucker

Youngsville, NC
Joie Howard

Zebulon, NC
Marie H. Moore

CHS Staff
Sandra Alexander
Anne Beasley
Joyce Blankenship
Edna Blevins
Vickie Chamberlain
Linda Collins
Sandy Cook
Jerry Duggins
Joan Duncan
Judy Gallagher
Betty Godwin
Jane Goodson
Diane G. Guy
Leslie Hall
Judy Harrison-Barry
Anita Hensley
Patsy Holland
Claire Hurst
Pat Jarvis
Shirley Johnson
Jean Little
Teresa McGraw
Lori Mashburn
Roberta Monosoff
Claudia Murray
Charma Pickett
Debbie Powell
Gloria Powell

Grace Ramsey
Francie Rieser
Louise Robinson
Mary Alice Sisk
Doris Smith
Freida Stewart
Linda Taylor
Ann Tietz
Ken Tutterow
Anna Tye
Judith Upchurch
Edith Votta
Reatha H. Ward

Restaurants
Chuckanut Manor - Bow, WA
Holly Inn - Pinehurst, NC
J. Basul Noble's - High Point, NC
Providence Cafe - Charlotte, NC
Sugar Magnolias - High Point, NC

Out-of-State Contributors
Connie Andersen - Atlanta, GA
Mary K. Asma - Covington, VA
Amy Bentley - Rochester, MI
Betsy Bentley - Rochester, MI
Brenda Booth - Knoxville, TN
Virginia Cates Bowie - Richmond, VA
Gay Brunton - Huntington, WV
Frances S. Crawford - Gloucester, VA
Elsie G. Dame - Gloucester, VA
Ineva Dill - Ocilla, GA
Elaine Dusold - Canajoharie, NY
Nelson Davis Edwards - Louisville, KY
Bill Flowers - Manakin-Sabot, VA
Velma Harding - Keysville, VA
Robert, Anne, Jed, Daniel, & Suzanne Hoyer - Plymouth, NH
Rita Lischwe - Chesterfield, MO
Margaret F. Lowery - Jackson, MS
George McClelland - Funkstown, MD
Olive Price McKeever - Gainesville, GA
Elizabeth McLean - Spokane, WA
Bobbie Nell Pass - Louisville, MS
Betty J. Patterson - Grove City, PA
Dewise Richards - Hampton, SC
Gigi Shapiro - Houston, TX
Ann M. Shiver - Atlanta, GA
Hazel P. Sipe - Cheraw, SC
Lana Staben - Baltimore, MD
Dorothy B. White - Jackson, MS
Virginia Wilson - Memphis, TN
Nan Zimmerman - Spartanburg, SC

Karen Weaver
Kim Wheat-Robinson
Lucille Williams

Other Contributors
Carole Hadley
Ada Sue Jackson
Jean McFarland
Sara McPhail
Morton Robins
Ann Schultz
Lucile Sharp
Carolyn Stewart

We sincerely hope that none of the many individuals who contributed recipes has been inadvertently overlooked.

Index

277

Prints and Note Cards

(All rights reserved by artist.)

Carolina Blessings and **The First Nursery**, two unframed
limited edition watercolor prints, signed and numbered (1,000 each)
by the artist, Cynthia H. Poole, may be obtained from

The Children's Home Society of North Carolina
P.O. Box 14608
Greensboro, NC 27415-4608
1-800-632-1400

	Amount
Each Print - $45.00 *(each approximately 24" x 21")*	
Send _____ prints of *Carolina Blessings*	$ _____
Send _____ prints of *The First Nursery*	$ _____
Send _____ packs of note cards @ **$9.50 ea.** *Assortment of artwork from the divider pages (10 cards per pack - 2 color, 8 black & white)*	$ _____
6% State Tax (NC residents only)	$ _____
Postage/handling: $7.50 each print	$ _____
Postage/handling: $2.00 ea. pack note card	$ _____
Matting and Framing *(For cost, consult Cynthia Poole at 910-789-6057.)*	$ _____
Total	$ _____

Make checks payable to The Children's Home Society of North Carolina.

Name _____ Phone _____

Address _____

City _____ State _____ Zip _____

☐ Charge my   ☐ VISA ☐ MC

Card # _____ Expiration Date _____

Signature _____

Reorder Form

Name _____

Address _____

City/State/Zip _____

Telephone _____

_____	Copies @ $17.95 each	$ _____
_____	6% tax @ $1.08 each *(NC residents only)*	$ _____
_____	Shipping & handling *(See fee schedule)*	$ _____
	Total	$ _____

☐ Additional donation to CHS $ _____

☐ Check enclosed, payable to CHS of NC/Cookbook

☐ Please charge my ☐ VISA ☐ MC

Card # _____ Expiration Date _____

Signature _____

1995 Shipping/Handling Fees

1 book $2.50
2-5 books.............................3.50
6-11 books 4.50
1 case (12 books) 6.00

Please send to: **The Children's Home Society of North Carolina**
P.O. Box 14608
Greensboro, NC 27415-4608

Profits from the sale of these cookbooks support the programs of The Children's Home Society of North Carolina.